Cambourne New Settlement

Iron Age and Romano-British Settlement on the Clay Uplands of West Cambridgeshire

By
James Wright, Matt Leivers, Rachael Seager Smith, and Chris J. Stevens

Cambourne New Settlement

Iron Age and Romano-British Settlement on the Clay Uplands of West Cambridgeshire

By
James Wright, Matt Leivers, Rachael Seager Smith and Chris J. Stevens

with contributions from
Michael J. Allen, Phil Andrews, Catherine Barnett, Kayt Brown, Rowena Gale, Sheila Hamilton-Dyer, Kevin Hayward, Grace Perpetua Jones, Jacqueline I. McKinley, Robert Scaife, Nicholas A. Wells, and Sarah F. Wyles

Illustrations by
S.E. James

Wessex Archaeology Report No. 23

Wessex Archaeology 2009

Published 2009 by Wessex Archaeology Ltd
Portway House, Old Sarum Park, Salisbury, SP4 6EB
http://www.wessexarch.co.uk/

British Library Cataloguing in Publication Data
A catalogue record for this book is available from the British Library

ISBN 978-1-874350-49-1
ISSN 0962-5778

Produced by Julie Gardiner
Cover design by Karen Nichols

Printed by Henry Ling (Dorset Press) Ltd, Dorchester

Front cover: Face from the rim of a Romano-British flagon or jug

Back cover: Lower Cambourne: aerial view from the west showing central area under excavation; medieval ridge and furrow overlies Late Iron Age and Romano-British enclosures. Romano-British pewter vessels found together in a pit at Lower Cambourne

Wessex Archaeology Ltd is a registered charity No. 287786

Contents

(Volume 1)

Specialist Appendices
(Volume 2: CD)

Artefacts
Prehistoric pottery, *by Matt Leivers*
Late Iron Age pottery, *by Grace Perpetua Jones*
Romano-British pottery, *by Rachael Seager Smith*
Saxon pottery, *by Rachael Seager Smith*
Glass, *by Rachael Seager Smith*
Metalwork, *by Kayt Brown*
Coins, *by Nicholas A. Wells*
Struck and burnt flint, *by Matt Leivers*
Worked stone, *by Matt Leivers and Kevin Hayward*
Shale, *by Matt Leivers*
Worked bone, *by Matt Leivers*
Ceramic building material, *by Kayt Brown*
Fired clay, *by Kayt Brown*
Slag, *by Phil Andrews*
Human bone, *by Jacqueline I. McKinley*
Animal bone, *by Sheila Hamilton-Dyer*
Marine shell, *by Sarah F. Wyles*

Ecofacts
Charcoal, *by Rowena Gale*
Charred plant remains, *by Chris J. Stevens*
Waterlogged plant remains, *by Chris J. Stevens*
Molluscs, *by Michael J. Allen*
Pollen, *by Robert Scaife*
Sediments, *by Catherine Barnett*

These reports are also available online at:

http://www.wessexarch.co.uk/projects/cambridgeshire/cambourne/publication/reports

List of Figures

List of Plates

List of Tables

Contributors

Michael J. Allen, Allen Environmental Archaeology, Redroof, Green Road, Codford, Wiltshire BA12 0NW

Phil Andrews, Wessex Archaeology, Portway House, Old Sarum Park, Salisbury, Wiltshire SP4 6EB

Catherine Barnett, Wessex Archaeology

Kayt Brown, Wessex Archaeology

Rowena Gale, Bachefield House, Kimbolton, Leominster, Herefordshire, HR6 0EP

Sheila Hamilton-Dyer, 5 Suffolk Avenue, Shirley, Southampton, SO15 5EF

Kevin Hayward, Birch Vale, Plantation Close, Curridge, Thatcham, Berkshire RG18 9DJ

S.E. James, Wessex Archaeology

Grace Perpetua Jones, Wessex Archaeology

Matt Leivers, Wessex Archaeology

Jacqueline I. McKinley, Wessex Archaeology

Rachael Seager Smith, Wessex Archaeology

Robert Scaife, Heyside, Dodpitts Corner, Main Road, Newbridge, Isle of Wight, PO41 0YR

Chris J. Stevens, Wessex Archaeology

Nicholas A. Wells, 4 Daisy Street, Canton, Cardiff CF5 1EP

James Wright, 24 St Mark's Road, Salisbury, Wiltshire SP1 3AZ

Sarah F. Wyles, Wessex Archaeology

Acknowledgements

It is 20 years since the start of Wessex Archaeology's involvement with the new settlement known as Cambourne, and many people have contributed to the project, culminating in this publication.

The work was commissioned by the Cambourne Consortium which consists of TaylorWimpey and Bovis Homes. Wessex Archaeology would particularly like to thank David Chare, Project Director of Chare Associates Ltd, and Maurice Gordon, Resident Engineer of WSP, for their assistance throughout the course of the project. Robert Westlake of Westlake Surveys and John Joy of WSP supplied details of survey stations and the survey control, and their help is acknowledged. Karl Kropf of Roger Evans Associates Ltd supplied data used in the terrain models. The fieldwork was monitored by Andy Thomas, Simon Kaner and Louise Austin of Cambridgeshire County Council Heritage Section (CCHS).

Much of the fieldwork was managed by Mark Roberts, with the remainder by Andrew Manning, Chris Moore, Niall Oakey, Mick Rawlings, Reuben Thorp, and Kit Watson. The fieldwork was directed by Vaughan Birbeck, Rachel Every, Dave Godden, Andrew Manning, Gail Wakeham, and James Wright, and supervised by Cornelius Barton, Jo Best, Zoë Clarke, Barry Hennessy, Dave Murdie, Paul Pearce, Chris Swaine, and Steve Thompson, with dedicated teams from Wessex Archaeology working in often appalling ground conditions, particularly during the winter of 2000/2001. The assistance of Gordon Everitt and Mike Davis with metal detectors is gratefully acknowledged.

The post-excavation assessment, managed by Julie Gardiner, was based upon individual site reports written by James Wright (Lower Cambourne, Poplar Plantation), Dave Godden (Monk Field Farm and Little Common Farm), Rachel Every (The Fields), Jo Best (The Grange), and Andrew Manning (other sites). Finds and environmental assessments were undertaken by several of the contributors to this volume as well as by Emma Loader (metalwork) and Claire Ingrem and Naomi Sykes (animal bone) of the Centre for Human Ecology and Environment (CHEE), Department of Archaeology, University of Southampton Sarah F. Wyles supervised the environmental processing and undertook preliminary identifications of the molluscs as well as assessing the charred and waterlogged plant remains, charcoal and marine shell. Sheila Hamilton-Dyer would like to thank Ian Baxter and Lorraine Higbee for access to unpublished reports. Caroline McDonald kindly provided information about pewter plates from Chelmsford recorded through the Portable Antiquities Scheme. Finds have been photographed for publication by Elaine A. Wakefield.

Lisa Brown and subsequently Jörn Schuster managed the post-excavation and publication programme. James Cheetham, Jens Neuberger, and Simon Skittrell were responsible for setting up the GIS analysis and Stephanie Knight carried out preliminary work on the animal bone assemblage. Pippa Bradley provided helpful comments on draft versions of the structural texts, Chris Stevens collated and edited the environmental contributions, and Phil Andrews and Andrew Powell undertook final revision and editing of the publication report.

Abstract

This publication presents the results of 12 excavations carried out by Wessex Archaeology within the Cambourne Development Area, a new settlement to the west of Cambridge. The site lies on the clay 'uplands' forming the watershed of the Bourn Brook and the Great Ouse, on land not favourable to settlement and only occupied at certain times when population or agricultural pressure demanded.

The excavations revealed evidence for intermittent human occupation of the Cambourne landscape from at least the Middle Bronze Age to the present day. Ephemeral evidence of short-lived Bronze Age occupation has been recorded from three sites, all lying close to watercourses or within partly-silted palaeochannels.

From the Middle Iron Age the Cambourne landscape was settled by small farming communities occupying roundhouses, perhaps initially unenclosed but subsequently set within enclosures linked by droveways to extensive field systems. The full spatial extent of these farmsteads is not known but the economy seems to have been based largely on stock rearing with some arable agriculture. Apart from the largest and most complex site investigated, at Lower Cambourne, the Late Iron Age seems to have seen something of a recession with abandonment of earlier settlements. This may have been partly due to increased waterlogging making farming less viable.

From the middle of the 1st century AD new settlements began to emerge, possibly partly stimulated by the presence of Ermine Street. Within a century or so the area was relatively densely occupied with what appear to be planned settlements consisting of roundhouses set within enclosures and field systems. Several sites were remodelled in the later Romano-British period, most clearly that at Lower Cambourne where two rectilinear enclosures were established, though none of these farmsteads seems to have been very prosperous and there is little evidence that they benefited from trade along Ermine Street. Of particular interest, however, were three 'placed deposits' at Lower Cambourne, comprising pewter vessels, glass vessels, and the iron elements of a plough. Stock raising and some arable cultivation seem to have formed the main constituents of the economy in the Romano-British period, as it did in the later Iron Age.

Occupation at Lower Cambourne may have continued into the early 5th century and here, as well as at four other sites, there are a few enigmatic features and very small quantities of finds which indicate some Early–Middle Saxon activity. There appears then to have been a hiatus until the 12th or 13th century when the entire area was taken into arable cultivation and this has left the ubiquitous traces of medieval ridge and furrow agriculture, the earthworks surviving into the 20th century.

Foreign Language Abstracts

Zusammenfassung

In diesem Band werden die Ergebnisse von zwölf Ausgrabungen vorgelegt, die von Wessex Archaeology im Bereich der Cambourne Development Area, einer neuen Ansiedlung westlich von Cambridge, durchgeführt wurden. Die Fundplätze liegen auf den lehmigen Höhenzügen ('clay uplands'), die die Wasserscheide zwischen dem Bourn Brook und der Great Ouse bilden. Die dort vorhandenen siedlungsungünstigen Böden wurden nur zu bestimmten Zeiten besiedelt, wenn Bevölkerungs- oder landwirtschaftlicher Druck dies erforderten.

Die Ausgrabungen zeigen, daß die Landschaft im Bereich von Cambourne, mit einigen Unterbrechungen, von der mittleren Bronzezeit bis heute besiedelt war. Einige wenige Hinweise auf kurzlebige Besiedlung während der Bronzezeit fanden sich auf drei Fundplätzen, die alle in der Nähe von Wasserläufen oder teilweise verfüllten ehemaligen Bachläufen lagen.

Seit der mittleren Vorrömischen Eisenzeit wurde die Gegend von Cambourne von kleinen bäuerlichen Gemeinschaften besiedelt, die in Rundhäusern lebten. Diese waren anfangs wohl nicht umzäunt, wurden aber im Laufe der Zeit in Einfriedungen errichtet, die über Feldwege mit einer ausgedehnten Feldflur verbunden waren. Die vollständige räumliche Ausdehnung dieser Gehöfte ist nicht bekannt, aber sie waren wohl vor allem auf Viehwirtschaft und nur zu einem geringeren Teil auf Ackerbau ausgerichtet. In der späten Vorrömischen Eisenzeit scheint eine Rezession stattgefunden zu haben, die zur Aufgabe früherer Siedlungen führte. Ausgenommen hiervon blieb nur die größte und komplexeste der untersuchten Siedlungen, Lower Cambourne. Diese Rezession war vielleicht zu einem gewissen Grade auf zunehmende Vernässung der Wirtschaftsflächen zurückzuführen, was einen Rückgang der landwirtschaftlichen Erträge zur Folge hatte.

Seit der Mitte des 1. Jahrhunderts n. Chr. wurden neue Siedlungen angelegt, was vielleicht zu einem Teil durch die Errichtung der römischen Ermine Street angeregt wurde. Innerhalb eines Zeitraums von ungefähr einhundert Jahren fand eine relativ dichte Aufsiedlung der Gegend mit scheinbar planmäßig angelegten Siedlungen statt. Diese bestanden aus innerhalb von Umzäunungen errichteten Rundhäusern sowie dazugehörigen Feldfluren. Mehrere Siedlungen wurden in der späten Römischen Kaiserzeit umgestaltet, am deutlichsten zeigt sich dies in Lower Cambourne, wo zwei rechteckig eingefriedete Gehöfte angelegt wurden. Diese scheinen allerdings nicht besonders wohlhabend gewesen zu sein, und es fanden sich nur wenige Hinweise darauf, daß sie von den Handelströmen entlang der Ermine Street profitiert haben. Von besonderem Interesse waren jedoch drei Deponierungen von Zinngeschirr, Glasgefäßen und den eisernen Komponenten eines Pflugs, die in Lower Cambourne gefunden wurden. Wie schon in der späteren Vorrömischen Eisenzeit scheint auch in der Römischen Kaiserzeit Viehwirtschaft, mit einem geringeren Anteil Ackerbau, den Hauptbestandteil der Lebensgrundlagen ausgemacht zu haben.

Die Besiedlung von Lower Cambourne dauerte wahrscheinlich bis in das frühe 5. Jahrhundert an, und sowohl hier als auch an vier anderen Siedlungstellen fanden sich einge nicht immer eindeutig interpretierbare Befunde sowie eine nur sehr geringe Anzahl Funde, die früh- bis mittelangelsächsische Aktivitäten belegen. Nach einem Hiatus, der bis in das 12. oder 13 Jahrundert hinein anhielt, wurde dann die gesamte Gegend ackerbaulich erschlossen, was sich durch die überall nachweisbaren Spuren mittelalterlicher Wölbäcker zu erkennen gibt, die sich als Geländemerkmale bis in das 20. Jahrhundert hinein erhalten haben.

Übersetzung: Jörn Schuster

Résumé

Cet ouvrage présente les résultats de 12 fouilles entreprises par Wessex Archaelogy dans le cadre du développement de la zone de Cambourne, une nouvelle occupation à l'ouest de Cambridge. Le site se trouve sur les 'hautes terres' crayeuses entre les zones de partage des eaux du ruisseau Bourn Brook et de la rivière Great Ouse, sur des terres peu propices à une occupation et fréquentées à certaines périodes, quand la pression sur la population ou l'agriculture l'exigeait.

Les fouilles révélèrent des témoignages d'occupation humaine intermittente du paysage de Cambourne qui s'étendent au minimum de l'âge du bronze moyen jusqu'à nos jours. On a retrouvé, sur trois sites, des témoignages éphémères d'occupation de courte durée à l'âge du bronze, tous ces sites se situaient à proximité de cours d'eau ou à l'intérieur de paléo-chenaux partiellement envasés.

A partir de l'âge du fer moyen, la campagne de Cambourne était exploitée par de petites communautés agricoles qui occupaient des maisons rondes, peut-être ouvertes à l'origine, elles furent plus tard implantées dans des enclos reliés par des sentiers de bouviers à de vastes systèmes de champs. Nous ne connaissons pas l'étendue totale de ces fermes, mais l'économie semble avoir en grande partie reposé sur l'élevage de bétail accompagné de quelques terres labourées. Mis à part le plus grand, et le plus complexe, des sites étudiés, à Lower Cambourne, la période finale de l'âge du fer semble avoir été témoin d'une récession avec l'abandon des occupations antérieures. Cela pourrait être en partie dû à l'augmentation de la saturation en eau des terres, ce qui rendait l'agriculture moins viable.

A partir du milieu du premier siècle après J.-C. de nouvelles occupations commencèrent à apparaître, peut-être en partie encouragées par la présence d'Ermine Street. En l'espace de plus ou moins un siècle, la zone devint assez densément peuplée avec ce qui semble être des occupations planifiées consistant en maisons rondes nichées dans des enclos et des systèmes de champs. Plusieurs sites furent remodellés à la période romano-britannique tardive, ceci est particulièrement évident pour celui à Lower Cambourne où deux enclos rectilignes furent établis, bien qu'aucune de ces fermes ne semble avoir été très pospère et qu'il y ait peu d'évidence qu'elles aient profité du commerce le long d'Ermine Street. D'un intérêt particulier, cependant, étaient trois 'dépôts disposés' à Lower Cambourne qui comprenaient des récipients en étain, des récipients en verre et des parties en fer d'une charrue. L'élevage de bétail et quelques terrescultivées semblent avoir formé les principaux constituants de l'économie à la période romano-britannique, comme ils l'avaient été à la fin de l'âge du fer.

Il se peut que l'occupation à Lower Cambourne se soit prolongée jusque dans les débuts du cinquième siècle et ici, tout comme dans quatre autres sites, il existe quelques traits énigmatiques et de très petites quantités de trouvailles qui témoignent d'une activité au début et au milieu de la période saxonne. Ensuite, il semble qu'il y ait eu un hiatus jusqu'au douz ième ou treiz ième siècle, période pendant laquelle toute la zone passa en cultures labourées ; ce qui laissa les omniprésentes traces d'agriculture médiévale à sillons et billons, leurs vestiges ayant survécu sur le terrain jusqu'au vingtième siécle.

Traduction: Annie Pritchard

1. Introduction

James Wright

Project background

The Cambourne Development Area, covering approximately 600 hectares, lies 12 km west of Cambridge and the same distance from St Neots on the Cambridgeshire/Bedfordshire border (Fig. 1). The Cambourne development, a new settlement first proposed in the 1980s under the name of Swansley Wood, was to be situated between the A1198 (Ermine Street) and the A428. However, a Public Inquiry held in 1990 asked for the settlement area to be moved further from the A1198. Outline planning permission was subsequently granted by South Cambridgeshire District Council in April 1994 for the development of a new settlement within the parishes of Bourn and Caxton centred on NGR 532200 259500. The original master plan for Cambourne was published in May 1995. Development started in 1998, with access roads being rapidly followed by construction of the business park, a school, and much of Great and Lower Cambourne (Pls 1 and 2). Work was also undertaken on an eco-park, country park, and tree planting. Following changes in central government guidelines and the take-up rate of the first houses, the original master plan was updated by Randall Thorp, principally affecting Great and Upper Cambourne.

The Cambourne Consortium of TaylorWimpey and Bovis Homes undertook the development. Wessex Archaeology, retained by the Cambourne Consortium as their archaeological consultants, produced a staged programme of archaeological work to investigate the area of the Cambourne New Settlement to be affected by the proposed phases of the development.

A programme of archaeological work was undertaken prior to the commencement of development. A study was made of relevant documentary evidence and cartographic sources before fieldwork started. Aerial photographs were examined and previous excavation reports from around the area of the proposed development were consulted. Fieldwalking of the western part of the Development Area in 1989 proved unpromising and, subsequently, a 2% sample of the area of each development phase was evaluation with trial trenches (Fig. 2). Based on the results of the previous stages of archaeological fieldwork, Wessex Archaeology produced detailed research aims and methods for excavation, set out within a summary Research Design for the development as a whole (Wessex Archaeology 2000).

The development of roads and houses and the associated landscaping necessitated initial topsoil stripping and levelling, so the potential for preservation *in situ* was limited. Accordingly, it was proposed to carry out open-area excavations in the areas of archaeological significance identified during the evaluation. The potential survival of Iron Age, Romano-British, and Saxon remains was considered to be high. Specific issues to be addressed included:

- How and when was the area first cleared of woodland, and once cleared how did development proceed?
- How did human activity develop through time in relation to topographic features?
- How do changes in the settlement activity relate chronologically and spatially to social groups, land use and division, and environmental changes?
- When and how did major boundaries first develop, and did their function change over time?
- What were the routes and patterns of communication in prehistory, and how did the development of Roman roads affect the social network?
- How significant were the changes at the end of the Romano-British period, and what factors led to the formation of the Late Saxon and medieval settlement pattern that still survives?

Archaeological and historical background

Preliminary archaeological investigations of the Cambourne Development Area were carried out by Wessex Archaeology on behalf of the Richard Wood Partnership (Wessex Archaeology 1989). More recently, a summary of the documentary sources for Caxton and Bourn has been produced by W.H.H. van Sickle on behalf of Terry Farrell & Co (van Sickle 1995) and, subsequently, Susan Oosthuizen has undertaken an important study of Cambridge's medieval fields (Oosthuizen 2006) and detailed work on the agricultural development of the Bourn valley since the Late Saxon period (Oosthuizen 2008).

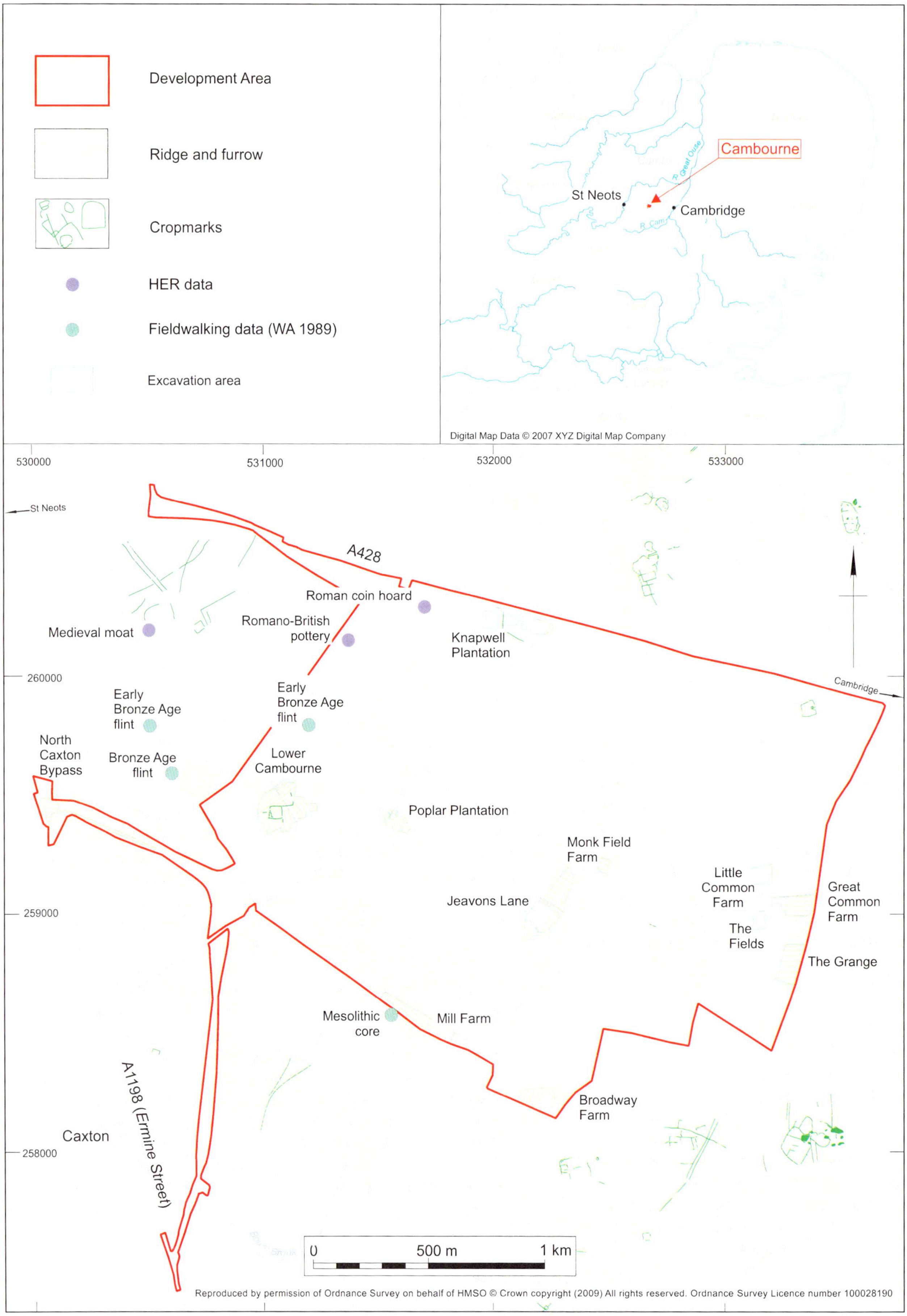

Figure 1 Site location, showing cropmarks (including medieval ridge and furrow), Heritage and Environment Records, fieldwalking results, and excavated sites

Plate 1 Cambourne from the west. The North Caxton Bypass is bottom right and the A428 upper left; the cruciform-plan runways of Bourn airfield, upper centre left, mark the eastern boundary of the Cambourne Development Area.

Cropmark evidence has been mapped and interpreted by Air Photo Services Ltd on behalf of Wessex Archaeology (Cox and Deegan 1996; Deegan 1996).

Prior to the start of the Cambourne development little was known about the archaeology of the area. It had been assumed that the clay subsoil was not amenable to prehistoric agriculture and that the area had not been settled. As recently as 30 years ago the *Victoria County History* declared that the clay uplands of western Cambridgeshire were not suitable for arable agriculture until the Romans brought in a heavy plough capable of turning the intractable soils (*VCH* Cambridgeshire, I, 303).

The Cambridgeshire Historic Environment Record (HER) was consulted but contained few records within the Development Area (Fig. 1). A Romano-British pottery scatter is recorded at NGR 53137 26016 close to the western boundary and a Roman coin hoard at NGR 5317 2603, although the accuracy of the grid location of the latter has been questioned. Other records within the HER relate to cropmarks and finds from fieldwalking or to post-medieval farmhouses and other buildings unaffected by the present proposals. For convenience, significant finds recovered during fieldwalking during the early stages of archaeological work are included in Figure 1.

Documentary evidence is summarised in van Sickle (1995) and the Royal Commission for Historical Monuments in England (RCHM(E)) (1968). It indicates that, prior to enclosure (in 1835), the area under investigation lay within a network of the common fields of Caxton and Bourn parishes. This was confirmed by cropmark and aerial photographic evidence, which shows ridge and furrow cultivation throughout the Development Area (Fig. 1).

All available aerial photographic evidence was mapped and interpreted for the area between NGR 530000 258000 (at the south-west) and NGR 534000 260000 (north-east). This comprised the agricultural land between Caxton, Bourn, Bourn Airfield, and the A428 Cambridge to Bedford road. Sites located immediately outside this area were also included (Cox and Deegan 1996). The study revealed a number of small ditched enclosures within the survey area which (on the basis of comparable examples elsewhere) were thought probably to represent Iron Age or Romano-British farmsteads (Fig. 1). In particular, two major cropmark complexes, comprising trackways, enclosures and possible field plots, were plotted immediately north of the village of Bourn, both lying outside the Development Area to the south-east. Independent research, funded by the RCHM(E), in

Plate 2 Cambourne from the east. The trees of Poplar Plantation are right of centre, with the excavation there in progress on the near side. The site of the Lower Cambourne excavation is immediately to the left of the new buildings in the centre of the photograph © Air Photo Services Ltd 2001

the claylands of the Bourn area has demonstrated that modern ploughing is eroding the traces of medieval ridge and furrow cultivation that hitherto masked cropmarks of earlier features, allowing the observation of the traces of earlier activity (Palmer 1996). Consequently, Air Photo Services Ltd was commissioned to carry out a new photographic sortie in late July 1996 (Deegan 1996). This revealed one ditched enclosure in the south-west of the Development Area. A previously unknown enclosure was also recorded to the south-east of the Development Area, and known enclosures were mapped in greater detail.

Recent evaluation excavations at two sites *c.* 4.75 km to the south-east at Highfields, Caldecote (NGR 5349 2583 and 5354 2587) revealed extensive management of the landscape in the form of two field systems. One of these proved to be of Late Iron Age/early Romano-British date with an associated settlement or farmstead, the other was laid out after the Roman Conquest (Oakey 1996; Leith 1997; Kenney 2007). In addition, the recently published results of a series of excavations undertaken in 2005 in connection with the A428 Caxton to Hardwick Improvement Scheme, along the northern edge as well as to the east and west of the Development Area, have been extensively referred to in the publication here (Abrams and Ingham 2008).

Geological and topographical background

The Development Area lies within the north-east to south-west trending Jurassic and Cretaceous deposits that extend from Yorkshire, Lincolnshire, and Norfolk to Dorset. To the west a *c.* 20 km wide exposure of Jurassic Oxford Clay forms a relatively flat landscape. To its east are the Jurassic Corallian Limestone and a narrow band of Kimeridge Clay. Further east Cretaceous deposits commence, and a narrow band of Lower Greensand is succeeded by Gault Clay. Cambourne lies over the Gault, and *c.* 15 km to its east is the Chalk. The clays form a generally flat landform, while the Chalk is more varied in height and slope. The drift geology consists of a blanket of

Boulder Clay often incised by river valleys which contain terrace gravels, alluvium and peat. In the Great Ouse and Cam or Granta valleys *c.* 20 km to the north-east are the nearest deposits of alluvium and peat surrounding the Wash.

In the Development Area the solid geology is not closely mapped as it is sealed by glacial drift deposits. However, in the north-west of the Development Area the solid geology is believed to comprise clays of the Upper Jurassic period unconformably overlain to the south-east by Sands and Sandstones of the Lower Cretaceous. The drift geology of the Development Area comprises Upper Tills or Boulder Clay derived largely from Triassic Marls. It is predominantly yellowish-brown clay with erratics of chalk, flint, some shale, carboniferous sandstone, and igneous and metamorphic rocks. There is localised variation across the Development Area with a concomitant effect on soils. The soils are mapped as the Hanslope Series, typically calcareous pelosols with clayey, water retentive topsoils that are prone to seasonal waterlogging and drought; they are often poorly drained, especially where the plateau is level (Soil Survey 1984, 190–1). Waterlogging and drying were encountered during the excavations but are likely to have always been a problem. Because the upper soil horizons are well structured and moderately permeable some rainwater is absorbed but prolonged heavy rain results in the lateral flow of excess water, and it is clear that considerable efforts to control drainage were taken in the Iron Age and Romano-British periods at some of the sites excavated.

Cambourne lies in the Cambridgeshire Western Clay Uplands which reach heights of *c.* 70 m aOD. It is on a plateau between the Great Ouse to the north and the Bourn Brook to the south (Fig. 2). It is not centrally located on this plateau and includes more of the south-draining catchment area of the Bourn than of the Great Ouse. Streams flowing both north and south have incised wide shallow valleys into the plateau. The Bourn drains east to join the Cam, which flows north before joining the Great Ouse and reaching the North Sea via the Wash.

The present settlements in the area follow the Bourn Brook (Bourn, Caxton, and Toft) to the south and/or are located along roads (Caxton on the A1198 and Eltisley and Hardwick on the A428). Measuring approximately 3 km east–west and 2 km north–south, the development lies just south of the A428 and comprised almost exclusively agricultural land divided into relatively small fields bounded by hedgerows with few trees. Arable agriculture was still being practised in some fields at the time of the development, but large areas had not been cultivated for several years and were fallow. Ploughing with conventional and mole ploughs was undertaken and many ceramic field drains had been laid to alleviate waterlogging. During evaluation and excavation the remains of land drains and traces of mole ploughing were frequently encountered; they demonstrate the drainage problems that the heavy clay soils create. Mole ploughmarks could penetrate 0.2–0.3 m below the level of machining during evaluation/excavation.

There was one surviving farm, Monk Field Farm, within the Development Area; more are shown on the Ordnance Survey (OS) map of 1891 along the eastern limit of development, including Little Common Farm, Great Common Farm, and Mill Farm. Fourteen residential properties remained, as did a number of abandoned agricultural buildings. The Development Area was relatively clear of woodland in comparison with adjacent areas, in particular compared with the south-west, which is the northern end of the Bedfordshire Greensand Ridge, or the ridge between St Neots and Cambridge. Three woods exist, all larger than shown on the 1891 OS map. The policy of the Cambourne Consortium of preserving natural features and habitats and using, where practicable, existing drainage has meant that the three woods, many hedges, and field boundaries have not been investigated archaeologically.

Fieldwork methods

A rapid walkover survey and limited fieldwalking were undertaken at the start of the project. Both techniques were found to be of limited value; the only visible earthworks were the medieval ridge and furrow already plotted from aerial photographs, while many of the fields were not suitable for fieldwalking. Small watching briefs were maintained on archaeologically less sensitive areas, particularly during infrastructure works, and some geophysical survey by fluxgate gradiometer was also undertaken.

The main evaluation technique adopted was that of trial trenching by mechanical excavator (Fig. 2). Trenches were typically 2 m wide and 50 m long, usually arranged in a grid pattern aligned north–south and east–west. The evaluation work was carried out in stages, from February 1999 and continued to August 2006, to match the infrastructure work areas and then subsequently the phased Development Areas which the infrastructure served. The trenches covered between 2% and 3% of each development plot, and *c.* 800 trial trenches with a total length of 40 km were excavated over the Development Area.

It was found during the evaluations that there were very few isolated features, and that ditches, pits, etc, were closely grouped around settlements. For such areas, in consultation with the Archaeological Officer for Cambridgeshire County Council, a Written Scheme of Investigation (WSI) was prepared proposing preservation by record of the presumed

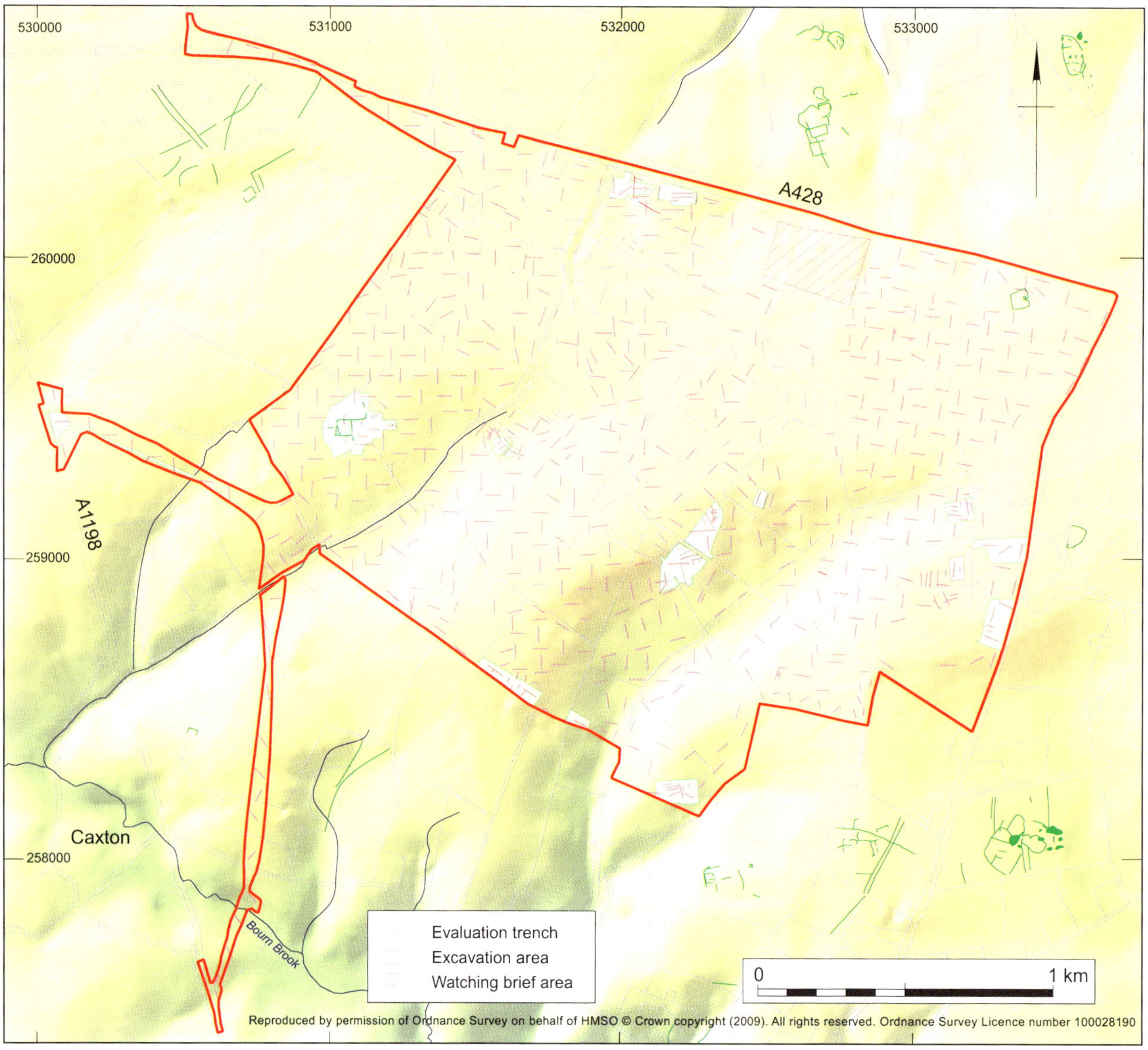

Figure 2 Terrain model of Cambourne, showing location of evaluation trenches and excavated sites

settlements. Twelve areas contained concentrations of ditches, pits, and post-holes with associated pottery and were selected for open area excavation (Figs 1 and 2). Only areas where development was taking place were excavated, so some sites were not fully exposed; for instance the North Caxton Bypass was 10 m wide and 500 m long and a complete understanding of the archaeology to the north and south of the road was not achieved. Similarly, at Jeavons Lane, an existing road ran through the site but as this was not being disturbed it was not excavated. Mill Farm was on the southern edge of the development and Knapwell Plantation on the northern edge; in both cases archaeological features and artefacts may extend beyond the excavated areas.

Two broad stages of mitigation were proposed for each site investigated, allowing a re-evaluation of progress towards achieving the project's research aims. First, the archaeology of each site was characterised in terms of broad structures, dating, sequence, and land-use, by stripping and planning and excavating a preliminary systematic sample of the archaeological features. The results of this work informed the second stage which involved a more detailed level of sampling in order to provide evidence for how people lived and used the landscape.

Each excavation area was stripped of topsoil and subsoil by means of 360° tracked excavators with toothless buckets, under the constant supervision of an experienced archaeologist (Pl. 3). After topsoil stripping, a pre-excavation site plan was produced using a Total Station Theodolite. On completion of the overall site plan, an appropriate strategy for the investigation and recording of the archaeological features and deposits was agreed between Wessex Archaeology and the Cambridge County Council Archaeology Office.

The following minimum strategy was employed at each site:

Plate 3 Topsoil stripping at Lower Cambourne in winter

- all ditch terminals were excavated and all significant relationships defined and investigated; in addition sufficient lengths of each ditch were excavated to establish its date, character, and function across its full length within the stripped area, especially with consideration given to the recutting of ditches;
- 90% of ring gullies on most sites were excavated;
- at least 50% was excavated of all pits, hearths, or similar features;
- excavation of other features attempted, as a minimum, to establish their stratigraphic relationship to other features, their nature, extent, date, and function.

All artefacts were retained from excavated contexts unless they were undoubtedly of modern or recent origin. In these circumstances sufficient material was retained to establish the date and function of the feature. The presence of modern artefacts was, however, noted on context records. All finds were washed, counted, weighed, and identified; selected assemblages were assessed and analysed further.

Bulk soil sampling (10 litres minimum) from appropriate deposits was undertaken for artefactual, economic, environmental, and dating (radiocarbon) data. Environmental soil sampling was principally directed towards recovering charcoal and charred plant remains. All procedures were in accordance with Wessex Archaeology's environmental and artefact sampling policy.

All archaeological features and deposits were recorded using Wessex Archaeology's *pro forma* recording system which includes a continuous unique numbering system. Detailed plans of individual features were produced at 1:20 and sections were drawn at 1:10. The Ordnance Datum (OD) height of all principal features and levels was calculated and plans/sections were annotated with OD heights. A full photographic record was maintained using both colour transparencies and black and white negatives (on 35 mm film). The photographic record illustrates both the detail and the general context of the principal features, finds excavated and the site as a whole.

Post-excavation programme

There are over 30 unpublished client reports for various elements and phases of the Cambourne project, the earliest being the initial fieldwalking (Wessex Archaeology 1989). Reports on the large number of evaluations undertaken are listed in an appendix to the bibliography but are not otherwise referenced in this volume. There is a project design for the excavations (Wessex Archaeology 2000), and interim statements of results were prepared covering

Table 1 Site-wide phasing

Phase	*Date range*	*Sub-phase*
0	Natural: palaeochannels & undated tree hollows	
1	Bronze Age (MBA–LBA)	
2	Midle/Late Iron Age ('later Iron Age')–early Romano-British: *c.* 400 BC–mid/late 2nd century AD	Phase 2A: unenclused Iron Age Phase 2B: enclosed Iron Age Phase 2C: early Romano-British
3	Mid–late Romano-British: *c.* AD 150/200–400	Phase 3A Phase 3B
4	Saxon: 410–11th century	
5	Medieval: 1066–1499	
6	Post-medieval–modern: 18th–20th centuries	

all of the sites investigated (Wessex Archaeology 2003; 2004a; 2004b). Finally, there is an assessment report and project design for post-excavation assessment, analysis, and publication (Wessex Archaeology 2005).

Assessment and analysis initially comprised a detailed examination of site records and the preparation of intra-site narratives. A database and Global Information System (GIS) were constructed as aids to the programme of analysis. Finds and environmental analyses and reporting were undertaken on artefact or ecofact assemblages from individual sites where detailed study and publication were recommended at the assessment level.

A rationalised phasing (Table 1) has been applied to all of the 12 sites excavated at Cambourne. Phase 2 has been assigned a broad period, divided into three sub-phases, Phases 2A and 2B spanning the Middle–Late Iron Age which have proved difficult to clearly distinguish on ceramic and other artefactual grounds, though there appears to have been a change from unenclosed to enclosed settlement within the 'later Iron Age'. This term is employed in this report to encompass this

PHASE	1 (MBA-LBA)	2A (M/LIA)	2B (M/LIA-ERB)	2C (ERB)	3A (M-LRB)	3B (M-LRB)	4 (Saxon)	5 (Med)	6 (P-med-mod)
North Caxton Bypass						✓		✓	✓
Lower Cambourne	✓	✓	✓	✓	✓	✓	✓	✓	✓
Poplar Plantation			✓					✓	✓
Mill Farm	✓					✓		✓	✓
Knapwell Plantation		✓	✓	✓		✓	✓	✓	✓
Jeavons Lane			✓			✓	✓	✓	✓
Broadway Farm			✓					✓	✓
Monk Field Farm						✓	✓	✓	✓
Little Common Farm		✓	✓					✓	✓
The Fields			✓		✓			✓	✓
Great Common Farm						✓		✓	✓
The Grange						✓	✓	✓	✓

Figure 3 Report-wide phasing scheme (sites by phase)

Plate 4 Excavations in progress at Lower Cambourne in 2000/2001, the wettest winter on record

period. Phase 2 also includes the early Romano-British period, as sub-phase 2C, to reflect the fact that the arrival of the Romans had no obvious effect on the morphology and nature of the existing settlements, with no clear changes becoming apparent until the middle of the 2nd century AD (Phase 3). The phases represented on each of the 12 excavated sites are shown in Figure 3.

Layout of this volume

Chapter 2 presents a description by individual site of the archaeological components, ordered by phase. The sites are described from west to east. Chapters 3–6 give a synthetic account of the development of Cambourne from the Mesolithic period through to medieval times. This draws together the stratigraphic, artefactual, and environmental evidence and places it in a local and regional context.

Detailed reports on the artefact and ecofact assemblages are provided as specialist appendices available in Volume 2 which is published on CD (inside the back cover of this volume) and online at: http://www.wessexarch.co.uk/projects/cambridgeshire/cambourne/publication/reports. The artefact reports are arranged by material, and the ecofact reports by material and, within each material category, by site. The excavation archive will be deposited at the Cambridgeshire County (Council) Archaeological Store.

2. The Sites

James Wright

North Caxton Bypass

The route of the northern part of the North Caxton Bypass runs from west of the Crow Dean track (NGR 530900 259000) to the A1198 north of Caxton (NGR 530050 259450) (Fig. 1). It crosses two ridges and a stream, all tending to the south-west (Fig. 2), and ranges in height from 59 m to 61 m aOD.

The site was situated at the western end of the Bypass route, at the junction with the Ermine Street Roman road, presently the A1198, approximately 300 m north of the village of Caxton. The site comprised a 10 m wide strip, 460 m in length, together with a larger area 100 m by 40 m at the west end adjoining the A1198 (centred on NGR 530400 259500) (Fig. 4). At the time of the excavation the site was under arable cultivation.

In addition to the archaeological features noted, part of a palaeochannel was recorded (Phase 0), at least 16 m wide and 0.55 m deep, at the eastern end of the excavated area. Romano-British pottery was recovered from the surface. A nearby stream/drain flows south-west to Caxton where it joins the Bourn Brook.

Phase 1 – Bronze Age

Despite the lack of dating evidence from a small roundhouse and a possible pen these have been included in this phase on typological grounds. The post-built roundhouse, and that from Lower Cambourne (below), both differ from all the other roundhouses within the Development Area in their lack of drip-gullies and their small size. The other roundhouses are at least 10 m diameter, have few if any post-holes but do have well defined drip-gullies. Similar small, post-built roundhouses have been shown generally to be earlier than Late Bronze Age/Early Iron Age, and accordingly the one from this site is included in Phase 1.

The roundhouse (RH30092) and a possible pen (30212) were identified in the middle of the site, beneath a ridge and furrow headland of up to 0.7 m depth (Fig. 4). The relationship between the roundhouse and pen is uncertain, the latter may have continued under the northern edge of the site.

The roundhouse was approximately 5.5 m in diameter, defined by seven regularly spaced post-holes *c.* 2 m apart (one is assumed to be beyond the stripped area, to the south), with diameters of 0.26–0.3 m and depths of 0.15–0.28 m. Two internal features were recorded, although only one (post-hole 30093) is likely to have been structural in nature. No evidence was found for an associated drip-gully or an entrance. The spacing between two post-holes on the south-eastern side (traditionally the most likely area for an entrance) was slightly larger, at 2.3 m, although this was also the case on the north-western side of the structure. A sample obtained from the single fill of post-hole 30080, on the south-east side, contained fragmented wood charcoal, probably dispersed or discarded fuel debris, and small amounts of charred grain.

Partly enclosing or overlapping with the northern half of the roundhouse was a possible pen (30212), measuring 14 m by 4 m, comprising a roughly rectangular arrangement of 10 post-holes, 0.28–0.4 m in diameter and 0.2–0.5 m deep. The post-holes were irregularly spaced, but the three in the west (30165, 30145, and 30143) were more substantial, with 30165 measuring 0.75 m by 0.5 m by 0.45 m deep.

Phase 3 – Romano-British

Romano-British features were present throughout the length of the site. They comprised a regular network of ditches/field boundaries and a group of pits in the south-east (Fig. 4).

A total of 17 ditches was recorded, mainly concentrated in the western half of the site. Most of the ditches, which were, on average, 0.7–0.8 m wide and 0.25–0.3 m deep, were 18–25 m apart, sealed by ploughsoil and orientated either NNW–SSE or NNE–SSW. At the western end of the site, one ditch (30018) ran WNW–ESE, forming part of a common boundary, with at least one other ditch (30015), creating a series of narrow fields to the south. The ditches at this end of the site are broadly parallel to Ermine Street but, further to the east, this is not generally the case, possibly for topographic reasons. Ditch 30214, the easternmost of the 'parallel ditches' towards the west end of the site, contained cereal processing waste. Ditch 30209 terminated within the site, possibly forming an access point between fields.

Ditch 30219, to the east of the Phase 1 roundhouse, was notable in that its irregular position within the field system and orientation (broadly

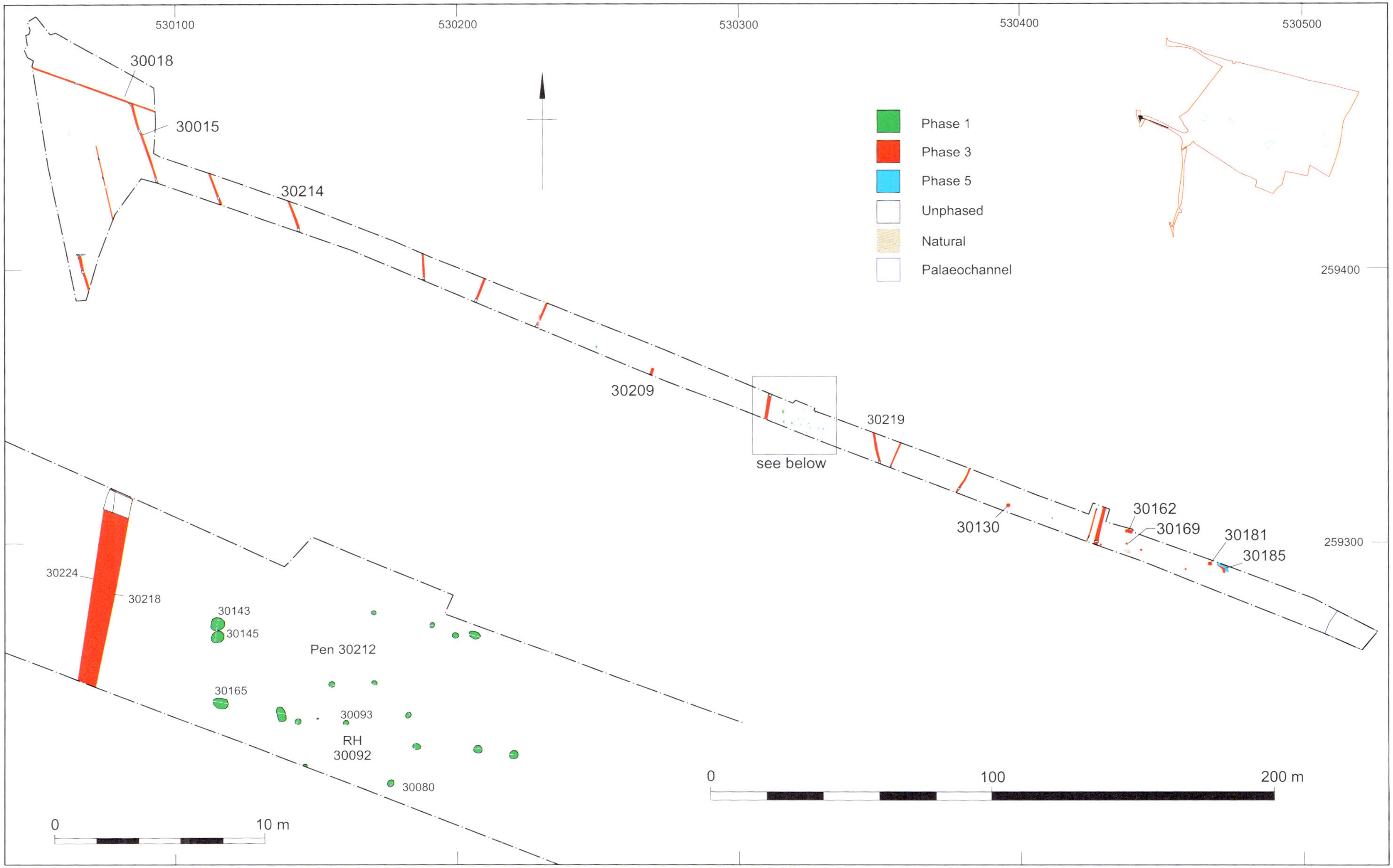

Figure 4 North Caxton Bypass: Bronze Age (Phase 1) and Romano-British (Phase 3) features

parallel to Ermine Street) appears to separate it from the surrounding field pattern. To the west of the roundhouse were two contiguous, parallel ditches (30218 and 30224), with an uncertain relationship. Five of the ditches produced small quantities of datable material, consisting mainly of Romano-British sandy grey coarsewares. A small quantity of abraded Iron Age pottery was also present.

Towards the eastern end of the site was a group of discrete features, including three pits containing large quantities of fire-reddened stones: pits 30162 (2.45 m by 1.1 m and 0.48 m deep), 30169 (0.76 m by 0.6 m and 0.23 m deep), and 30181 (1.3 m in diameter and 0.22 m deep). Pit 30181 produced much of the pottery recovered from the site and its dark, charcoal-rich fill also contained animal bone and a relatively large quantity of cereal processing waste. Pits 30169 and 30162 contained some cereal processing waste and small quantities of pottery. To the west, pit 30130 contained small sherds of pottery, animal bone, and fired clay. Charcoal from pits 30130 and 30181 indicates fuel debris from domestic hearths. A large irregular pit or ditch terminus (30185), at least 4.3 m in length, 2.8 m wide and 0.63 m deep, lay immediately east of pit 30181 and continued under the northern edge of the site. This feature contained a concentration of burnt stone and charcoal as well as a single piece of iron slag. The impression gained in this part of the site is of occupation close by, with waste from hearths being tipped into pits. An occupation site here would match the positions of other settlement sites within the Development Area, which are often located on the on south-west facing slopes of valleys.

Phase 5 – Medieval

Ridge and furrow was present, aligned almost parallel to the site (Fig. 1). As noted above, it was discontinuous near roundhouse 30092 where the headland ridge had been.

Lower Cambourne

Lower Cambourne was the largest and most complex of the sites excavated within the Development Area (Fig. 1), and incorporated areas designated as School Lane, Lower Cambourne Green, Lower Cambourne Collector Roads, and Lower Cambourne 15 & 16. The site lay in the west of the Development Area, centred on NGR 531080 259460, at 63 m aOD on a gentle, south-east facing slope between the crest of a ridge and a stream (Fig. 2). It comprised an approximately rectangular area measuring 210 m by 150 m (3.3 ha).

Features of Phases 0–5 were present, Phase 0 comprising natural features and undated tree hollows. Phases 1 (Bronze Age) and 4 (Saxon) had few features and most activity was divided between Phases 2 (Iron Age–early Romano-British) and 3 (mid–late Romano-British). Phase 2 is sub-divided into Phases 2A, 2B, and 2C, Phases 2A and 2B producing only Iron Age pottery and Phase 2C producing a mixture of Iron Age and early Romano-British material. The change from Phase 2 to 3 is represented by a major realignment of enclosures, and has been dated on the evidence of coins to the second half of the 2nd century AD.

It should be emphasised here that the excavation of this site was made more complex by it being done in several stages, often in difficult conditions, with some parts being flooded during periods of prolonged rainfall. This has made resolving the phasing a considerable challenge, particularly where features were shallow, contained little or no dating evidence, or where stratigraphic relationships could not be established. Therefore, the sequence that is presented here, particularly for Phases 2 and 3, is subject to some uncertainty. What follows is based on the stratigraphic evidence where this exists, artefact dating and, in some cases, the spatial relationship of certain features, notably some of the smaller ditches. Other features could only be assigned to a broad Phase 2 and here, particularly, there is scope for other sequences of features to that presented below.

Metal detectors were used to maximise the recovery of objects, many of which would otherwise have been lost. Approximately 140 coins and 16 brooches were retrieved from stratified deposits and three-dimensionally recorded. Their distribution shows strong patterning (see below) and it is presumed that the areas of their loss reflect the areas of the site being occupied or used during the period of currency of the coins. This patterning has been used to help clarify the stratigraphic sequence and augment the information provided by the analysis of pottery, other artefacts, and ecofacts.

Phase 0 – Undated and natural features

A palaeochannel (850) ran from north to south down slope for at least 57 m and was *c.* 10 m wide and 0.85 m deep (Fig. 5). The only stratigraphic relationships occurred where undated tree hollows could be seen within its fill of silty loam (the only feature on the site to contain such material). Its fill was possibly a relic of an earlier, aeolian soil that had overlain the calcarcous

Figure 5 Lower Cambourne: Bronze Age (Phase 1) features and palaeochannel

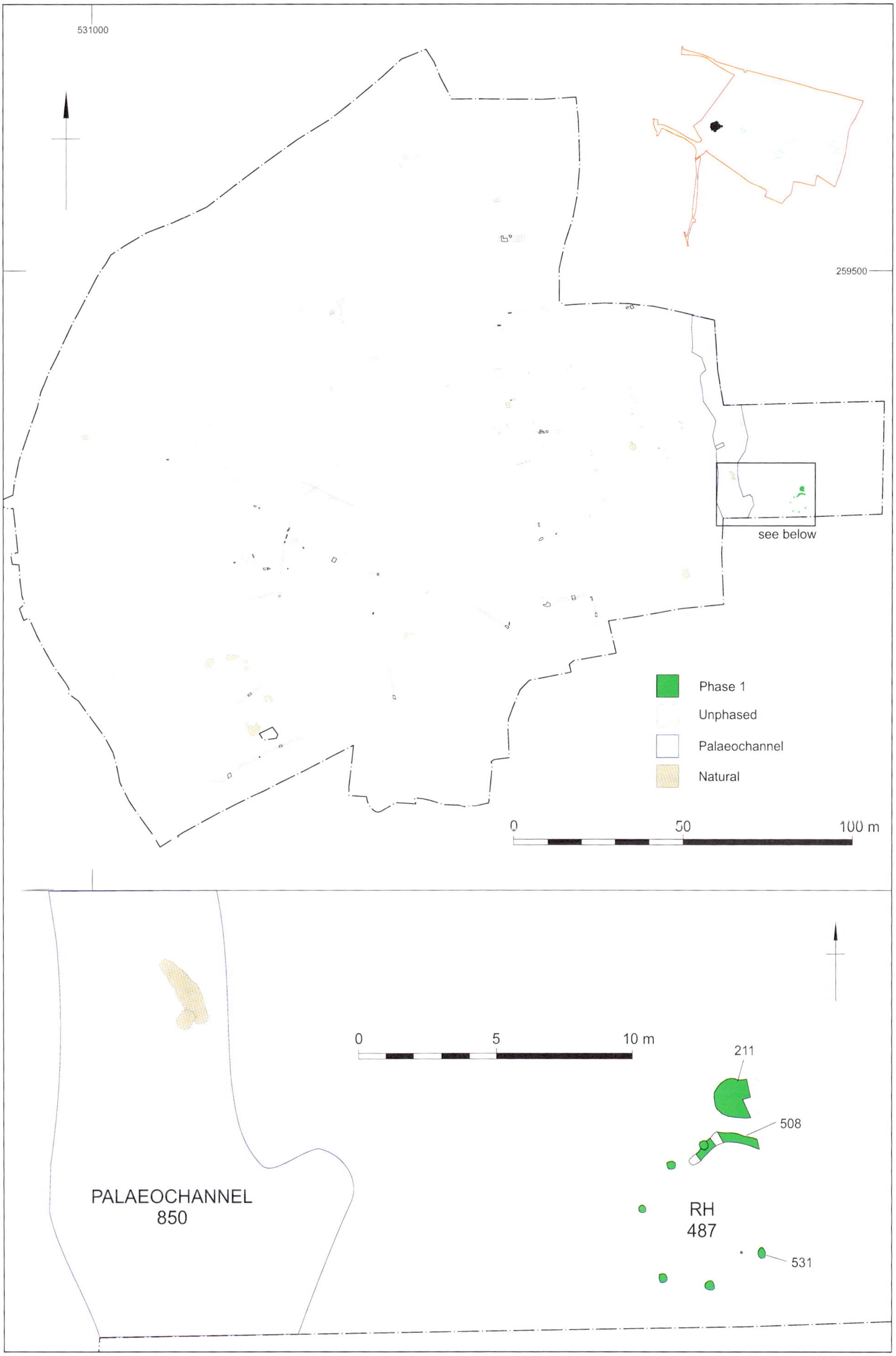
531000
259500
see below
Phase 1
Unphased
Palaeochannel
Natural
0
50
100 m
0
5
10 m
211
508
531
PALAEOCHANNEL
850
RH
487

Plate 5 Lower Cambourne: post-built roundhouse 487 (Phase 1)

clay and been eroded after tree clearance to survive only in this negative feature. A 2.9 m wide segment was excavated through the palaeochannel and though charcoal was observed near the base no artefacts or ecofacts were recovered.

Phase 1 – Bronze Age

There is no direct dating evidence for this phase and no Bronze Age pottery was recovered. A total of 135 pieces of worked flint was, however, retrieved and the flakes and scrapers may be of Bronze Age date, although a later period is also possible. All the features assigned to this phase occurred in the extreme east of the site (Fig. 5).

A small post-built roundhouse (487) (Pl. 5) was atypical of the other roundhouses on this site, being the only one that had post-holes but no drip-gully, and it was not obviously associated with any of the excavated enclosures. Although no dating evidence was recovered from it, it is tentatively assigned to the Bronze Age. A similar, undated roundhouse at North Caxton Bypass was also assigned a Bronze Age date.

Roundhouse 487 was represented by seven post-holes, five of them in a ring *c.* 5 m in diameter and a gully; medieval ridge and furrow ploughing had cut away the eastern side of the structure. Post-hole 531 was representative of the others, oval in shape, measuring 0.37 m by 0.28 m and 0.21 m deep. It contained two fills: clay probably used as post-packing and the possible fill of the post-pipe, containing some burnt stones; similar stones were recovered from the upper fills of the other post-holes and also from nearby pit 211. No artefacts were recovered but environmental samples from four of the post-holes contained waste from cereal processing and, in contrast to most of the samples within the Development Area, very few weed seeds. This may reflect a different method of cereal processing, possibly being undertaken on a smaller scale, but it does emphasise the difference between this post-built roundhouse and those defined by a drip-gully.

Gully 508, to the north of the roundhouse, was 0.3 m wide, up to 0.13 m deep and extended slightly across the circle formed by the post-holes. Pit 211 was oval, at least 1.6 m long by 1.6 m wide and 0.35 m deep. It is possible that a stream still existed in the palaeochannel during this phase, perhaps seasonally, and that the roundhouse was built close to the source of water that this may have provided.

Phase 2 – Middle/Late Iron Age–early Romano-British

The sequence of this phase (Fig. 6) is complicated by the fact that although the enclosures and roundhouses were broadly contemporary, the roundhouses routinely produced Iron Age pottery and the enclosure ditches Romano-British pottery. The Romano-British pottery (mostly 1st–2nd centuries AD) was not confined to tertiary fills but was often in primary fills, and it is assumed that this is because the enclosure ditches were regularly cleaned out, a supposition supported by the size of the ditches, often *c.* 3 m wide and over 1 m deep. It seems that when the ditches were cleaned out they were enlarged, as few re-cuts were observed during excavation.

Although few 1st century AD coins were present among the 137 recovered, the 16 brooches are all of this date. Over half of these brooches were recovered from Enclosures A and B, the two D-shaped enclosures (Phase 2B/2C), and all but one of the 2nd century coins came from within or immediately adjacent to Enclosure B, which also produced early Romano-British pottery (Fig. 7). The absence of coins from Enclosure A suggests either different uses of the two enclosures or that the western enclosure was in use during the 1st century AD but had been abandoned by the 2nd century. The majority of later coins came from Phase 3 Enclosures G and H. It appears, therefore, that Phase 2 occupation was concentrated in Enclosures A and B and continued there until possibly as late as the end of the 2nd century.

Phase 2A

The drip-gully of roundhouse 1343, which had a projected diameter of *c.* 14 m, is the only feature that can be shown to have been in use before the enclosures were constructed (Fig. 8). Although only less than a quarter of the gully survived on its southern side, its presumed northern side was respected by Enclosure A ditch 3111 (Phase 2B), which shows a marked change of course around it, indicating that the roundhouse was probably standing when the enclosure was constructed. Iron Age

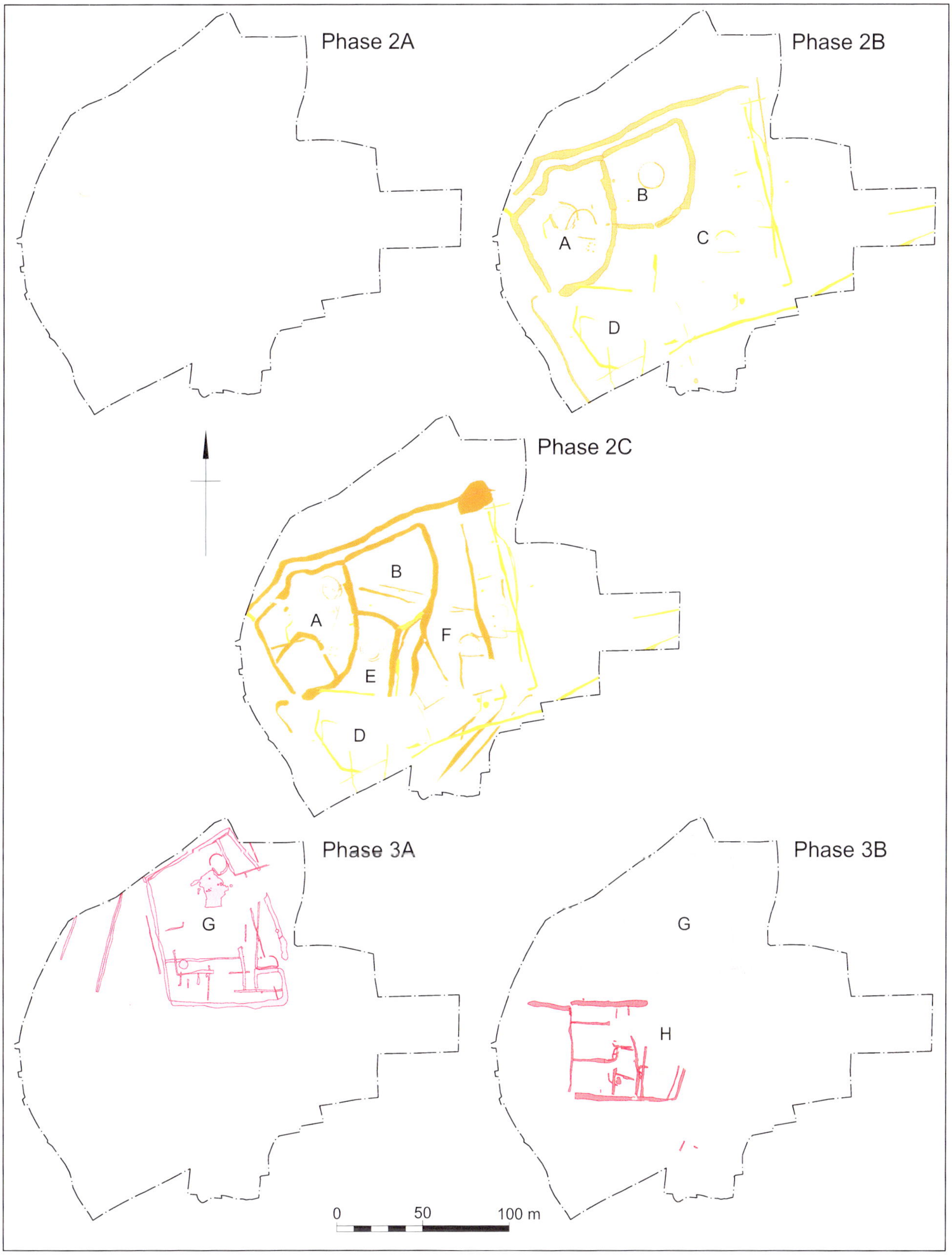

Figure 6. Lower Cambourne: sequence of later Iron Age (Phases 2A and 2B), Late Iron Age/early Romano-British (Phase 2C), and Romano-British (Phase 3) enclosures

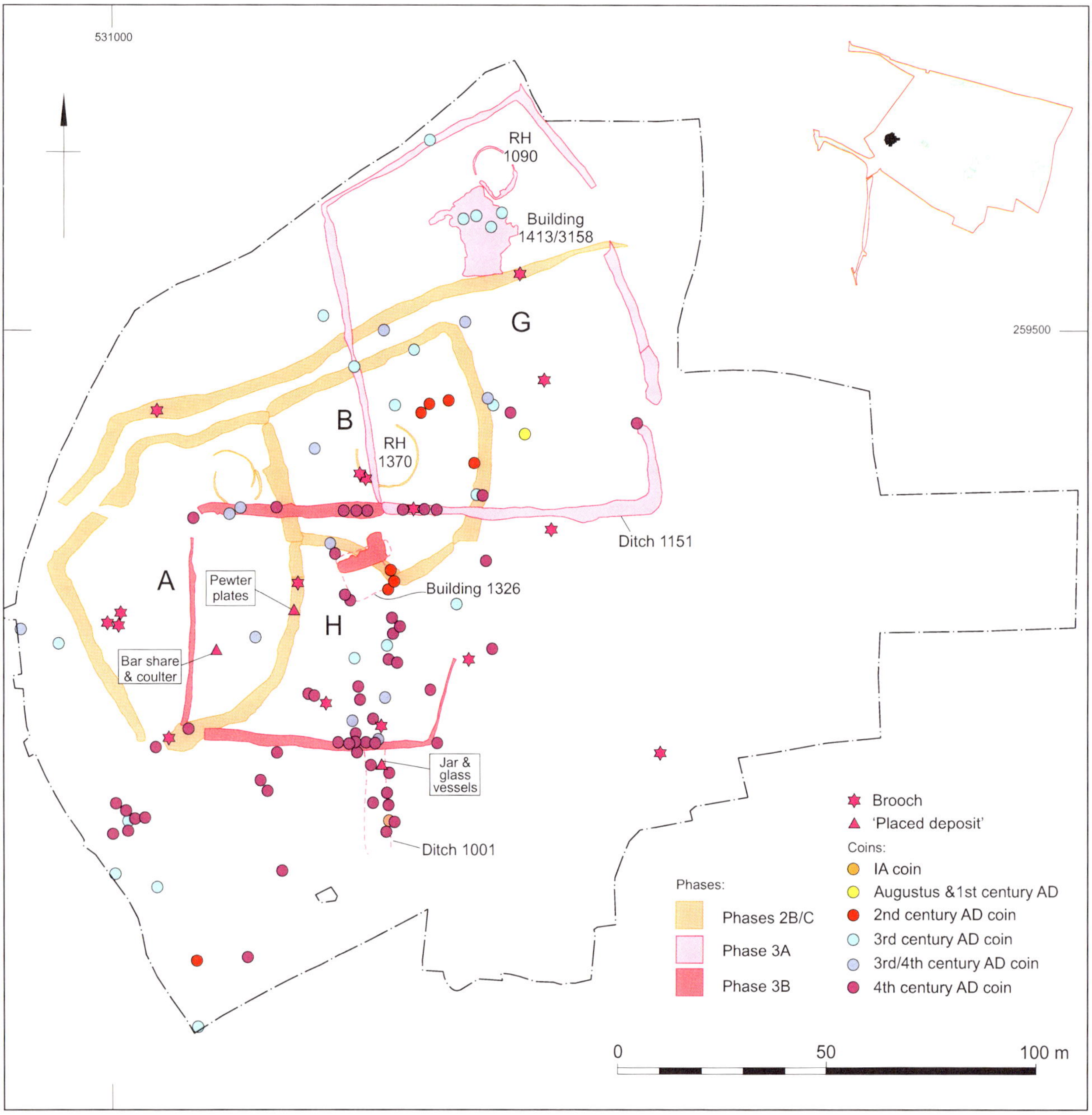

Figure 7 (above) Lower Cambourne: later Iron Age (Phase 2) and Romano-British (Phase 3) enclosures – distribution of brooches, coins, and 'placed deposits'

Figure 8. (opposite) Lower Cambourne: later Iron Age (Phases 2A and 2B) enclosures, droveways, roundhouses, and associated features

pottery, animal bone, and worked and burnt flint were recovered from the drip-gully. A single, intrusive sherd of post-medieval pottery was present in one context which also produced *c.* 100 g of Iron Age sherds.

The phasing of roundhouse 5406, less than 10 m to the south, is uncertain. It might also belong to Phase 2A, but its proximity to roundhouse 1343 and its central location within Enclosure A, suggests that it may belong to Phase 2B; it is described further below.

Phase 2B

As noted above, roundhouse 1343 was apparently still standing when a D-shaped enclosure (Enclosure A) was constructed (Fig. 8). However, it is unclear why this enclosure was laid out so that the ditch on its northern side had to be dug around the roundhouse. A second, central, roundhouse, 5406, that may have replaced roundhouse 1343, lay within the centre of Enclosure A. It, in turn, was succeeded by what is

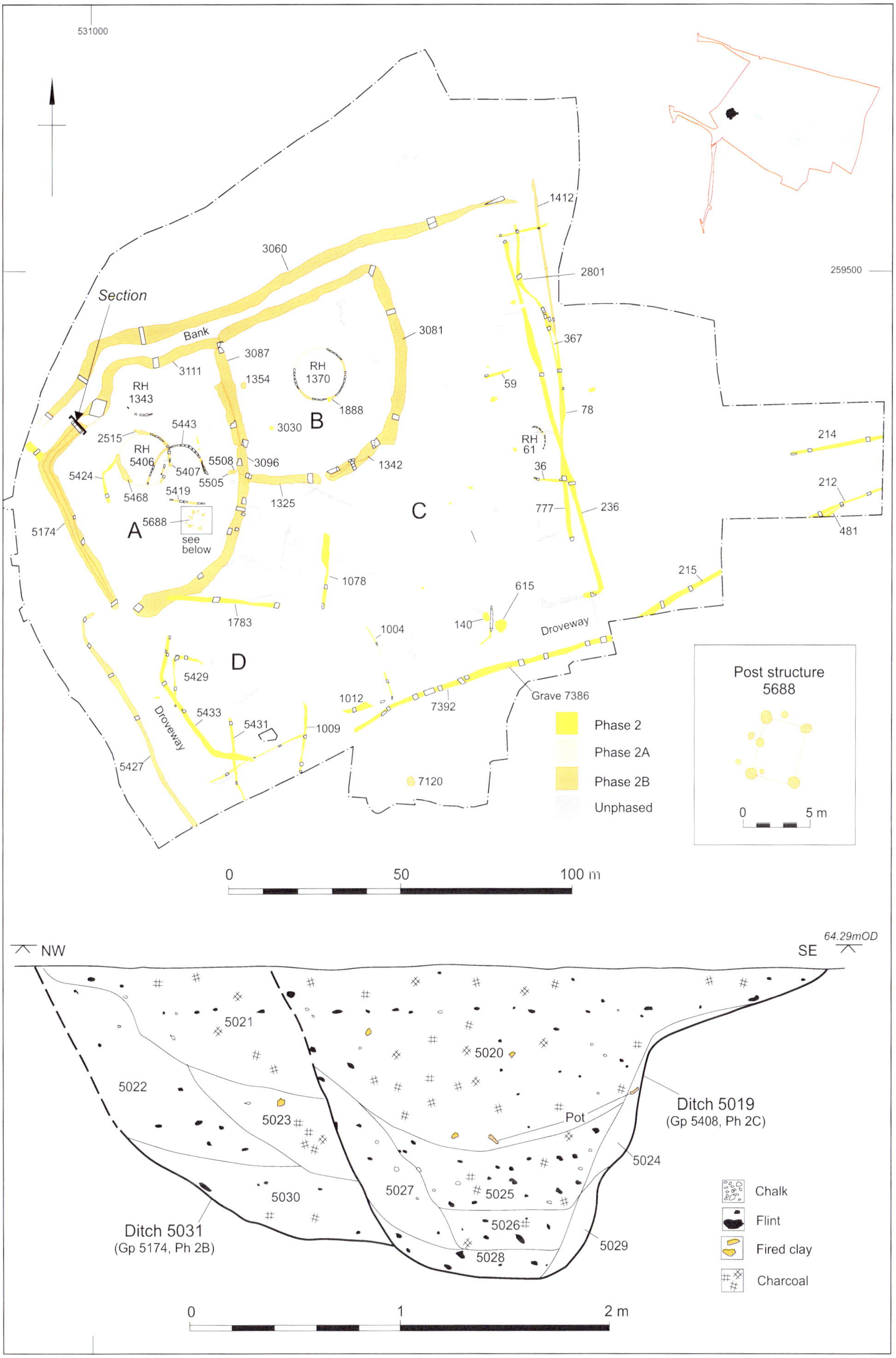
531000
259500
Section
Bank
3060
3081
3087
3111
RH 1343
RH 1370
1354
1888
3030
B
5443
2515
RH 5406
5407
5508
3096
5505
5424
5468
5419
1342
1325
5174
A
5688
see below
C
1412
2801
367
59
78
RH 61
36
777
236
214
212
481
215
1078
615
140
1783
1004
Droveway
D
5429
5433
5431
1012
7392
Grave 7386
1009
5427
Droveway
7120
Phase 2
Phase 2A
Phase 2B
Unphased
Post structure 5688
0
5 m
0
50
100 m
NW
SE
64.29mOD
5021
5022
5020
5023
Pot
Ditch 5019
(Gp 5408, Ph 2C)
5024
5027
5025
5030
5026
Ditch 5031
(Gp 5174, Ph 2B)
5028
5029
Chalk
Flint
Fired clay
Charcoal
0
1
2 m

interpreted as a shelter (5419 and 5443), possibly associated with a four-post structure (5688) and several other features, all of which are assigned to Phase 2B.

Possibly contemporary with Enclosure A was a slightly smaller D-shaped enclosure (Enclosure B) to the east, also containing a central roundhouse (1370). At the same time a substantial ditch (3060), running parallel to the north edges of Enclosures A and B, and a series of smaller ditches to the south, appear to have formed a large sub-rectangular enclosure (Enclosure C), which incorporated the two D-shaped enclosures and another (Enclosure D), less clearly defined and of irregular shape, in its south-west corner. One or two trackways may also belong to this phase.

Enclosure A and roundhouse 5406

Enclosure A covered an area of just under 0.25 ha. Its ditches (3087, 3096, 3111, and 5174) were generally between 2.5 m and 4 m wide and up to 1.5 m deep, with steep sides and rounded bases (see Fig. 8). However, the southern terminal of curved ditch 3096 defining its eastern side was *c.* 6 m wide and 2 m deep where it flanked the 5 m wide entrance in the southern corner of the enclosure, perhaps functioning also as a waterhole for animals. Pottery from the ditches largely reflects their recutting and subsequent infilling in Phase 2C rather than their construction and use in Phase 2B.

The entrance was approached from the south by a *c.* 10 m droveway defined by ditches 5427 and 5433, probably a spur which led off an east–west droveway exposed along the southern edge of the site. These ditches were relatively insubstantial, being 1.4 m wide and up to 0.4 m deep. The eastern ditch (5427) was recut at least twice but there was no sign of the western ditch having been recut.

Roundhouse 5406 was represented by short, truncated gullies (2515 and 5468) which indicated that it was *c.* 14 m diameter, possibly with a south-east facing entrance. Approximately 1 kg of Middle Iron Age pottery, animal bone, and fired clay were recovered from these gullies. They were cut by Phase 2C sub-enclosure ditch 5418 (Fig. 9), C-shaped gully 5443 (see below) and several later, Phase 3 ditches. Close to the presumed entrance was pit 5407, 0.18 m deep, which produced Middle Iron Age pottery, animal bone, fired clay, worked flint, and burnt, probably local, stone.

C-shaped gully 5443, together with straight gully 5419 lying 5 m to its south, may have defined a shelter or possibly a small enclosure *c.* 17 m wide. Gully 5443 contained mostly Middle Iron Age pottery and a smaller quantity of Late Iron Age sherds, as well as a burnt and part-worked igneous rock of unknown origin, *c.* 0.5 kg of fired clay, animal bone, and cereal processing waste. The fired clay suggests a wattle and daub structure, although most of this material was recovered from the northern part of the gully and may have derived from the demolition of one of the roundhouses. The south-east end of gully 5443 had been recut before it went out of use and was cut by ditch 5418 (Phase 2C). It is noteworthy that the layout and orientation of this shelter or enclosure is very similar to a Phase 2C structure in Enclosure F (see below).

To the south of the shelter was a sub-rectangular structure (5688) measuring 4.2 m by 3.2 m, with post-holes at the four corners and a fifth in the middle of one of the longer sides. Several other, smaller post-holes that might have been associated with the structure lay in the vicinity. Middle Iron Age pottery was recovered as was some waste from cereal processing.

Pits 5505 and 5508 close to the eastern edge of the enclosure produced Middle Iron Age pottery and probably also belong to this phase. Both pits were oval in plan, approximately 1.2 m by 1 m and 0.3 m deep, and contained fired clay and animal bone. Nearby were three similarly shaped pits, none with dating evidence, although one contained burnt stone.

Enclosure B and roundhouse 1370

Enclosure B, which covered a roughly D-shaped area of *c.* 0.2 ha abutting to the north-east side of Enclosure A, was defined by ditches 1325, 1342, and 3081. The ditches were between 2.7 m and 4.2 m wide and 1.3 m and 1.5 m deep, with steep sides and rounded bases. As with Enclosure A, pottery from the ditches is predominantly of a later phase (Phase 2C).

The earliest feature within Enclosure B, though possibly pre-dating it, was a keyhole-shaped hearth or kiln (1888), cut by roundhouse 1370. It was 1.7 m long, 1m wide and 0.43 m deep, and had been lined with a 0.35 m thick layer of clean bluish grey clay. Above the clay were four fills, all of which were recorded as ashy, but which contained no significant amounts of charcoal or charred plant remains. The only finds were a single sherd of Middle Iron Age pottery and a relatively small amount of animal bone.

Roundhouse 1370, which was 15 m in diameter, was centrally located inside the enclosure with a good view of the surrounding area. Its drip-gully, generally 0.4 m wide and 0.2 m deep, was truncated by later features particularly to the north-west; there was no evidence of an entrance to the east. Finds included Middle Iron Age pottery, animal bone, fired clay, and some fuel-ash slag.

Enclosure C

Parallel to and 10 m from the northern side of Enclosures A and B was a further substantial ditch (3060), with a bank between this and the enclosure ditches. This bank, an estimated *c.* 3 m high, survived at least in part into Phase 3, as shown by Phase 3 ditch 1369 (see below and Fig. 10) narrowing where it cut through the bank. The ditches and bank formed an earthwork 115 m long and *c.* 10 m wide which may have been dug to create a barrier to divert water away from the enclosures (and into Phase 2C pond 2716), but its length and size also would have made it an impressive feature in the surrounding landscape and it is possible, therefore, that it also served as a statement of status.

Ditch 3060 formed the north side of Enclosure C, which had overall dimensions of 120 m by 150 m and which enclosed Enclosures A and B within it. Enclosure C was bounded to the east, in part, by a much less substantial ditch (1412) which extended south for *c.* 50 m of the eastern end of ditch 3060. This boundary been recut on several slightly differing alignments, by ditches 78, 236, 367, and 777, together these being traced for just over 100 m. At the south ditch 236 turned to the west for 15 m where it terminated on the north side of a possible droveway, aligned ENE–WNW, which led into the south-east corner of the enclosure.

Approximately 12 m to the south, ditches 212, 215, and 7392 may have formed the southern side of the droveway, the latter forming the southern boundary of Enclosure C. An oval grave (7386; see Fig. 8) cut into the fill along the southern edge of ditch 7392, was approximately 1 m by 0.5 m, aligned west–east, and contained a crouched burial of an adult female aged *c.* 35–50 years (Pl. 6).

On the east side of Enclosure C was a truncated probable drip-gully, 61, with a projected diameter of *c.* 10 m. This survived to a maximum width of 0.25 m and a depth of 0.03 m and most probably represents a roundhouse. Two nearby pits contained some Romano-British pottery as well as Iron Age material, while a nearby post-hole contained half of a cylindrical loomweight. It is considered most likely that the roundhouse and pits belong to Phase 2B.

The east side of the Enclosure C was broadly parallel to palaeochannel 850 approximately 40 m to the east, but few features were recorded between them and this area appears to have been avoided, perhaps because it was still seasonally flooded. Ditch 214, east of the palaeochannel, may have formed part of the droveway's north side.

Enclosure D

Several shallow gullies among the complex of features in the south-west corner of Enclosure C may have defined a further, relatively small, irregularly shaped enclosure (Enclosure D) measuring *c.* 55 m by a maximum of 50 m. These included gullies 1004, 5433, and possibly 1783, the latter cutting Enclosure A ditch 3096. Gully 5433 also formed the east side of the droveway approaching the entrance to Enclosure

Plate 6. Lower Cambourne: grave 7386 (Phase 2B)

A. Other interpretations of these gullies are, however, possible, though it appears that various north–south aligned gullies (1009, 1078, 5429, and 5431) in this area were probably part of a different layout and are unlikely to have been contemporary with Enclosure D.

Phase 2C

Much of the earlier, Phase 2B layout was retained, with Enclosures A and B remodelled (Fig. 9). Enclosure C and the associated droveway to the south were replaced by a new arrangement of enclosures (E and F) with their own associated droveway; Enclosure D may have been incorporated within this arrangement. New roundhouses were constructed, in Enclosures A and E, though none of these overlapped the sites of earlier roundhouses and did not, therefore, directly replace them.

Enclosure A

Enclosure A was retained, although marked by some recutting of the ditches: ditch 3111 was recut as ditch 3080, ditch 3087 as 3089/1154, and ditch 5174 as 5408 (see Fig. 8). However, its internal layout was altered, with ditches 5404 and 5418 dug to create a sub-enclosure immediately inside the entrance, separate from the larger, northern part of the enclosure. Ditch 5418 was 3 m wide, compared with 2 m for ditch 5404, but both were 1.1 m deep, and there was a 2.3 m wide entrance gap between their terminals. Both ditches contained mostly Iron Age pottery with a small amount of Late Iron Age/early Romano-British material in the upper fills.

Roundhouses 1155 and 3067, in the northern part of the enclosure, overlapped but their sequence could not be established. Both were cut by Phase 3 ditches and further truncated by medieval ridge and furrow. Pottery recovered from them was fragmentary, with an average weight of 4 g, and comprised a mixture of Iron Age and 1st or 1st/2nd century Romano-British sherds. Roundhouse 1155 would have been slightly larger with a diameter of *c.* 13 m, compared to *c.* 11 m

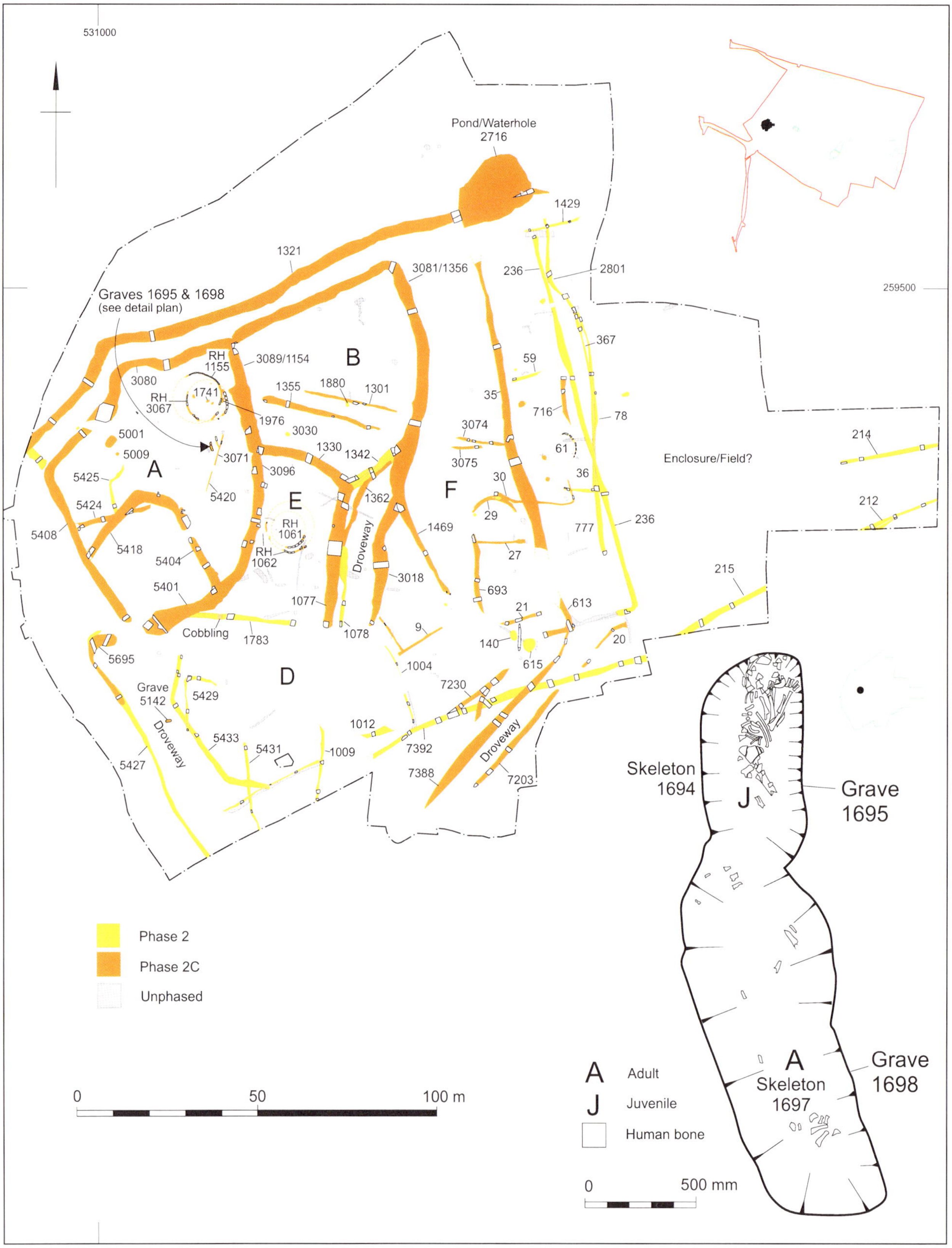

Figure 9. Lower Cambourne: Late Iron Age/early Romano-British (Phase 2C) enclosures, droveways, roundhouses, and associated features

Plate 7. Lower Cambourne: grave 5142 (Phase 2C)

for roundhouse 3067. Their drip-gullies were a maximum of 0.23 m wide and 0.18 m deep, but in neither could the locations of the entrances be established. However, the east side seems improbable in both cases because of the proximity of enclosure ditch 3089/1154, and a south-facing entrance is more likely.

There were several small pits or large post-holes in or around the roundhouses. Most were shallow and undated but pit 1741, which could have been in the centre of either roundhouse, contained a disturbed but possibly articulated ?animal burial. Pit 1976 may also have been an internal feature and contained Iron Age pottery and animal bone.

Two inhumation burials were recorded approximately 5 m to the south of the roundhouses. Both north–south aligned graves (1695 and 1698) were shallow, surviving to a depth of only 0.1 m (see Fig. 9). Although the graves overlapped it was not possible to determine their sequence. Only a few bones of an adult survived in grave 1698, with a juvenile of *c.* 5–6 years age in grave 1695. The few small sherds of pottery, recovered mostly from grave 1698, were a mixture of Iron Age and Romano-British in date. A third shallow grave (5142) lay between droveway ditches 5427 and 5433 to the south of the enclosure; this contained the skeletal remains of a male of over 45 years age (Pl. 7). Although it produced no datable material, it is tentatively assigned to this phase.

Enclosure B

A slight realignment in the south of this enclosure, with ditch 1330 replacing ditch 1325, may have been to facilitate drainage. The only features of this phase identified within the enclosure were two almost parallel ditches, 1301 and 1355. Ditch 1301 was *c.* 0.6 m wide and had a maximum depth of 0.5 m, whereas ditch 1355 was slightly larger at 1.4 m wide and between 0.5 m and 0.85 m deep. Both ditches produced a mixture of Iron Age and early Romano-British pottery, animal bone, and fragments of fired clay. Although parallel to ditch 1330, and possibly continuing as ditches 3074 and 3075 outside the enclosure to the east, there was no indication of why they were dug, probably towards the end of Phase 2C; they were both cut by Phase 3 ditches, while ditch 1301 cut Phase 2B roundhouse 1370.

It was not possible to determine when the various ditches running south from Enclosure B were dug, but it was probably at the same time, or shortly after, the south side of enclosure was remodelled. Ditches 1077, 1078, and 1362 to the west, and ditches 1469 and 3018 to the east all ran downslope away from the enclosure, and appear to have formed a droveway, perhaps linking Enclosures B and D. The ditches were up to 2.6 m wide and 1.3 m deep. Pottery was of Iron Age and early Romano-British date, with a small quantity of later Romano-British and some Saxon sherds in the upper fills. Other finds included animal bone, fired clay, several iron objects (probably nails), fuel ash slag, and burnt stone.

Enclosure E

Enclosure E was bounded by Enclosure A to the west, Enclosure B to the north, Enclosure D to the south and the droveway to the east. It measured *c.* 50 m by 35 m. The only access was through a 7.5 m wide gap east of ditch 1783 which separated it from Enclosure D. Ditch 1783 was heavily truncated by Phase 3 ditches but survived to a maximum width of 1.6 m and was 1.1 m deep. It contained Iron Age and Late Iron Age/early Romano-British pottery and a complete cow carcass.

Near the centre of Enclosure E was part of a drip-gully (1061), 0.5 m wide and 0.3 m deep, probably the heavily truncated remains of a roundhouse *c.* 11 m in diameter (Pl. 8). It contained a mixture of Iron Age and early Romano-British pottery, animal bone, fired clay, flint, and shell. One metre to its south was a slightly shorter length of gully (1062), with a projected diameter of *c.* 14 m, probably representing a second roundhouse, although the relationship

Plate 8. Lower Cambourne: roundhouses 1061 and 1062 (Phase 2C)

between the two is unclear. Both gullies were cut by Phase 3 ditches.

There were several pits (not numbered on plan) in or around the two roundhouses. The smallest measured *c.* 1 m diameter and was 0.2 m deep, with the largest measuring 2 m by 1.6 m and 1 m deep. Small amounts of undiagnostic Romano-British pottery, animal bone, and fired clay were present in some of these pits, with over 2 kg of pottery, some of 1st or 2nd century date, coming from pit 1931, the largest in the group.

Enclosure F

To the east of Enclosures B and E and the associated droveway was an area, bounded on the east side by ditch 35, which has been designated Enclosure F. Ditch 35, which was at least 80 m in length, possibly continuing to the south as ditch 613, lay at *c.* 90° to ditch 1321 to the north at the point where the latter drained into pond/waterhole 2716, at the enclosure's north-east corner. The pond/waterhole was *c.* 15 m in diameter and 1.1 m deep, its base metalled with rounded cobbles. It contained Romano-British pottery, some 1st or 2nd century date and some 2nd century or later, and may have been dug in Phase 2C, continuing in use into Phase 3.

The southern boundary to Enclosure F may have been defined by a droveway ditch (7388, see below) in which case the enclosure would have had an irregular shape, measuring possibly as much as 130 m long and 50 m wide.

On the west side of ditch 35, was a possible shelter or small enclosure formed by curvilinear gully 29 and straight gully 27 to the south. Gully 29 was between 0.5 m and 1.1 m wide and had a maximum depth of 0.6 m, while gully 27 was approximately 1 m wide and 0.25 m deep. This structure has tentatively been assigned to Phase 2C, though it might be earlier. At approximately 12 m across it was slightly smaller but otherwise similar in layout and orientation to the Phase 2B structure in Enclosure A (see above). Middle Iron Age pottery was recovered from gully 29, although some 1st–2nd century Romano-British sherds were also present. Ditches 693 and 21 to the south may also have been associated with this structure, as might ditches 9 and 7230 further to the south-west, all perhaps defining small pens.

Various isolated pits were probably dug at this time, including two immediately to the south of ditch 21. Pit 140 measured 3.7 m by 2 m and 1.8 m deep, and was waterlogged towards the base. Although scraps of preserved timber were noted none was large enough to retain, and some Iron Age pottery, animal bone, fragments of fired clay, and an unidentified iron object were the only artefacts recovered. A larger pit (615), to the south-east, was sterile.

It is possible that Enclosure F was flanked to the east by a square or rectangular field, possibly 120 m by at least 115 m, that extended beyond the limit of excavation to the east. The palaeochannel, approximately 60 m east of the enclosure, may have survived as a lower-lying, periodically wet area within this field. Running north-east into the south-west corner of the field was a droveway, *c.* 60 m long and 5 m wide, defined by ditches 613/7388 and 20/7203. A few shallow pits or scoops, and possibly two lengths of gully, may have been the only contemporary features within the field, but this remains uncertain.

Phase 3 – Mid–late Romano-British

In the middle–late Romano-British period the site was totally remodelled and the earlier, Phase 2 enclosures replaced by a new arrangement of rectilinear enclosures (Fig. 10). However, the droveway along the south of the site was retained in a modified form, whilst the eastern boundary to the enclosures remained in approximately the same location as it had been in Phase 2, reflecting the presence of the lower lying, probably occasionally flooded area to the east.

Phase 3 has been divided into two sub-phases. The start of Phase 3A, comprising a rectangular enclosure (Enclosure G) and buildings in the northern half of the site, appears to be in the latter part of the 2nd or the early 3rd century. Phase 3B, represented by a rectangular enclosure (Enclosure H) and building in the southern half of the site, seemingly belongs to the 4th century. The Phase 3A and 3B enclosures did not overlap and it seems certain that they probably co-existed in Phase 3B as part of a single entity.

The coin distribution (see Fig. 7) provides one of the principal chronological indicators for this sequence. In contrast the concentration of 2nd century coins within or immediately adjacent to Phase 2 Enclosure B (see above), over half of the 3rd century coins were found within Enclosure G containing presumed building 1413/3158 and roundhouse 1090 (Phase 3A). Only two of the 4th century coins were recovered from north of east–west ditch 1151 (Phase 3A/3B), and most were from within Enclosure H (Phase 3B) containing presumed building 1326, or from the large drainage ditch, 1001 (Phase 3), immediately to the south.

Phase 3A

Enclosure G

Enclosure G was sub-rectangular, measuring up to 100 m north–south by 70 m east–west, and was bounded by ditches 79, 1151, 1369, 1411, and 1418. The ditches were 1.5–2.6 m wide and 0.65–0.95 m

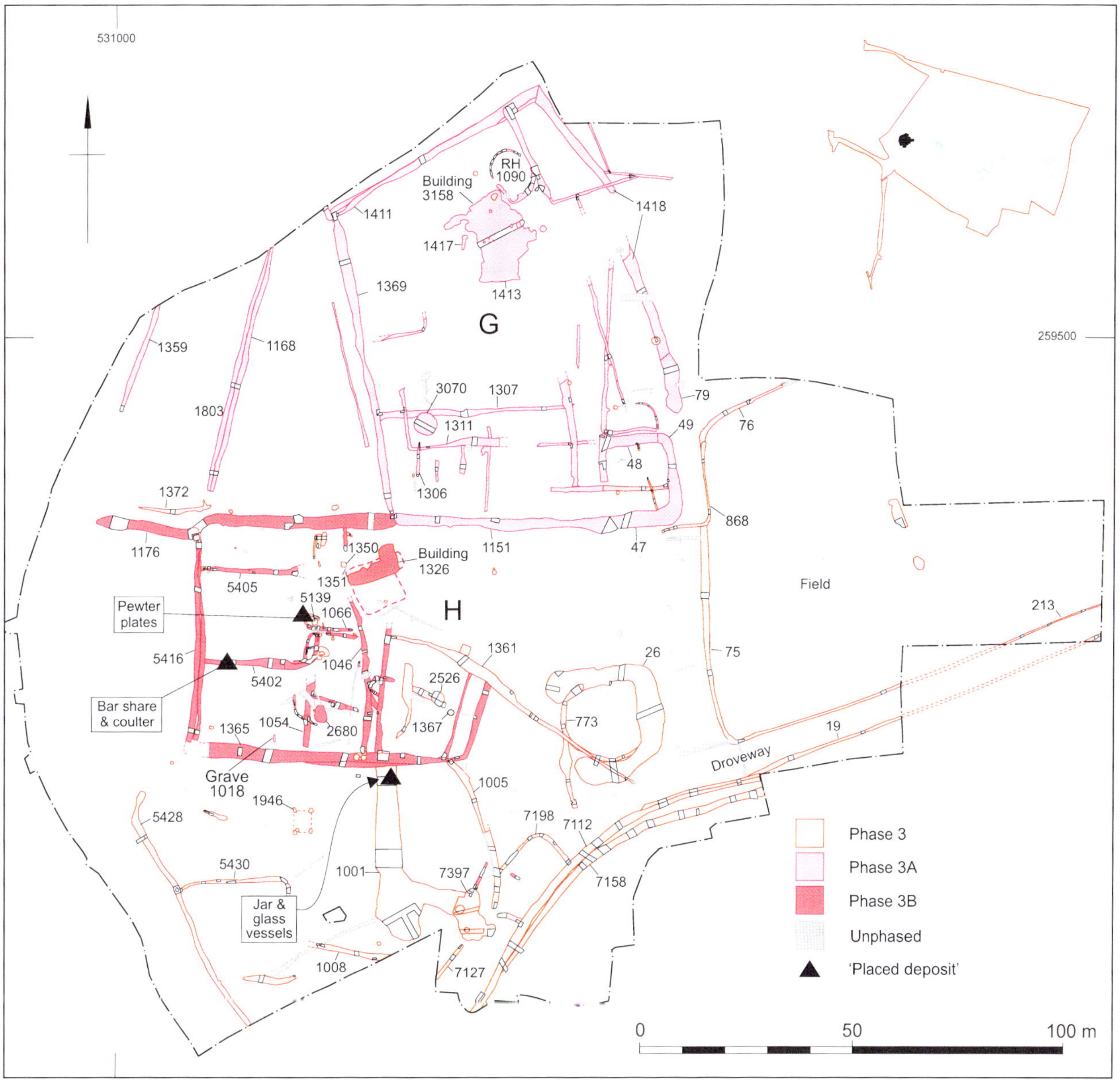

Figure 10. Lower Cambourne: mid–late Romano-British (Phase 3) enclosures, droveways, buildings, and associated features

deep and contained pottery of mid-2nd–3rd century date.

Roundhouse 1090 was situated in the north-east corner of the enclosure. It comprised two segments of drip-gully, well-defined in the north but less clear in the south, with a projected diameter of *c.* 10 m. Gaps to the ENE and WSW respectively, indicate the likely location of one or more entrances. Although a ditch lay immediately to the north-east, and a rectangular building (3158) immediately to the south-west, neither was necessarily contemporary with roundhouse 1090, despite being assigned to the same phase. Pottery of 2nd–4th century date, animal bone, some fired clay, and iron objects, mostly nails, were the main artefacts recovered from the fills of the gullies.

A possible rectangular building (3158) was indicated by a slightly irregular sunken area measuring 14.5 m by 7.5 m and up to 0.4 m deep, representing a structure or surface associated with one. A slot excavated through it revealed three shallow post-holes, three possible stake-holes, and a gully running approximately parallel to the long axis, all filled and sealed by a shallow spread of dark soil (1413) which produced 1.5 kg of pottery dated to the 2nd–3rd century. A lift key and four 3rd century coins were also present, whilst many of the 84 iron artefacts recovered by metal-detecting were nails. Two quern-

Plate 9. Lower Cambourne: excavating ditches 1365 (Phase 3B) and 1783 (Phase 2C)

stones and small quantity of animal bone comprised the remainder of the finds from this feature.

A keyhole-shaped oven (1417) lay 4 m west of building 3158 and 13 m from roundhouse 1090. Oriented almost north–south, the northern end was bowl-shaped with a diameter of 1.2 m and a depth of 0.5 m, and the flue was 2.5 m long, 0.7 m wide and 0.3 m deep. The clay into which the oven had been dug was scorched red and black, especially in the bowl, and this was where most charcoal and cereal processing waste were found. A little over 300 g of fired clay was recovered and this is likely to have formed the lining or dome of the oven.

The southern boundary of the enclosure, ditch 1151, ran east–west. At its eastern end it widened and deepened and, with ditches 47, 48, and 49 created what may have been a square animal pen measuring *c.* 15 m by 15 m internally. The ditches were 1.7–5.5 m wide and 0.7–1.4 m deep. The eastern ditch, 49, cut Phase 2 ditch 236, and the southern ditch, 47, cut Phase 2C ditch 35. Most of the pottery was of 2nd–3rd century date but a few prehistoric sherds were present and the very dark, upper fill of the southern side of the enclosure contained over 100 g of Saxon pottery. A similar, sub-square, pen formed by ditch 26 lay 30 m to the south of Enclosure G (and a lesser distance to the east of Enclosure H, Phase 3B).

Some remodelling within Enclosure G is evident in its south-western corner where L-shaped ditch 1311 was cut by ditches 1306 and 1307, the latter in turn cut by pit 3070. Ditch 1311 ran parallel to the two ditches forming the south and west sides of the enclosure and was 0.6– 2 m wide and 0.2–0.5 m deep. It contained Romano-British pottery, animal bone, fired clay, and some shell.

Ditch 1307, up to 1.85 m wide and 0.8 m deep, formed a T-junction with enclosure ditch 1369 and extended eastwards for approximately 45 m. It is likely that at least some of the other north to south ditches in the immediate area were dug at the same time to form smaller sub-enclosures, plots, or pens.

With a diameter of over 5 m, pit 3070, perhaps a well, was excavated to 1.2 m and then augered to reveal at least another 0.9 m of fill. Almost 2 kg of pottery and 1.6 kg of animal bone were recovered and, amongst the pottery, was an entire Horningsea jar of 2nd–3rd century date. The two latest fills of this feature contained relatively large amounts of cereal processing waste.

Immediately to the west of Enclosure G were two small fields or further enclosures, partly defined by parallel ditches 1168 (recut as 1803) and 1359, which extended to the north beyond the limit of excavation. Ditch 1168/1803, and associated ditch 1372, appeared to respect ditch 1176 defining the north side of Phase 3B Enclosure H, and perhaps the latter was a recut of an earlier, Phase 3A ditch of which nothing survived. The arrangement of ditches

1168/1803 and 1372, as well as later ditch 1176, indicates an entrance to the fields or enclosures from the south-west and also demonstrates that the use of Enclosures G and H overlapped.

Phase 3B

Enclosure H

Enclosure H, a sub-rectangular enclosure measuring *c.* 65 m by 50 m, lay to the south-west of Phase 3A Enclosure G. It was defined by ditch 1176 to the north, perhaps a re-cut or extension of Phase 3A ditch 1151, ditch 5416 to the west and ditch 1365 to the south and part of the east side (Pl. 9). These ditches increased in size down slope to the south-west, with ditch 1365 being up to 3m wide and 1.2 m deep. Ditches 1365 and 5416 were subsequently recut, the pottery from them comprising a mixture of 1st–2nd century and undiagnostic Romano-British sherds. Access to the enclosure appears to have been through a wide gap at the north end of the east side, between ditches 1151 and 1365.

The western part of Enclosure H was further subdivided by ditches 1054, 5402, and 5405, and to the east of 1054 by other ditches on a slightly different alignment, including 1066. Ditch 5402, 2.1 m wide and 0.6 m deep, cut Phase 2 ditches 5401 and 5404. Placed in the base of ditch 5402, towards its west end, were the coulter and tanged bar share from a plough; its significance is discussed further below.

That drainage in this area was probably a problem is demonstrated by ditch 1001, to the south of Enclosure H, one of whose principal functions appears to have been to carry water away from the enclosure, perhaps to a waterhole at its southern end. This ditch would also have formed a substantial boundary extending between Enclosure H and a droveway to the south (see below). It was 4.5–6 m wide, becoming wider down-hill to the south, and between 1.6 m and 1.8 m deep with an irregular profile and a flat, undulating base (Pl. 10). It was cut through a relatively stonefree clay at the top but at the

Plate 10. Lower Cambourne: ditch 1001 (Phase 3B)

Plate 11. Lower Cambourne: cobbling 1326, excavated on a 1m grid pattern (Phase 3B)

base exposed small boulders in the clay. The fills were in places laminated and sometimes separated by lenses of fine calcareous sand, and were certainly water lain. Just over 13 kg of pottery, 7 kg of animal bone, and nearly 1 kg of fired clay were recovered from the ditch, along with small quantities of ceramic building material, shell, and several iron and copper alloy objects. There were five 4th century coins, with two others found nearby, and a single Iron Age coin.

The wider, southern end of this ditch had more shallowly sloping sides and cobbling had been spread over an area of approximately 9 m by 7 m along its southern edge, presumably to ease access to the waterhole there. Pit 7397, to the south-east, also appears to have been part of ditch 1001 and may have served as a further waterhole.

In the north-eastern part of Enclosure H, a shallow cut, 3079, measuring *c.* 13 m by 3.5 m with a north-east to south-west orientation, was filled by was an area of rough cobbling (1326) that extended over it. The cobbling, which had been truncated along its south-eastern side by medieval ridge and furrow (Pl. 11), had been spread in part over Phase 2 ditches and elsewhere over natural clay, its extent to the west apparently defined by a curving ditch, 1046. The alignments of both the ditch and the cobbling were

Plate 12. Lower Cambourne: grave 1018; inset shows ring on finger (Phase 3B)

slightly askew to the orientation of Enclosure H. Sealing the cobbling was a *c.* 0.1 m deep deposit of dark soil. Investigation by way of a chequerboard pattern of 1 m squares showed no differentiation within this deposit, nor were post-holes or beam-slots revealed within or below the cobbling.

The interpretation of the cobbling is therefore uncertain, and although no clear structural remains were identified in Enclosure H, it shows some similarity to the site of the possible rectangular building in Enclosure G (Phase 3A) to the north-east. The dark soil produced *c.* 26.5 kg of artefacts, almost half of which comprised pottery that spanned the Romano-British period, but included late 3rd–4th century material and one small early Saxon sherd. Animal bone, fired clay, ceramic building material, many nails, and miscellaneous iron fragments (totalling 129 iron objects) and a rotary quern-stone were also recovered. Notable items included a single fragment of window glass, an iron lift key, a copper alloy spoon bowl, and a bone comb. Whatever the function of the cobbling, therefore, the relatively large quantity of finds and the composition of the assemblage are noteworthy.

A north–south aligned grave (1018) lay 1.7 m inside the south side of the enclosure. It was 1.65 m long and 0.48 m wide but only 0.1 m dccp, and contained the supine skeleton of an adult female of *c.* 35–55 years, with the head to the south (Pl. 12). A copper alloy ring was found on a finger of the right hand.

A substantial sub-square post-hole (1350), near the northern edge of the enclosure and adjacent to cobbling 3079, measured 1.3 m by 1.2 m and was 0.8 m deep with near vertical sides. Its fills comprised post-packing and an associated post-pipe, indicating a post *c.* 0.6 m in diameter, suggesting a large, free-standing post, possibly a totem of some form. It contained a 4th century coin, some late 3rd–4th century pottery and small quantities of fired clay and animal bone. Adjacent, undated pit 1351 was 0.46 m in diameter and 0.37 m deep with vertical sides, its lowest fill containing some vesicular fuel ash slag, and the remainder comprising largely this material, with a total of 2.6 kg present.

Oval-shaped pit 2680, in the southern part of the enclosure, measured 2.3 m by 2.1 m and was 0.7 m deep. It contained two 4th century coins, Romano-British pottery of probable post-2nd century date, animal bone, ceramic building material, fired clay, and shell, as well as a residual mid–late 1st century AD brooch.

In the eastern part of the enclosure were at least two pits. Pit 1367, which cut through the fills of Phase 2C ditch 3018, was 1.7 m diameter, 0.7 m deep and produced later Romano-British pottery with some fired clay and animal bone. Pit 2526, to the north-wesl, was larger at 6 m by 5.6 m, but only 0.5 m deep; this also cut the earlier ditch and contained a similar range of material.

Enclosure 26

To the south-east of Enclosure H, on the northern edge of a droveway, was the substantial ditch (26) of a sub-square enclosure, open on its west side. It truncated part of what may have been a sub-circular enclosure, covering much the same area, with a projected diameter of 17 m, defined by 1 m wide ditch (773). Ditch 26, in contrast, was between 5 m and 6 m wide and up to 1.3 m deep, with shallowly sloping sides possibly caused by trampling of the edges. Its dark grey upper fill contained pottery dating from the Iron Age through to the Saxon period. Its size and character is comparable to ditch 1001, 40 m to the west, and it is possible that the two were contemporary, perhaps associated with animal husbandry. It had similarities in form to the sub-enclosure at the south-east corner of Enclosure G, 30m to the north (above).

Droveway

The droveway along the south-east edge of the site was extensively remodelled, but it continued to follow the alignment of that established in Phase 2B, and presumably continuing through Phases 2C and Phase 3A. The droveway was defined to the east by ditches 19 and 213, *c.* 6 m apart, which extended over a distance of at least 100 m. To the west, where the sequence and layout of ditches was more complex, the droveway turned to the south-west, possibly to avoid ditch 1001, and continued beyond the limit of excavation.

Ditch 19, the southern of the droveway ditches, continued at the west as ditch 7112, perhaps recut and slightly realigned as 7158. The droveway's northern ditch (213) also bounded a field to the north (see below) and did not continued beyond it; to the south-west the north side of the droveway may be represented by ditch 7127, and the 65 m gap between them would have allowed access to Enclosures G and H, as well as sub-square enclosure 26. Subsequently, this arrangement may have been modified by a funnel-shaped arrangement of ditches, 1005 and 1361, which could have defined a broad, north-western extension to the droveway. This was at least 20 m wide and appeared to cut across the south-east corner of Enclosure H and the south-west corner of the enclosure 26. Ditch 7198 may also have been part of this new arrangement.

To the west of ditch 1001 a recut (5428) of the Phase 2 western droveway ditch formed the south-western limit of a possible sub-enclosure to the south of Enclosure H. Several ditches, including 1008 and 5430, may have been internal divisions, though it is clear that not all were contemporary. In the north-east of this area was a four-post structure (1946) measuring 5.1 m by 3.8 m.

Plate 13. Lower Cambourne: pewter plates during excavation (Phase 3B)

In the eastern part of the site was a probable sub-rectangular field, defined by droveway ditch 213 to the south, ditch 75/868 to the west and ditch 76 to the north, and measuring 75 m by at least 100 m but extending beyond the limit of excavation. Ditches 76 and 868 appear to represent a later modification to the field's boundary and their layout indicated the continued existence of Enclosure G to the north-west.

Placed deposits

Of particular interest were three placed deposits, made towards or at the end of Phase 3B within or adjacent to Enclosure H (Fig. 10). All are of certain or probable late Romano-British date, comprising pewter plates, glass vessels inside a pot, and two iron parts (bar share and coulter) of a plough. The pewter

Plate 14. Lower Cambourne: excavating pot containing glass vessels (Phase 3B)

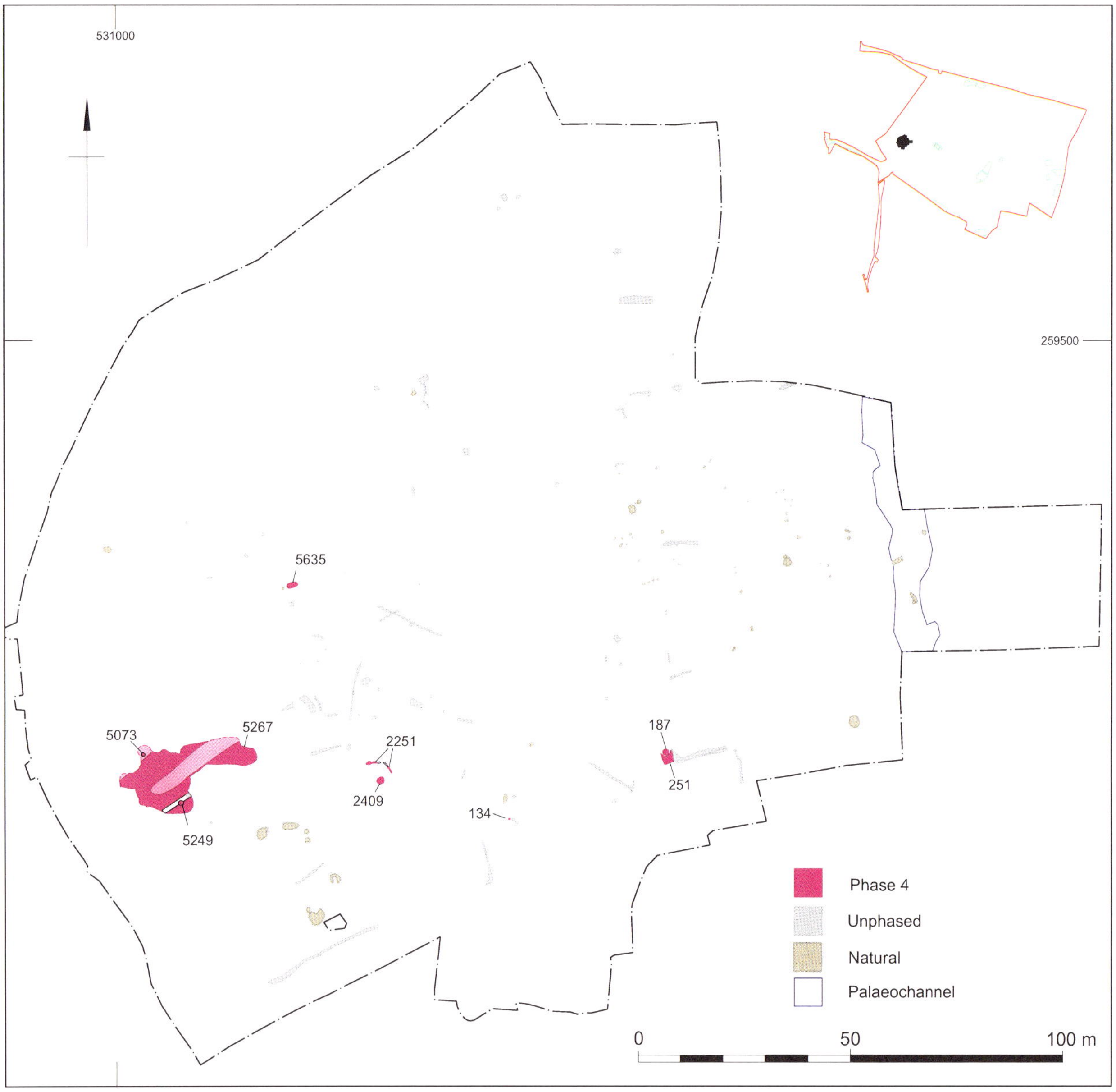

Figure 11. Lower Cambourne: Saxon (Phase 4) features

and plough parts were both located at the intersections of Phase 3B and earlier ditches within the western half of the enclosure, while the pottery jar and glass vessels were buried in ditch 1001 immediately to the south of the enclosure.

Oval pit 5139, which contained three pewter vessels – a large circular plate, an octagonal plate, and a smaller, deeper, circular dish – laid on its base, measured 1.1 m by 0.7 m and 0.6 m deep, (Pl. 13). Its single fill indicated that it had probably been backfilled immediately after deposition of the objects. Pit 5139 cut through the fills of Phase 2 enclosure ditch 5401, close to where it was intersected by Phase 3B ditch 1066.

A large jar containing five glass vessels was probably also placed in a pit, cut into the top fill on the eastern side of ditch 1001, although no cut was identified (Pl. 14). The jar is an unusual form but broadly similar rim forms, also with pie-crust decoration, are known from late Romano-British layers in Cambridge (Pullinger *et al.* 1999, pl. cxxxvii, 1000 and 1001). The glass vessels – a jug and four bottles, all probably used for serving at table – were all late 3rd or 4th century in date.

The tanged bar share and coulter of a plough had been placed adjacent to each other parallel to the line of Phase 3B ditch 5402 near its base, at the point where it cut Phase 2 ditch 5404. Whether these objects were left exposed or were covered is unknown, but it does seem clear that they were placed in an open ditch rather than in a pit cut through its fills.

Plate 15. Lower Cambourne: cobbled 'causeway' over hollow 5267 (Phase 4); Phase 2C cow burial in foreground

Phase 4 – Saxon

While few features can unequivocally be assigned to this phase on the basis of finds, three vertically-sided pits cut through large, silted up ditches all contained late Romano-British pottery and two contained sherds of Saxon date (Fig. 11). It is possible they were wells, dug to exploit water draining along the former ditches.

Pit 187, 0.97 m in diameter and 0.84 m deep, cut Phase 2C ditch 613, 1 m east of Phase 3 ditch 26. It contained over 1 kg of animal bone and pottery that was mostly Saxon in date. To the south, and respecting the cut, was cobbled layer 251, over which was a 0.08 m thick layer containing some residual 1st–2nd century pottery. Sealing both this layer and the pit were two layers containing mostly Saxon pottery.

Pit 2409, 70m to the west of pit 187, was 1.75 m in diameter, 1.63 m deep and cut all the fills on the western side of ditch 1001. It contained 3rd or 4th century pottery and one Saxon sherd from half way down. Other materials included animal bone, shell and stone. A possible shelter or windbreak, 3 m to the north, was represented by curvilinear gully 2251 which contained a small amount of later Romano-British pottery.

Further west, pit 5249, which was 1.6 m in diameter and 1.1 m deep, was cut through the final silting of an extensive shallow hollow (5267), formed at the junction of several earlier ditches. The few finds recovered from the pit included two sherds of unspecific Romano-British pottery but nothing later. A Saxon spearhead was recovered from the upper fill of the hollow and nearby was a 'causeway', across the edge of the hollow, comprising a 1.5 m long, 1.2 m wide area of large, even-sized, neatly laid cobbles (Pl. 15).

Other features assigned to this phase include another pit (5073), cutting the silted up hollow; it was 0.8 m in diameter and 0.7 m deep, and contained some Romano-British pottery and a complete quern stone lying flat on the base. In addition, a small pit (5635) and a possible post-hole (134), contained Saxon pottery, as did the upper fills of several Phase 2 and Phase 3 ditches in this area.

Phase 5 – Medieval

In common with the other sites at Cambourne, there appears to have been a hiatus of perhaps several centuries following the late Romano-British/Saxon periods before the site was used again. During the

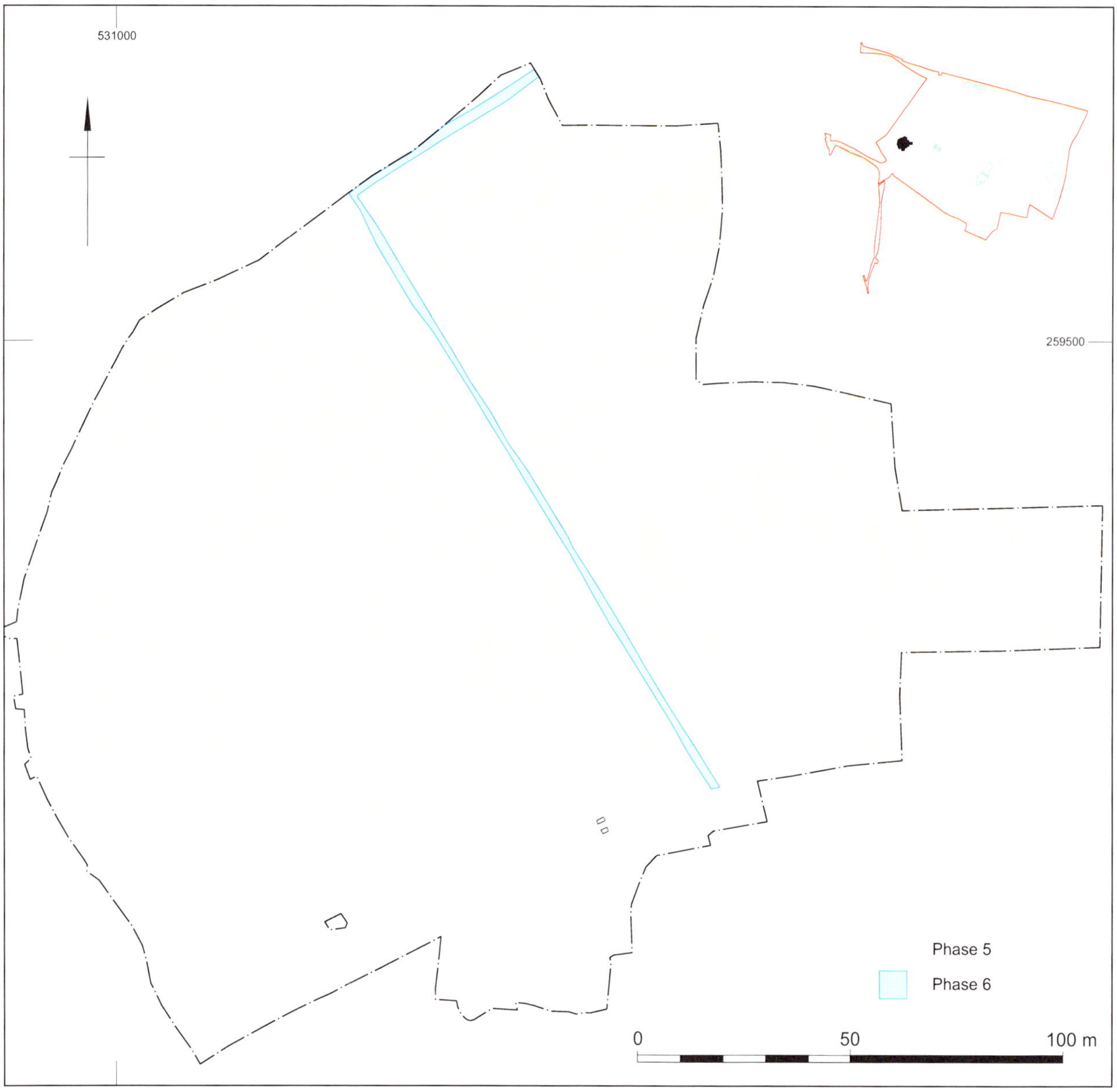

Figure 12. Lower Cambourne: medieval (Phase 5) and post-medieval/modern (Phase 6) features

medieval period, most likely in the 12th century, the distinctive pattern of ridge and furrow ploughing was established (Fig. 12). Two separate alignments of furrows were present at Lower Cambourne, with a narrow headland between them. The furrows can clearly be seen to broaden approaching the headland, possibly as the plough team started to turn.

Phase 6 – Post-medieval/modern

Many ceramic field drains were exposed. These often ran along the deepest parts of the medieval furrows, indicating that these were still visible in the 19th or 20th century. A post-medieval ditch ran south-east to north-west across the site, before turning to the north-east and continuing beyond the limit of excavation. This lay parallel to the southern pattern of furrows but crossed those to the north at 90°, before turning to run parallel with them. This ditch is shown on Ordnance Survey maps and is likely to have been dug in the 18th or 19th centuries.

Poplar Plantation

The site, located *c.* 100 m south of Poplar Plantation, a copse near the centre of the Development Area, was centred on NGR 531590 259385 (Fig. 1). It comprised an irregular area approximately 80 m by 55 m (*c.* 0.35 ha), lying immediately east of School Lane; a stream issuing from near the copse flowed south-west to join the Bourn Brook. The site sloped gently westwards down to the stream and varied in height between 62.5 m and 64.3 m aOD (Fig. 2).

During the exceptionally wet winter of 2000 construction traffic working School Lane had been forced to drive over the western part of the site which was subsequently re-machined to remove any wheel ruts. A 1 m baulk was left either side of a post-medieval or modern ditch which bisected the site.

Nearly all the features were assigned to Phase 2B, and comprised an enclosure ditch, field and droveway ditches, a small number of pits and possibly three roundhouse drip-gullies. A single, possibly Phase 3 ditch was also present, as well as Phase 4 ridge and furrow and one Phase 6 (modern) pit.

Phase 2B – Later Iron Age–early Romano-British

There was clearly more than one episode of activity during this phase, with the laying out of enclosures and field ditches accompanied by, and preceding, the construction of circular structures, probably roundhouses, and various other ditches and gullies (Fig. 13).

Enclosure

A large, irregularly-shaped enclosure, part of it outside the site to the north-east, was defined by ditch 72001/72002 which was traced some 130 m within the site, enclosing an area of *c.* 0.2 ha measuring approximately 52 m by 42 m. Nine sections were excavated across the ditch, three of which could not be completed due to flooding. Those excavated near a droveway at the north-west showed a steep-sided, slightly rounded V-shaped profile. Along the southern and eastern sides of the enclosure the profile was wider and less steep sided. There were no gaps in the ditch to indicate the location of an entrance, suggesting the entrance lay outside the site to the north-east, although there may have been some form of access from the north-west, associated with a droveway (see below).

Ditch 72001 was 1.66 m wide and 1.08 m deep with a slightly asymmetric V-shaped profile, the north-western side being slightly steeper (see Fig. 13). The three lowest fills (72102, 72103, and 72104) were all pale grey or pale yellowish-grey with reddish-brown mottles, contained relatively few stones apart from small pieces of chalk, and derived from erosion of the ditch sides. Above them, fills 72105 and 72106 had both slumped from the south-east and did not extend the full width of the ditch; they were respectively greyish and yellowish-brown in colour and 72106 contained some medium-sized stones. Above these and slumping from the north-west was greyish-brown fill 72111; two sherds of Middle Iron Age pottery came from these lower fills. Above them and extending the whole width of the ditch was fill 72107, a greyish-brown silty clay containing Middle Iron Age pottery, fired clay, animal bone, and a small iron blade. Above was redeposited clay 72108, and above that 72109, a mid–dark greyish-brown fill possibly derived from eroded topsoil and containing only animal bone. The final charcoal-rich fill (72110) also contained animal bone.

Only one ditch section showed any evidence for recutting. In another section, on the west side, there were many cobbles slumping into the ditch from the north-west. These were not present in any other excavated section, although similar cobbles were present in nearby pits 72009 and 72010, and may have formed a surface around them.

Internal features

Sections of curving gullies within the interior of the enclosure are interpreted as the remains of drip-gullies, indicating the presence of possibly three roundhouses. None survived as complete circuits. Although it appears that one roundhouse replaced another at the west end of the enclosure, it could not be established whether roundhouse 72314, 3–4 m to the east and cut by ditch 72018, was earlier than or contemporary with one or both of these.

The two length of drip-gully comprising roundhouse 72314 formed a projected circle of 9.2 m diameter, the south-east part lying beyond the limit of excavation. At the south-west it was 0.48 m wide and 0.34 m deep with steep to very steep sides and a flat, slightly sloping base, while at the north it was 0.74 m wide and 0.18 m deep with a shallow U-shaped profile. Much of it was filled with redeposited natural containing some charcoal flecks, burnt flint, fired clay, and Middle Iron Age pottery. Either cut by or respecting the drip-gully to its immediate north was a small area of flint and chalk cobbling (not illustrated).

In the west of the enclosure were two overlapping probable roundhouses, one represented by the five short curving segments of gully (72020), the other by curving gully 72140. Four more lengths of curving gullies (72021, 72146, 72147, and 72236) may also have been parts of these two roundhouses. The 'best fit' would have two slightly overlapping circles, with gullies 72020, 72146, and 72236 forming a roundhouse *c.* 15.7 m in diameter, and gullies 72140, 72021, and 72147 forming one *c.* 12.5 m in diameter.

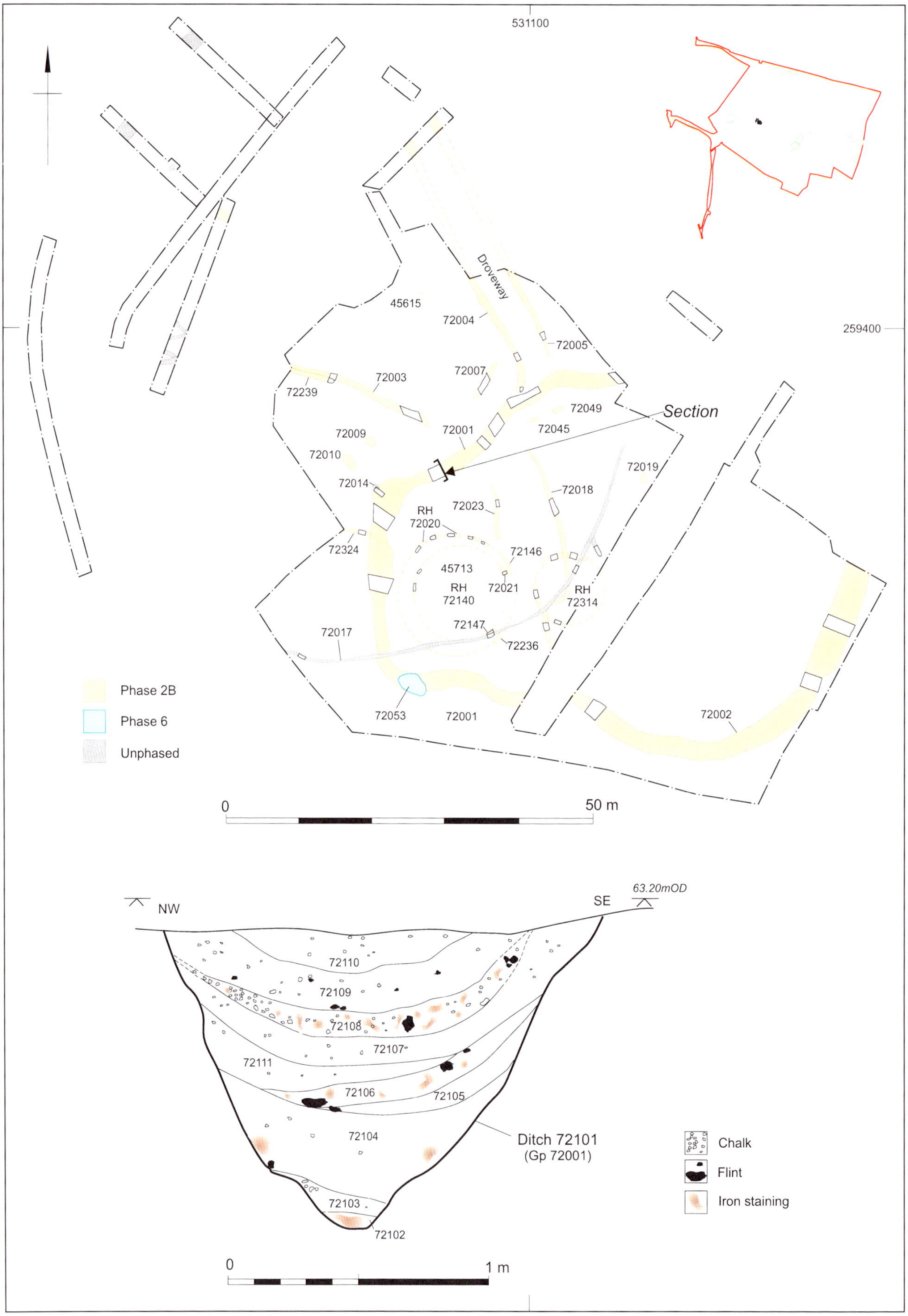

Figure 13. Poplar Plantation: later Iron Age (Phase 2B) and Romano-British (Phase 3) features

The only stratigraphic relationships were where gullies 72147 and 72236 were cut by a unphased gully (72017).

The gully segments of 72020 may have been the only surviving portions of an originally continuous drip-gully, but if so it must have been deeper at regular intervals. The best preserved part was 0.51 m wide and 0.22 m deep with straight edges and a flat base, and most of the other segments, from both roundhouses, were of similar dimensions. A small internal pit or posthole (45713), 0.62 m by 0.4 m by 0.34 m deep, may have been a roof support.

The interior of the enclosure was subsequently divided by ditch 72018, which separated the western third of the enclosure from the rest. It ran south-south-east for 20 m from near post-hole 72045 (one of a pair with 72049, see below), opposite western droveway ditch 72004, before turning west for 3.5 m and then south-south-east again. Ditch 72018 was 0.76 m wide and 0.41 m deep with straight sides sloping to a rounded base. It contained Middle Iron Age pottery, animal bone and fired clay. Although it post-dated roundhouse 72314, it may have been contemporary with either or both of the successive roundhouses to its west.

Ditch 72023, roughly parallel to ditch 72018 and 6.5 m to its west, only survived for a length of 7.3 m. It was 0.55 m wide and 0.22 m deep with straight sides and a flat base, and produced small quantities of Iron Age pottery and animal bone. Its location and proximity to the western roundhouses suggests that it may have been associated with one or both of them.

In the northern half of the enclosure, an oval pit (72019), measuring 1.42 m by 0.86 m and 0.4 m deep, contained pottery and animal bone.

Droveway

Approaching the north-western corner of the enclosure, but stopping short of the ditch was a droveway, defined by parallel ditches 72004 and 72005, set 3.9 m apart and extending for at least 35 m. The eastern ditch (72004), was 0.61 m wide, 0.34 m deep and had steep sides and a flat base; the western ditch (72005) was 0.73 m wide and 0.56 m deep. The fills of both ditches produced Iron Age pottery, fired clay, and animal bone.

Opposite the droveway and inside the enclosure were two keyhole-shaped post-holes (72045 and 72049). They were parallel to the enclosure ditch, *c.* 2 m from its inner edge, and 1.8 m apart. Both were approximately 1.8 m long, between 0.5 m and 0.7 m wide, and at least 0.3 m deep. The fills contained common large flints which appeared to be post-packing, and there was some evidence for post packing. It is possibly they represent some form of entrance structure, providing access to the enclosure from the end of the droveway.

Other external features

Also radiating from the western side of the enclosure, and probably contemporary with it, were two field ditches (ditch 72003, recut as 72239, and ditch 72324), both extending beyond the limit of excavation. Ditch 72003 was 0.9 m wide, 0.52 m deep and had a U-shaped profile, its recut (72339) being shallower and stopping 14 m short of the enclosure; both cuts contained Middle Iron Age pottery, fragments of animal bone and fired clay. Ditch 72324, which was 0.55 m wide and 0.26 m deep with a U-shaped profile, contained no finds.

A short length of ditch, 72007, *c.* 3 m outside the enclosure at the north-west, was aligned north-east to south-west. It was 1m wide and 0.67 m deep, with straight, steep sides and a 0.3 m wide, flat base. Its charcoal-rich fill contained Iron Age pottery, burnt stone, fired clay and some animal bone.

Lying 3.5 m north-west of the enclosure ditch were pits 72009 and 72010. Pit 72010 was the larger, sub-oval in plan measuring 2.53 m by 1.12 m and 0.78 m deep. Its lower and middle fills contained small amounts of pottery, animal bone and charcoal, but the penultimate fill contained larger amounts of pottery and animal bone and several large flint cobbles and chalk lumps. Similar stones were present in the nearby excavated section of the enclosure ditch and it is likely that there had been a localised area of cobbling in the vicinity. Pit 72009 was approximately circular, with a diameter of 1.3 m and 0.3 m deep. Although it produced no dating evidence it is included in this phase on the basis of its proximity to pit 72010 and the presence of cobbles in its lower fill which might have been part of the same spread recorded in pit 72010 and the adjacent ditch section.

Unphased

A curving ditch, 72017, crossed the western part of the site, terminating *c.* 3.5 m from its north-western edge. It cut roundhouse 72314 and gully 72018, and the top fills of the 1.2 m deep enclosure ditch, 72001, indicating that it had been dug after the enclosure had been abandoned and the ditch had silted up. It was 0.45 m wide and 0.22 m deep, with finds from it including two sherds of Iron Age pottery and a small quantity of animal bone, but most of this material is assumed to be residual. A small oval pit (72014), measuring 0.9 m by 0.56 m and 0.22 m deep, which cut the upper fills of enclosure ditch 72001, contained no dating evidence.

Phase 6 – Post-medieval – modern

The south-west corner of the enclosure ditch was cut by a large modern pit (72053).

Mill Farm

This site was located along the southern edge of the Development Area, approximately 1.2 km to the east and north-west of the villages of Caxton and Bourn, respectively (Fig. 1). The initial intention was to strip and excavate a single large area. However, the presence of newts (a protected species) close to the centre of the proposed excavation area necessitated the creation of a 100 m wide exclusion zone. In order to accommodate this, the site was stripped as two rectangular areas: a western area measuring 197 m by 30 m (*c.* 0.56 ha) and centred on NGR 531630 258590, and an eastern area measuring 64 m by 25 m (*c.* 0.15 ha) and centred on NGR 531860 258470. The ground sloped to the south-east across these areas (Fig. 2), falling from 65.6 m to 54.2 m aOD within the site.

Two principal phases of activity were identified: Phase 1 (Bronze Age features, cutting a palaeochannel) and Phase 3 (Romano-British enclosures and ditch systems) (Fig. 14). Other remains included possible modern plough scars (Phase 6) and several undated plough scars.

Phase 0 – Undated and natural features

The palaeochannel (40312), which occupied most of the eastern area, was at least 25 m wide and 0.5 m deep, aligned north-west to south-east. Within its northern half was a shallow, irregular, discontinuous layer (40310), between 2 m and 5 m wide and 0.02 m and 0.48 m thick. Its irregular shape and thickness, together with its silty nature, strongly suggests that it represents the last infilling episode of the palaeochannel, the artefacts from it indicating that this took place during Phase 1 (below).

Phase 1 – Bronze Age

The earliest phase of activity consisted of a number of post-holes, hearths, and gullies associated with the final silting up of the palaeochannel in the eastern area. An excavated segment through its upper fill (40310), in the middle of the trench, showed that this layer was *c.* 3 m wide and 0.2 m thick with sub-angular stones at the base; it produced 32 small sherds of Middle–Late Bronze Age pottery and a few small fragments of animal bone. In a second section, excavated to the north-west, it was 5.1 m wide and 0.48 m thick, producing eight pieces of lightly patinated and rolled worked flint, including an end scraper, fired clay, a burnt bone, and a stone rubber/quern-stone fragment; the rubber or quern-stone was an igneous rock, possibly a local erratic but if not then from either Whin Sill, Northumberland, or Shropshire.

Two intercutting gullies (40311 and 40321), up to 1.4 m wide and 0.5 m deep, cut the palaeochannel at the north and terminated close to feature 40304. Both gullies produced small quantities of Middle–Late Bronze Age pottery, gully 40311 also containing over 30 fragments of hazelnut shell. Feature 40304, which contained no dating evidence, was an irregular hollow or possible pond, 9.8 m long, 3.2 m wide and up to 1.5 m deep, all of its fills indicating natural silting, with a band of relatively large stones showing at least one episode of high energy infilling.

Other features in the south-eastern excavation area contained no dating evidence, although burnt stone was recovered, which is frequently found in Bronze Age contexts near watercourses, and so the features are tentatively included in this phase on this basis. These features included a second pair of intercutting gullies (40258 and 40259), up to 0.67 m wide and 0.4 m deep, located to the south-east of gullies 40311 and 40321. They were traced for *c.* 5 m before terminating and both cut the latest silting of the palaeochannel.

An oval hearth (40260) in the centre of the palaeochannel was 1.55 m long, 0.97 m wide and 0.12 m deep, and contained much heat-damaged stone and charcoal. Several small pits or possible post-holes were cut into the upper silty fill of palaeochannel 40312. Although at least 50% of their fills comprised burnt stone, none of the sides of the features showed signs of scorching or baking. The largest pit (40238), measuring 2.03 m by 1.67 m and 0.85 m deep, contained 21.4 kg of burnt stone, worked flint, a few fragments of animal bone, and fired clay. Pit 40231 was smaller (1.42 m by 1 m and 0.42 m deep) and contained animal bone, worked flint, and pieces of fire-cracked sandstone that looked like a dump of pot-boilers.

At the north-western end of the western excavation area were two adjacent hearths (40215 and 40219). Although neither produced any datable finds they are thought to belong to Phase 1. The smaller hearth (40215), 0.58 m in diameter and 0.08 m deep, produced little environmental evidence, but hearth 40219, 0.88 m in diameter and 0.25 m deep, contained brushwood-type charcoal.

Phase 3 – Mid–late Romano-British

All the Phase 3 features were in the western excavation area. A small sub-square enclosure in the south-east of the area appears to have been the focus of activity, with field and other boundary ditches extending to the north-west. The enclosure was remodelled and two clear phases of ditches were identified; these are presented as Phases 3A and 3B.

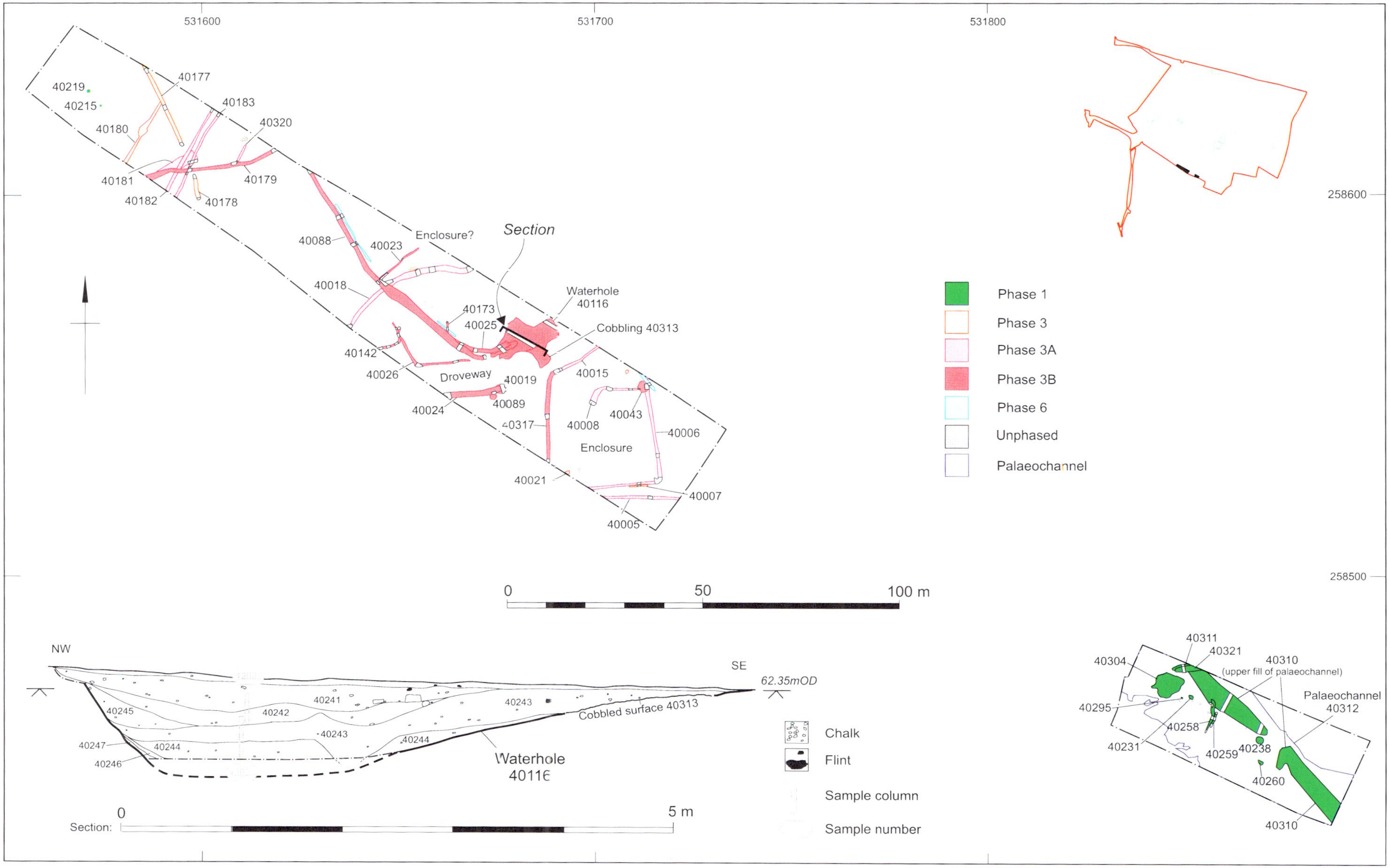

Figure 14. Mill Farm: Bronze Age (Phase 1) and Romano-British (Phase 3) features

Most of the finds came from the south-eastern end of the area, with none from north-west of ditch 40179.

Phase 3A

Ditches 40015 and 40008 were two of the earliest components of the small, square enclosure. It is likely that ditch 40015 continued to the south, on the same line as its later recut (40317), then turned east just outside the excavation area, then north as ditch 40006, with the terminus of ditch 40008 marking a wide entrance. The short, shallow ditch 40007 suggests maintenance of the southern boundary, while ditch 40005, which lay parallel to and outside the south side of the enclosure, may have formed a larger version of the enclosure or part of a field system.

Although the relationship between ditches 40008 and 40006 was destroyed by pit 40043 (which contained a large fragment of Puddingstone quern), it was evident that in its latest phase ditch 40006 continued north beyond the limit of excavation, by which time ditch 40008 may have fallen out of use.

Ditch 40015, which was 0.73 m wide and 0.24 m deep, contained Romano-British pottery, two iron objects, a considerable amount of grain and chaff, and fragments of a Neidermendig lava quern-stone in the top fill. Ditch 40008, a minimum of 0.54 m wide but broadening to 1.5 m in the south-west, was 0.2 m deep and contained Romano-British pottery, fired clay, and two pieces of lead. Many stones were recovered from one of the sections of ditch 40008, possibly used to consolidate a 'soft spot' where there was frequent movement of people and/or animals, reinforcing the suggestion that this ditch was allowed to go out of use.

The interior of the enclosure had been badly disturbed by ploughing, and only three pits, all approximately 1 m in diameter and 0.13–0.17 m deep, survived in the south-west and north-east corners, giving little indication of the enclosure's function or of possible activity areas.

Perhaps contemporaneous with it was 35 m long curvilinear ditch 40018 to the north-west, which may have formed part of a second enclosure or a field boundary. It was 1.2–2 m wide and 0.4–1.2 m deep. In one excavated section a deposit of over 6 kg of Romano-British finewares, including many whole or near-whole pottery vessels, had been placed on the base of the ditch. The four other sections produced only small amounts of pottery and some animal bone, although relatively large amounts of grain and chaff were recovered from one section.

Ditch 40181, further to the north-west, was at least 13.5 m long (continuing beyond the western edge of the excavation area), 2.6 m wide and 0.5 m deep, and its north-eastern terminal had a distinctive square shape. Its single fill produced no artefacts. It was cut by a pair of parallel ditches (40182 and 40183) *c.* 1 m apart; both were less than 0.15 m deep and neither produced any artefacts. Parallel to them to the south-east and also containing no artefacts, ditch 40320 was only 0.07 m deep. As these four ditches were cut by Phase 3B enclosure ditch 40179, they are included in this earlier phase.

Phase 3B

As described above, the square enclosure in the south-eastern end of the site was altered and its entrance remodelled, when its ditch(es) was recut. The west side was recut as 40317, ditch 40008 at the north was abandoned, and ditch 40006 on the east side was continued to the north beyond the limit of excavation. Ditches 40006 and 40317 were both slightly larger than their predecessors and both produced above average amounts of Romano-British pottery and some animal bone; ditch 40006 also produced a coin of 3rd century date.

At probably the same time, Phase 3A enclosure or field ditch 40018 to the north-west was replaced a new arrangement which included ditches 40179, 40088, 40026, and possibly 40023. It is difficult to determine the overall layout from the area exposed, but ditches 40026 and 40024 could have defined a funnelled droveway running east to the south-eastern enclosure, with ditch 40024, up to 1.5 m wide and 0.9 m deep, continuing the curving alignment of ditch 40015. Ditch 40024 produced small amounts of Romano-British pottery, animal bone, and fired clay, along with considerable amounts of grain processing waste. It was cut by pits 40089 and 40019, the latter, at its terminal, containing a 3rd or 4th century coin. Ditch 40026, meanwhile, along with ditches 40088 and 40179, may have formed the north side of an irregularly shaped enclosure.

It seems likely that ditch 40088 initially ran south-east in a straight line, before turning to the east (parallel to ditch 40024), with ditch 40026 therefore part of its original line. Subsequently, its southern part was realigned, cutting off the corner before possibly draining water into waterhole 40116 at its south-eastern end. The north-west part of ditch 40088 was 0.6 m wide and 0.2 m deep, but it became larger to the south-east, being 1.9 m wide and 0.8 m deep near the waterhole. Its cut had an irregular shape, perhaps a result of erosion from seasonal run-off. At the south-eastern end of this ditch there was a recut (40025) which was *c.* 1 m wide and 0.2 m deep.

The other ditches, most of which produced small quantities of Romano-British pottery, animal bone, and fired clay, were generally less substantial than ditch 40024, ditch 40179 being 1.24 m wide and 0.33 m deep, and ditch 40026 being up to 0.9 m wide and 0.2 m deep. Ditch 40023, which ran perpendicular and north-east from ditch 40088, was 1 m wide and 0.2 m deep.

Waterhole 40116 was *c.* 16 m long, 7.5 m wide, and 1.6 m deep (Fig. 14). Health and Safety constraints and waterlogging meant that its full profile was not revealed and its depth was only established by augering. Its northern side sloped at 45° but its southern side had a gentler slope; the base was roughly horizontal. Along the southern edge was a roughly cobbled surface of compacted stone rubble, 40313. Above a slump of sandy material (40247) and possibly tipped ashy hearth material (40246) along the north edge, there was a build-up of broadly horizontal silty clay fills (40244, 40243, 40245, 40242, and 40241), the uppermost cut by medieval ridge and furrow. Almost 2.5 kg of Romano-British pottery and 1.7 kg of animal bone, with a very small amount of fired clay, was recovered from the fills. Grain processing waste was also present, though in smaller quantities than from some of the Phase 3A ditches. Pollen from the waterhole suggested an open environment with few trees, but was not present in sufficient quantities for further analysis

Probable Phase 3 features

Several ditches and small pits are probably Romano-British but cannot be readily grouped into either of the two phases described above. In the north-west, probably contemporaneous ditches 40177, 40178, and 40180, which were all under 0.3 m deep, had no stratigraphic relationships with other features, and only ditch 40178 produced artefactual material – a small, abraded sherd of Romano-British pottery. In the centre of the area, and badly disturbed by ridge and furrow, an irregular L-shaped ditch (40142), which cut ditch 40026, contained a small quantity of Romano-British pottery.

Knapwell Plantation

The site was in the north of the Development Area next to the A428, centred on NGR 532100 260225 (Fig. 1). It lay at 65 m aOD, to the north of the relatively flat plateau between the Bourn Brook and the Great Ouse, and was the only site in the Development Area to lie within the Great Ouse drainage system (Fig. 2). At the time of the excavation it consisted of rough, untended ground.

The initial intention was to strip and excavate a single area of approximately 2.5 ha. However, during the course of stripping it became evident that fewer archaeological features were present than had been predicted by the evaluation. With the agreement of the County Archaeological Officer, the area proposed for stripping and excavation was reduced to two

Plate 16. Knapwell Plantation: machining in progress, revealing enclosure ditches

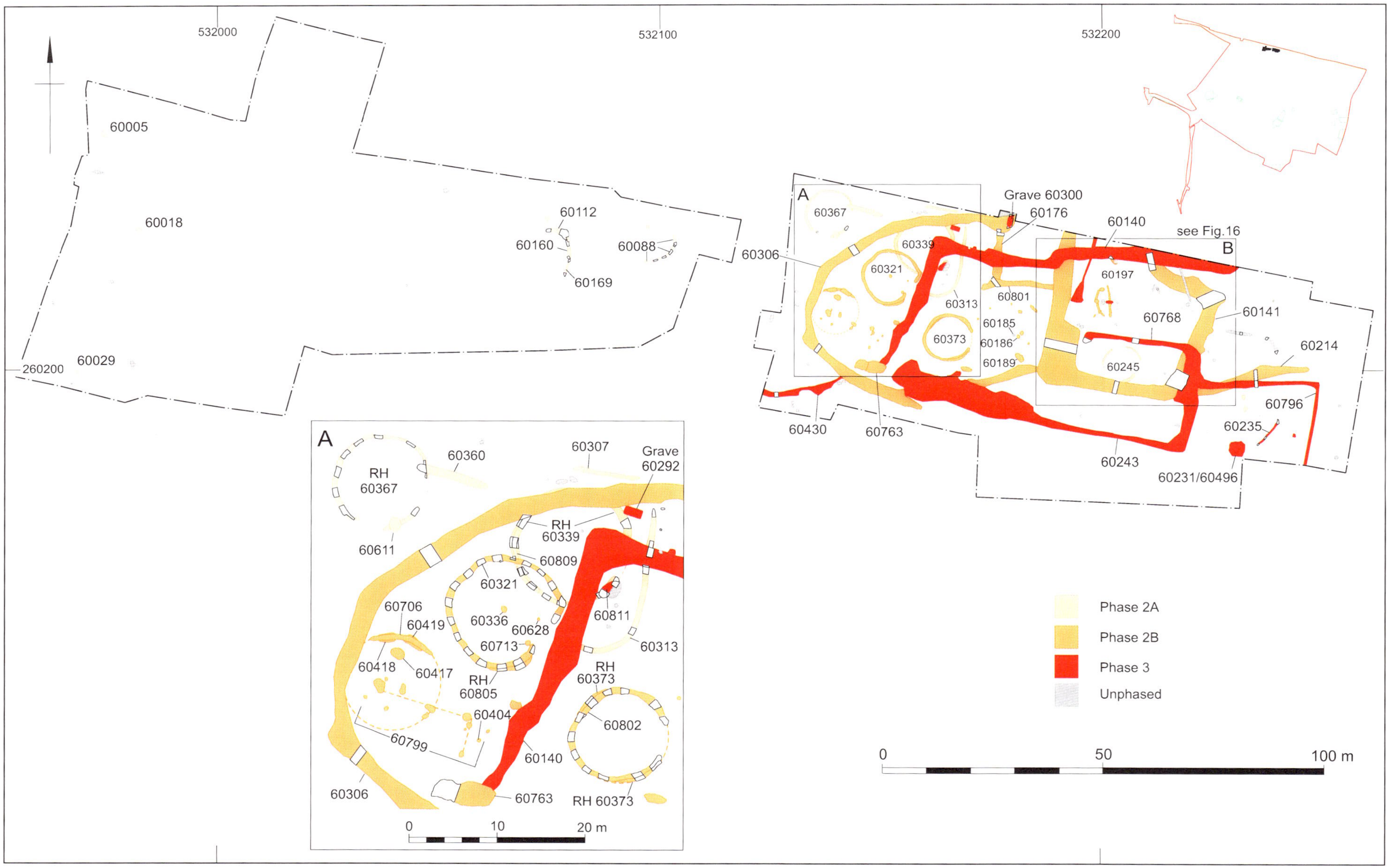

Figure 15. Knapwell Plantation: later Iron Age (Phases 2A and 2B) and Romano-British (Phase 3) features

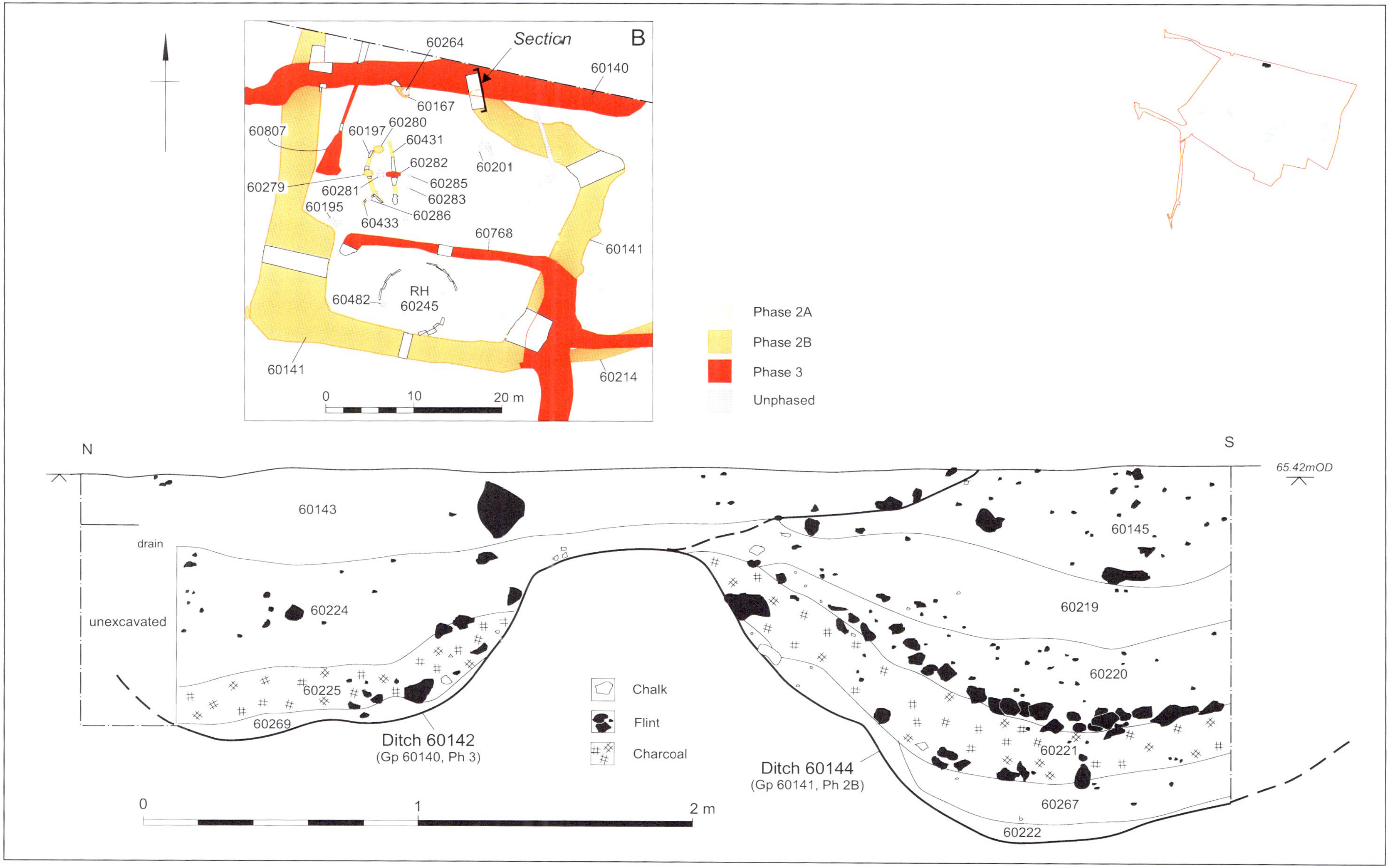

Figure 16. Knapwell Plantation: later Iron Age (Phase 2) and Romano-British (Phase 3) features

separate but adjacent areas totalling approximately 1.5 ha (Fig. 15). The western area measured 150 m by 65 m (0.82 ha), centred on NGR 532020 260235, with the eastern, which measured 135 m by 50 m (*c.* 0.72 ha) (Pl. 16), centred on NGR 532200 260210. A wide, modern service trench running parallel to the A428 was exposed during machining, and stripping of the remainder of the site was confined to the south of this disturbance. Excavation started in the exceptionally wet autumn of 2000 and had to be abandoned because of flooding; it recommenced four months later.

The eastern area contained almost all of the archaeology. The majority of the pottery was Iron Age in date with smaller quantities of Romano-British and some Early Saxon sherds present, usually in the upper fills of large ditches.

Phase 2 – Middle–Late Iron Age to early Romano-British

Phase 2 may initially have comprised unenclosed roundhouses; these were replaced by roundhouses, small pits and gullies within an enclosure (Figs 15 and 16). These are accordingly allocated to Phases 2A and 2B respectively.

Phase 2A

Roundhouse drip-gullies 60339 and 60367 had diameters of 12.9 m and 10.8 m respectively, the larger being also wider (0.8 m compared to 0.45 m) and deeper (0.5 m maximum compared to 0.2 m). Both appear to have had south-east facing entrances, although there was also a gap in the south of drip-gully 60367, and drip-gully 60339 had been cut by substantial enclosure ditches 60140 and 60306, making entrances elsewhere at least possible. Drip-gully 60339 had been recut (60809) along its western side.

Gully 60313, which was only 2 m to the east of 60339, and east–west gully 60307, may have been parts of an insubstantial enclosure that partly surrounded both drip-gullies. Gully 60313 was 0.35–0.6 m wide and 0.17–0.32 m deep.

Further to the east, drip-gully 60245 was cut through the centre by medieval ridge and furrow and survived as three separate segments, with a projected diameter of *c.* 8.5 m (Fig. 16). Although it had gaps to the east, south-west and north-west, it too may have had an east facing entrance. It produced Middle Iron Age pottery, animal bones, and small quantities of fired clay, and was cut by Phase 2B enclosure ditch 60141; it has therefore been included in this early phase. At the south-west the gully was 0.68 m wide and 0.35 m deep, about twice the size of the two other segments. An unphased feature (60482), *c.* 0.5 m diameter and 0.13 m deep, on the projected line of the gully may have been a post-hole or could represent a variation in its depth. The south terminal of its presumed east facing entrance produced charcoal, mostly of blackthorn (*Prunus spinosa*).

In the western excavation area were short curving gullies 60088 and 60112. Gully 60088 could be the surviving remains of a drip-gully of *c.* 9.5 m diameter. It was widest (0.58 m) and deepest (0.3 m) on the east side and became discontinuous to the west. Gully 60112, which together with gully 60160 and 60169, formed an irregular arc 11 m long producing Iron Age pottery, animal bone, and fired clay, was relatively substantial, measuring between 0.75 m and 1.8 m wide, and between 0.4 m and 0.97 m deep, with steep sides and a flat base.

Of the other unenclosed features in the western area, pit 60005 and tree-throw hollows 60018 and 60029 have been included in this phase. Circular pit 60005 was *c.* 1.45 m in diameter and 1 m deep. Although its southern side was vertical, its northern side had a gentler slope, the bottom *c.* 0.3 m comprising a vertical-sided cut 0.5 m in diameter. Although no lining was present this feature may have been a well. Most of its fills suggested gradual silting with some occupation debris towards the top. Tree-throw hollow 60029 contained small quantities of Iron Age pottery, while tree-throw hollow 60018 produced also a small quantity of animal bone, fired clay, and worked flint.

Phase 2B

Phase 2B saw the construction of a 0.2 ha, oval enclosure, 35 m at its widest point and *c.* 55 m long, defined on the north, west and south sides by ditch 60306. At its eastern end the ditch was probably cut by that of a small sub-square enclosure (60141, below), although it is possible the latter was a contemporaneous feature closing off the eastern end. Ditch 60306 was 2.2 m wide and 1–1.2 m deep, with a flattish base and sides that were steep at the base but more gently sloping higher up, presumably the result of erosion. It produced small amounts of Middle Iron Age pottery, animal bone, and fired clay.

Ditch 60176 formed a right-angle in the north-east of the oval enclosure, its southern (east–west) arm being recut (as 60801), and extended slightly to the west. Both cuts were 1.1 m wide and over 0.5 m deep, flooding preventing their full excavation. They produced Iron Age pottery and animal bone.

The oval enclosure contained two roundhouses, the larger at the north-west cutting Phase 2A roundhouse 60339, the smaller at the south; in both cases the drip-gullies had been recut. At the north-west, roundhouse 60805 was represented by a *c.* 5 m length of drip-gully, subsequently replaced by roundhouse 60321. The drip-gully of the latter was a slightly irregular circle, *c.* 12 m in diameter, flattened around its south-east facing entrance. It produced Middle Iron Age pottery, animal bone, small quantities of fired clay, and some fragments of fuel-ash slag. Internal post-holes on each side of the entrance may have held door posts or possibly internal supports. Post-hole 60713 was 0.6 m in diameter and 0.3 m deep while post-hole 60628, further inside the building on the north-east side, was oval in shape, measuring 0.27 m by 0.34 m and 0.42 m deep. Both contained Middle Iron Age pottery and fire cracked stones, along with small quantities of fuel-ash slag and fired clay. In the centre of the roundhouse was pit 60336, up to 0.16 m deep, containing no pottery but producing a large amount of fire-cracked stone.

To the south-east, the drip-gully of roundhouse 60373 was 10.8 m in diameter with an east facing entrance. It survived best south-west of the entrance where it had an estimated width of 0.9 m and a depth of 0.3 m. In addition to pottery, animal bone, and fired clay there was a fragment of a quern-stone in the gully terminus. The drip-gully recut (60802), which was of similar dimensions, contained Middle Iron Age pottery, animal bone, and fired clay. There were no internal features within this roundhouse.

To the west of roundhouse 60321, a short length of curving gully (60706) could have been part of the northern arc of a pre-enclosure drip-gully *c.* 10 m in diameter, truncated at the west by the enclosure ditch. However, the presence to its south of numerous pits and post-holes, grouped together as 60799, might suggest that this area was occupied by a building, the gully cutting one pit (60419) and, in turn, being cut by another (60418). The pits and post-holes in the group were generally less than 0.3 m deep, and some may have held posts supporting a fence or screen. Post-hole 60404 to the east was 0.25 m in diameter and 0.31 m deep with a possible post-pad in its base. Pit 60417, in contrast, measured 1.86 m by 1.26 m and 0.69 m deep. Some of the pits contained stones interpreted as pot boilers, and together these features may represent an activity area, although not one associated with food processing. Less than 5 m south of this group was pit (60763), 3.6 m long, 2.4 m wide and 1 m deep, which contained *c.* 1.6 kg of Iron Age pottery, 1.1 kg of animal bone, 0.4 kg of fired clay, a quern-stone, and several iron and copper alloy objects.

There was a similar cluster of pits to the east of roundhouse 60373. The largest, pit 60189 measuring 2.5 m by 1.4 m and 0.8 m deep, contained Middle Iron Age pottery weighing *c.* 0.8 kg and fire-cracked stones. Nearby pit 60186 also contained fire-cracked stones, but no other artefacts. Other pits in this area were small, contained no artefacts, and are described below with the unphased features, although they may belong to Phase 2.

Plate 17. Knapwell Plantation: ditch 60141

A small sub-square enclosure defined by ditch 60141, cutting or abutting the eastern end of the oval enclosure, measured at least 35 m by 34 m (Pl. 17). The ditch averaged 3.2 m wide (although wider in the south-west corner) and up to 1.2 m deep, with access from the north through a 15 m wide entrance; at the north-east it terminated on the southern edge of Phase 3 ditch 60140. It contained a wide range of pottery, from Iron Age to Early Saxon in date. However, in ditch section 60144 (Fig. 16) only prehistoric pottery was recovered from the lower fills (60222, 60267, 60221, 60220, and 60219); its uppermost fill, 60145, produced Romano-British pottery and a single Early Saxon sherd, along with much iron, some lead and several large fragments of quernstone. Quantities of cereal processing waste were recovered from fill 60267, near the base.

Within this enclosure and included in this phase, was curving gully 60197, 0.3–0.5 m wide and 0.13 m deep, forming an arc of projected diameter 9.5 m (see Fig. 16). It produced approximately 0.75 kg of Middle Iron Age and a small quantity of animal bone. Nearby were gully 60431 and pits 60279 and 60280. Gully 60431 was straight, aligned north to south, measuring 7.5 m long, 0.4 m wide and 0.15 m deep. Its charcoal-rich fill contained small amount of Iron Age pottery as well as fired clay and a fragment of iron. Pit 60279 was 0.5 m in diameter, 0.16 m deep and had a concave base, while pit 60280 was slightly larger, measuring 1.1 m by 0.7 m and 0.5 m deep; both produced Iron Age pottery, some animal bone, and fired clay.

An oval pit (60167), measuring 2.4 m by 1.26 m, lay within the entrance to the sub-square enclosure; it was excavated to a depth of 1.2 m and augering showed that it continued for at least a further 0.4 m. Its fills were a mixture of slumped natural clay with usually charcoal-rich tip lines and lenses. Finds comprised Middle Iron Age pottery, animal bone, fired clay, and some stone rubble. After silting up the pit was cut by Phase 3 enclosure ditch 60140 and small, unphased pit 60264, the latter containing a broken leaf-shaped arrowhead.

A group of four post-holes was identified within the north-eastern corner of the enclosure, but they formed no obvious structure and their phasing is uncertain.

Phase 3 – Mid–late Romano-British

During Phase 3 a 0.2 ha, sub-rectangular enclosure was superimposed on the earlier, Iron Age enclosures, defined by ditches 60140 and 60243. It had a 2.7 m wide entrance in its south-west corner and another, of unknown width, in the north-east corner (Figs 15 and 16). Ditch 60140, forming the enclosure's north and west sides, was 2 m wide. In one section (60142) towards the north-east (Fig. 16), the primary fill 60269 was overlain by the organic, probably cess-derived fill 60225, above which was a mixed mineral and organic fill, 60224, that showed signs of having been waterlogged for some time and which changed imperceptibly into fill 60143. Approximately 3 kg of predominantly Romano-British pottery was recovered from this section (there was some residual Iron Age material). Other finds included a 4th century coin of the House of Constantine, recovered from the surface of the ditch. Five metres beyond the south-western terminus of ditch 60140, and probably associated with it, was a less substantial ditch (60430) that continued to the south-west beyond the limit of excavation.

Few features within the enclosure can be shown to be of this phase. An internal division to the eastern half of the enclosure is suggested by east–west ditch 60768. This was traced for *c.* 27 m, with a slight turn to the south at its western end, and was 1.4–2 m wide and up to 0.5 m deep. The small quantity of pottery from it comprised a mixture of abraded Iron Age sherds and some Romano-British material. Pit 60282, which cut Phase 2 gully 60431 (Fig. 16), produced 0.2 kg of pottery, half of which was residual Iron Age material. Measuring 1.7 m by 0.6 m and 0.2 m deep, it contained a partial cow skeleton sealed by redeposited clay (Pl. 18). Oval pit 60811, which cut the southern terminus of roundhouse 60339 in the north-western corner of the enclosure, measured 2.7 m by 1.3 m and was 0.5 m deep, and produced 0.5 kg of pottery, the majority residual and of Iron Age date. Other undated pits in the area could have been either Phase 2 or 3, and are described below as unphased.

Also probably associated with the enclosure, was an L-shaped ditch (60796) which projected east from its eastern side, then turned south beyond the limits of excavation, partly enclosing an area at least 28 m by 18 m. It was 0.6–1.5 m wide and 0.4 m deep. Only three dated features were found within this area, the

Plate 18. Knapwell Plantation: partial cow skeleton in pit 60282

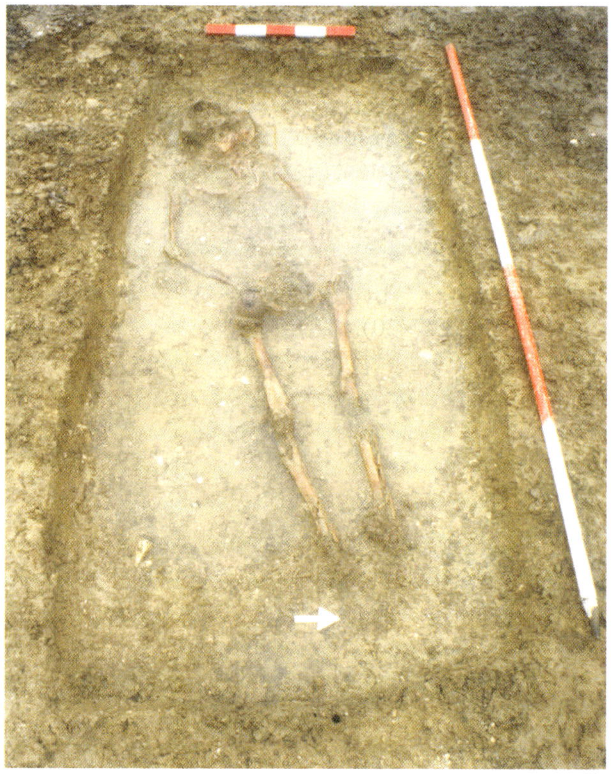

Plate 19. Knapwell Plantation: grave 60292

Plate 20. Knapwell Plantation: pottery vessel in grave 60292

largest being a centrally placed, steep-sided pit 60231, 4.2 m in diameter and 1.12 m in deep, with a *c.* 2 m wide flat base. There were no indications of its use, although large amounts of cereal processing waste were recovered from its primary fill; the pit also contained small amounts of pottery, fired clay, and some iron, and a 3rd century coin of Claudius II came from the top fill. It was recut as pit 60496, *c.* 1.3 m in diameter and 1 m deep. Nearby was a 0.4 m wide gully (60235) which produced no artefacts but contained the largest quantity of cereal processing waste recovered from the site.

Two inhumation graves were uncovered just outside the north-west corner of the enclosure. Grave 60300, measuring 1.15 m by 0.32 m and 0.3 m deep, was orientated approximately north–south and cut into Phase 2B enclosure ditch 60306, close to the northern limits of the excavation area. It had been badly disturbed by later activity, including a modern drain. The skeleton is that of a *c.* 35–54 year old male. Ten metres to the west was the second grave (60292, Pl. 19), oriented east–west, measuring 2.1 m by 1 m and 0.2 m deep. The skeleton, of a *c.* 40–50 year old female, was surrounded by iron nails, indicating a wooden coffin measuring 1.7 m by 0.6 m. The burial was accompanied by a complete 2nd–3rd century pottery vessel (Pl. 20).

Unphased

A number of features could not be easily assigned to either phase. They included pit 60185, east of roundhouse 60373, and pits 60281, 60283, 60285, and 60286 which lay close to Phase 2B curvilinear gully 60197. The largest, pit 60281, was oval and measured 0.98 m by 0.58 m and 0.39 m deep. The three smaller pits were only 0.1 m deep, with 60281 distinguished by a charcoal-rich fill. Pit 60195, 1 m in diameter and 0.16 m deep, was only a few metres to the south-west of gully 60197. Further to the east of 60197 was a very irregular feature (60201), 1.5 m long, 0.42 m wide, and 0.17 m deep. Both 60195 and 60201 contained large concentrations of fire-cracked stone, burnt flint, and charcoal, although with no obvious *in situ* burning.

Jeavons Lane

The site lay towards the centre of the Development Area, centred on NGR 532230 259040 (Fig. 1). It lay across the 65 m contour on the north-western side of a stream valley, less than 1 km from the valley head (Fig. 2). It was bisected by Monkfield Drive, which was still in use at the time of the excavation.

The excavation produced evidence for Iron Age and Romano-British activity throughout the site, mostly within the southern half. Small amounts of Iron Age pottery (Phase 2B) were recovered from three ditches, one forming a part of a possible D-shaped enclosure, and a number of discrete features. These were followed by a rectangular enclosure, a trackway, two probable rectangular buildings, and several clusters of pits and post-holes. This group produced 2nd–4th century pottery (Phase 3), most of it 3rd–4th century in date. Damage from medieval ridge and furrow was evident throughout the site.

Phase 2B – later Iron Age

This earliest phase of activity extended across both excavation areas and consisted of a possible D-shaped enclosure in the southern part of the site, parallel linear boundaries extending into the northern part, a curving ditch, and two ponds or waterholes (Fig. 17).

D-shaped enclosure

The possible large D-shaped enclosure was formed by ditches 80095, 80150, 80261, and possibly 80145, and extended beyond the limits of the site to the south. The excavated portion measured 94 m by 84 m (0.6 ha), but no internal features could be confidently assigned to it. Ditch 80261, forming the west side, ran for 96 m from the southern edge of the site to a terminal 8 m south of the western terminal of curvilinear ditch 80095, which formed the enclosure's north side. The latter ran for 105 m, first east then south-east, ending at a possible eastern entrance near to the southern edge of the excavation. Here there was a 10 m gap between it and ditch 80145, which continued to the south but was not excavated due to flooding in this lowest part of the site. Inside this eastern entrance was a curved ditch 80150, which also continued beyond the limit of excavation to the south. It was at least 38 m long and may have been part of the enclosure boundary or internal entrance arrangements. A change in direction of ditch 80095, to the north of the terminal of ditch 80150, may indicate that that the former was initially shorter, but extended when 80150 was abandoned and replaced by ditch 80145. Three ditches east of the eastern entrance (80149, 80159, and 80160) possibly formed a part of an associated stock control system, including a possible droveway; these, too, could not be excavated due to flooding.

The enclosure ditches were of broadly similar dimensions but contained relatively few artefacts, including Iron Age pottery. Ditch 80261 was *c.* 2.3 m wide and *c.* 0.6 m deep and contained only animal bone, a few sherds of (intrusive) Romano-British pottery, and a fragment of fired clay. The average width of ditch 80095 was 1.5 m but it was only *c.* 0.3 m deep; an iron hook, an iron fitting, and a small

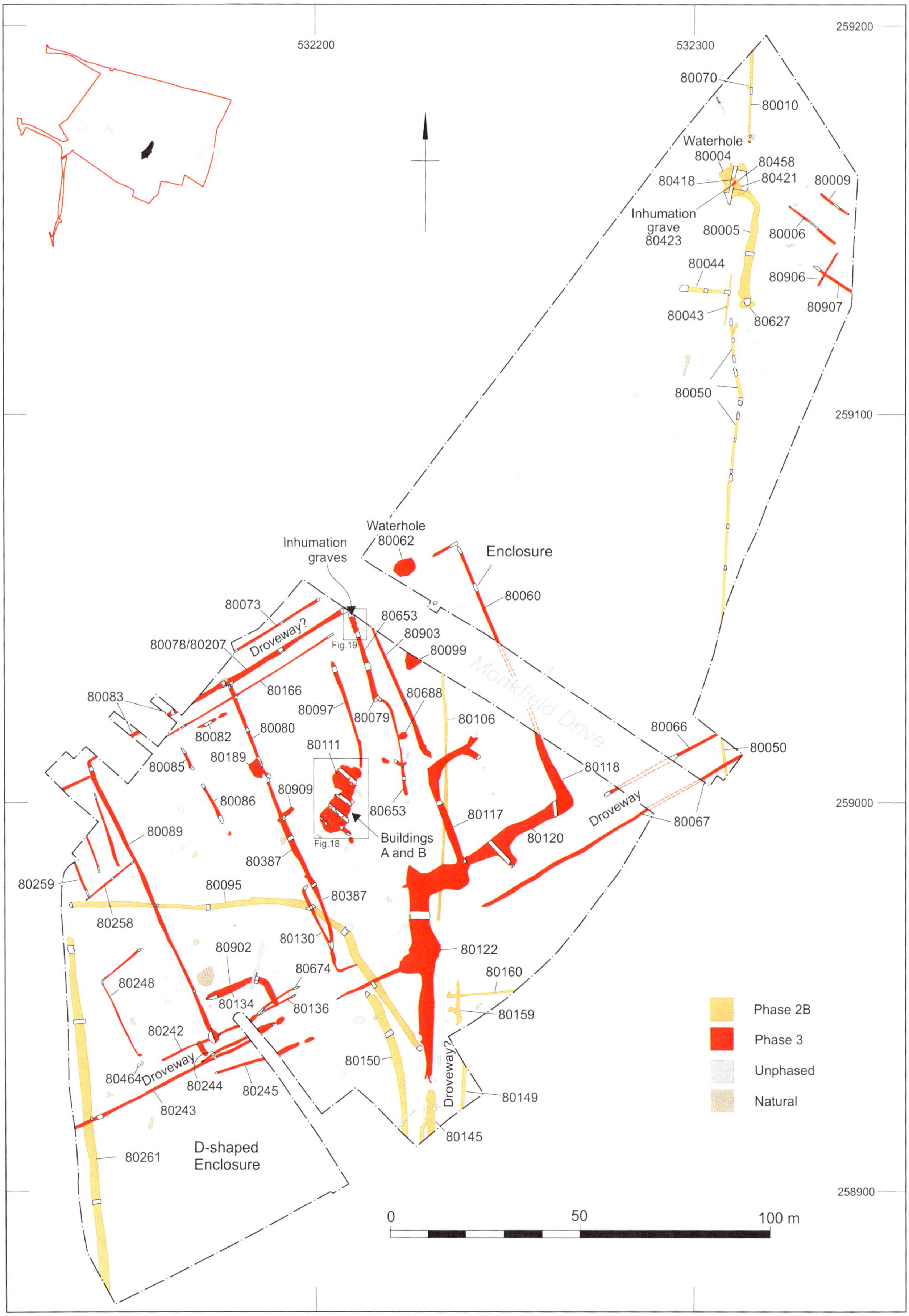

Figure 17. Jeavons Lane: Late Iron Age (Phase 2B) and Romano-British (Phase 3) features

amount of animal bone were the only artefacts recovered. Ditch 80150, which contained only animal bone, had a maximum width of 2 m and a depth of 0.8 m.

Other features
Elements of two parallel ditches, 71 m apart, were identified in the eastern half of the excavation area, aligned north–south, slightly against the slope. The western ditch (80106), which was up to 0.7 m wide and 0.6 m deep, ran for 64 m in the southern part of the excavation but was not recorded north of Monkfield Drive. No datable material was recovered, but it was cut by the Phase 3 ditches 80117 and 80120 (see below). Possible enclosure ditch 80145 appeared to continue its alignment to the south.

To the north-east, in the northern half of the excavation area, ditches 80050 and 80010, separated by a 45 m gap, had the same orientation, continuing to the south and north, respectively, beyond the excavation limits, with an overall length of 187 m. Ditch 80050 was at least 0.7 m wide and 0.4 m deep, with vertical sides and a flat base but, in contrast to ditch 80106, consisted of a series of butt-ended segments, in places separated by narrow gaps between 0.5 m and 2 m wide. It was cut by the Phase 3 droveway ditch 80067 at its southern end, and the small quantity of pottery recovered was all Iron Age in date. Cut by ditch 80010 was a pit (80070), 1.2 m in diameter and at least 1.76 m deep, containing no artefacts.

Part of the gap between ditches 80050 and 80010 was occupied by pond/waterhole 80004. This was irregular in plan, measuring 9.8 m by 7.8 m and 1 m at its deepest, with a shallow U-shaped profile. A narrow ramp had been created on the southern edge to provide access, and its edge had been stabilised with a compacted layer of small, rounded cobbles which extended around the perimeter and upper edges of the feature. Lenses of primary slumping were present at the edges but the principal fill (80415), with its heavy iron mottling, appeared to be a water-lain deposit. It is assumed that this pond was used for watering animals and, although no datable artefacts were recovered, its use was contemporaneous with ditch 80050. A grave and three pits were cut into the upper fill (Phase 3, below).

Also in the gap between ditches 80010 and 80050m was a substantial ditch (80005), 30 m long, 2 m wide and up to 1 m deep, which ran east for 5 m, downslope from the pond/waterhole, before turning south, its southern end cutting undated pit 80627. The only closely datable material, a very small sherd of Romano-British pottery from ditch 80005, could be intrusive; animal bone was also recovered. Running west from ditch 80005, near its southern end, was another ditch (80044), 13 m long, 1 m wide and 0.2–0.4 m deep containing animal bone and a small amount of fired clay, which cut a short length of north–south gully (80043), 13 m long, 0.45 m wide and 0.1 m deep, perhaps an element of boundary 80010/80050.

Phase 3 – Mid–late Romano-British

The main focus of activity in Phase 3 was centred on a rectilinear enclosure, measuring 110 m by 70 m, with droveways immediately to its north-west and south-east (Fig. 17). The enclosure seems to have been laid out with its major axis at 90° to the slope and it partially overlay the Phase 2B D-shaped enclosure. Pottery suggests activity between the middle of the 2nd century and the 4th century, with an emphasis on the late 3rd–4th centuries. Despite the probable loss of many discrete features to ploughing, both medieval and recent, there is sufficient evidence to suggest that the enclosure was associated with domestic occupation. Finds and environmental evidence also point to pastoral and agricultural activity.

Enclosure
The sides of the enclosure were formed by ditches 80060 and 80118 to the north-east, 80207 (with recut 80078) and 80083 to the north-west, 80089 to the south-west, and 80242, 80136 (with recut 80674), and 80120 to the south-east. The main entrance appears to have been in the south-eastern side of the enclosure, with two gaps between the ditches providing access to a southern droveway. With the exception of ditch 80120, these ditches (and the internal ditches, below) were insubstantial, up to 0.8 m wide and 0.4 m deep, although recut 80078 (of 80207) was 1.2 m wide and 0.5 m deep; they contained Romano-British pottery and animal bone, and a very small quantity of slag came from near the southern end of ditch 80089.

Ditch 80120, however, was 4.3–9 m wide, *c.* 1 m deep, and had gently sloping sides, especially towards the south-western end where an adjacent cobbled surface was present. Its size may reflect a combination of drainage and animals being moved and/or penned in this area, with resultant trampling, and its probable use at the south-west also as a waterhole (80122). It produced over 3 kg of animal bone and a 3rd century coin.

The enclosure was divided by two further ditches into three approximately equal parts, perhaps associated with stock control. Other shallow, internal ditches may indicate further sub-division and remodelling, although these could also be relatively early features, pre-dating the division of the enclosure. Towards the west, ditch 80130 had been recut and

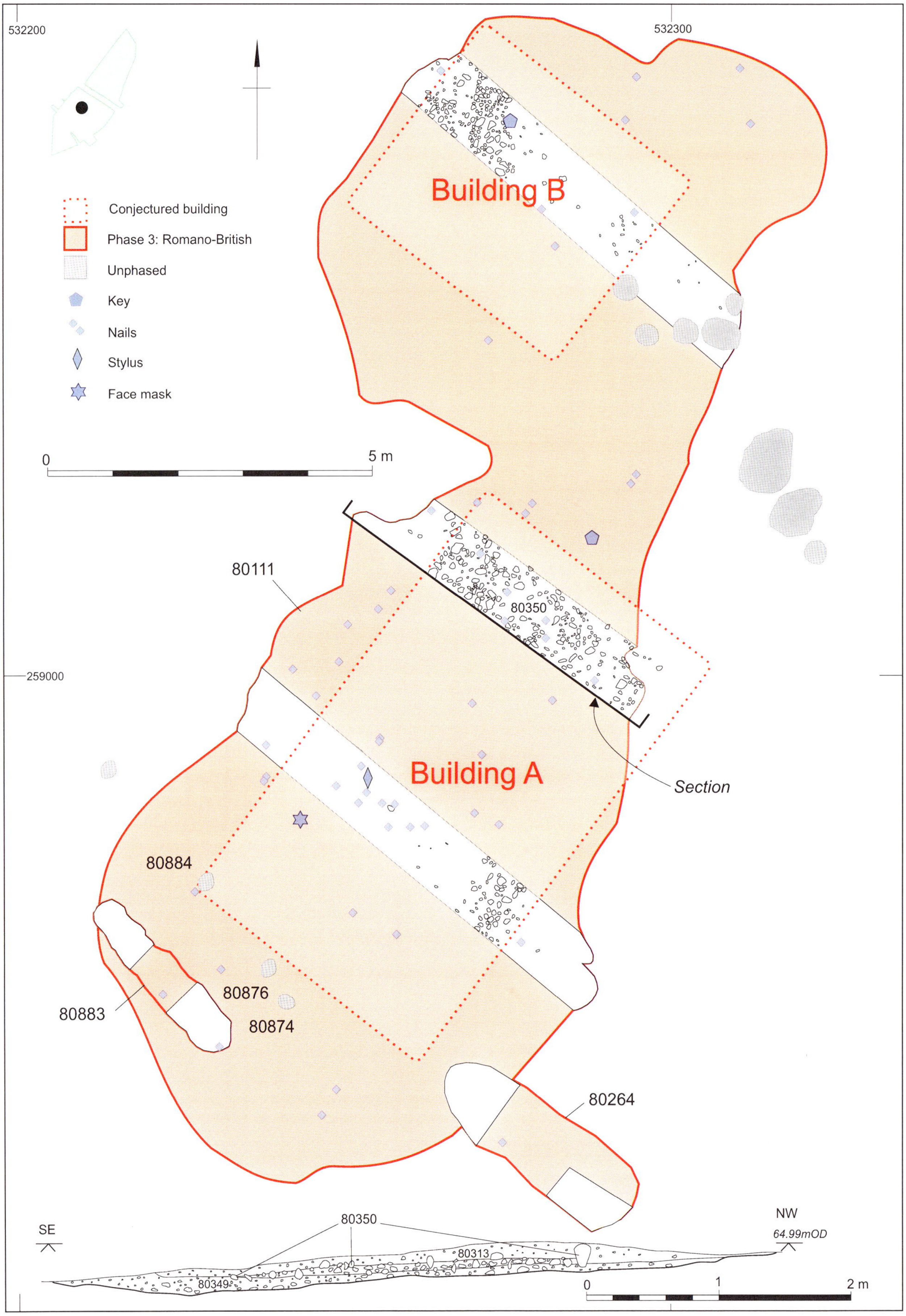

Figure 18. Jeavons Lane: Romano-British (Phase 3) buildings A and B

extended to the north as 80387 and 80080, separating the western and central divisions. Ditch 80166, which spanned the western and central divisions, no more than 5 m inside ditch 80078/80207, may have been contemporary with ditch 80130, perhaps pre-dating ditches 80080/80387. In the south-west corner of the enclosure, a recut, L-shaped ditch (80134/80902), formed a small sub-compartment. Shallow ditches 80085, 80086, with 80082 at 90°, may represent the modification of the western division.

To the east, ditches 80903 and 80117 separated the central and eastern divisions. Two parallel ditches within the central division (80097 and 80653) may have been associated with some remodelling of this area; the former, perhaps associated with Buildings A and B (see below), lay less than 10 m to the west of ditch 80653 which was replaced by ditch 80079. Three graves (80299, 80406, and 80467, Fig. 19), were inserted into the fill of ditch 80079 at its north end (see below). In the eastern division, ditch 80117, which was 1.4 m wide and 0.5 m deep, formed another sub-compartment, in the south-east corner of the enclosure, larger than that in the south-west corner.

In addition to some Romano-British pottery and animal bone, iron objects (two socketed tools, a plough-share, and shears) were recovered from ditches 80079, 80653 and 80903. A silver 2nd century coin and a 4th century coin were recovered from ditch 80134.

Rectangular buildings

In the centre of the enclosure's central division was a shallow irregular hollow (80111), measuring *c.* 18 m by *c.* 7 m and aligned NNE–SSW, filled with deposits sealing what are interpreted as the remains of two rectangular buildings, Buildings A and B (Fig. 18). Three slots were excavated across it.

Building A

The width of the larger building, aligned north-east to south-west, can be estimated at *c.* 4 m by the extent of cobbling in the southern part of the hollow, probably representing the remains of a floor surface. Plotting the positions of nails recovered by metal-detecting suggests that the line of the north-western wall coincides with the edge of the cobbles. The south-western end was probably marked by post-holes 80444, 80874 and 80876, and gully 80883 may have been a drainage feature just outside. The line of this wall may also be indicated by the positions of nails and an iron bar, which perhaps accumulated during the life of the building, finding a final resting place against or close to the outside of the wall, rather than being deposited when the walls collapsed. The cobbling in the south-western slot shows the likely alignment of the south-eastern wall. The building appears to have been some 7.5 m long, although the position of the north-eastern wall was not established and it is not certain whether the iron key recovered here came from inside or outside the building.

The cobbling comprised pieces of chalk and occasional flint nodules pressed into a 0.1 m thick dark soil layer (80349), and even through it into the underlying natural. It probably derived from the overlying layer, up to 0.15 m thick, of many medium and large rounded stones (layer 80350; Fig. 18). Above these was a second dark soil layer (80313). These soil layers produced the greatest quantity and variety of artefacts from the site, comprising almost 6 kg of 3rd–4th century pottery, 2 kg of animal bone, 1.2 kg of ceramic building material, including a few brick and *tegula* fragments, fired clay, shell, and objects of stone, iron, and copper alloy. Among the iron objects were over 50 iron nails and a barb spring padlock key. Among the domestic objects were a face mask from a 4th century flagon (probably curated after it had been broken), recovered close to the north-western wall, a copper alloy spoon probe from close to the south-western wall, the spatulate end of an iron stylus in the central area of the building, and two 3rd century coins.

Building B

This lay immediately to the north of Building A, possibly with the same orientation, and was also sealed by a spread of dark soil, 0.2 m thick. A slot excavated through it showed that this area had also been cobbled, although not as intensively as for Building A. The cobbling only survived in the north-west and here had been cut by a modern field drain; an iron lift key was recovered from within the cobbles. It is possible that this cobbling represented the floor of an ancillary building, of a less substantial scale than Building A. Its dimensions were difficult to establish, but it may have measured *c.* 4 m by 3.5 m. Again, relatively large quantities of 3rd–4th century pottery, animal bone, ceramic building material, and iron objects were recovered.

Other features within the enclosure

Several pits were excavated inside the enclosure. Pit 80189, which cut ditch 80080 (dividing the central and western divisions), was sub-rectangular, measuring *c.* 5 m by 3 m, and 1.05 m deep with steep sides and a flat base. Its fills showed signs of gleying, suggesting waterlogging. A considerable amount of 3rd–4th century pottery was recovered, as was animal bone, fired clay, ceramic building material, and several iron objects including hobnails and a hippo-sandal (a removable horseshoe). Cereal processing waste was also abundant.

Oval pit 80688, to the north-east of Building A, was 2.3 m long and 0.9 m deep with a V-shaped profile. Further north-east and partly under

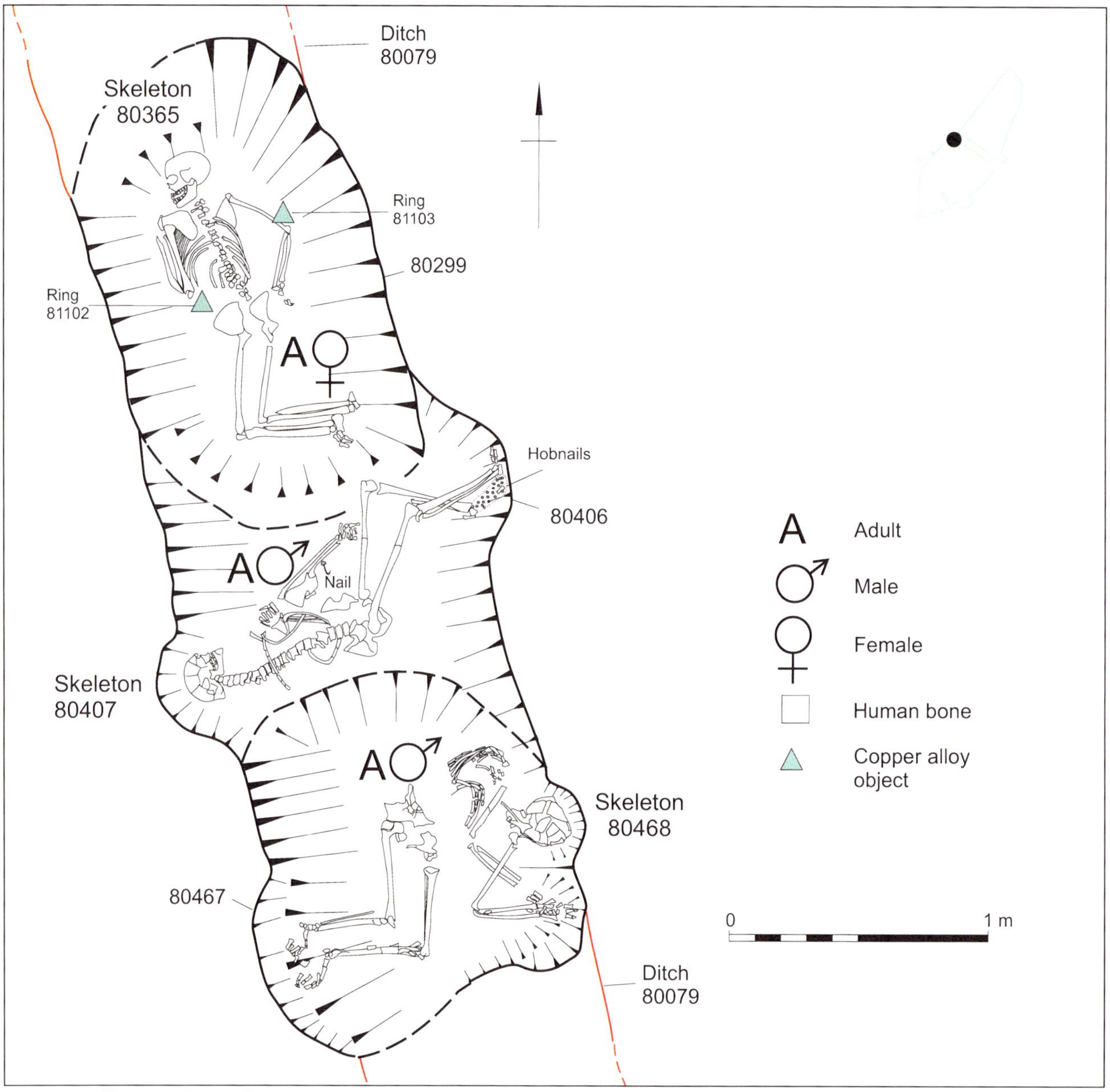

Figure 19. Jeavons Lane: Romano-British (Phase 3) burials in ditch 80079

Monkfield Drive was oval pit 80099, measuring at least 4.3 m by 3.2 m, and 1.65 m deep, which produced large amounts of late 3rd–4th century pottery, including a complete pottery vessel deposited upside down in the bottom, as well as animal bone, some fired clay, ceramic building material, and a bone pin.

Waterhole 80062 lay close to the north-east corner of the enclosure, possibly pre-dating it. It occupied a gap in enclosure ditch 80078/80207. This oval feature, measuring *c.* 6.8 m by 4.4 m and 1.07 m deep, was accessed from the south-west by a shallow, 3.5 m long ramp. Its fill produced a small number of 2nd or 3rd century sherds and a fragment of Romano-British ceramic building material.

Pens or fields

Attached to the south-west end of the enclosure were two small, sub-rectangular pens or fields. The northern, measuring 30 m by 15 m, was formed by ditches 80258 and 80259, and apparently divided into three strips by two shallow ditches running approximately parallel to enclosure ditch 80089. The southern pen, measuring 30 m by 20 m, was formed by ditches 80242 and 80248, and had gaps, possibly entrances, in the north-east and south-western corners. These insubstantial ditches contained little artefactual material.

In the north-east corner of the site were three short, parallel ditches (80006, 80009, and 80907) and a fourth (80906) at a right-angle to them. They were

Plate 21. Jeavons Lane: grave 80299

0.6 m wide and only 0.05 m deep. None produced any artefacts, but they have been tentatively assigned to Phase 3.

Droveway

Immediately to the south-east of the enclosure, and sharing a boundary with it, was a droveway that was up to 11 m wide and extended beyond the site's eastern and western limits. This was represented to the north-east by ditches 80066 and 80067, and to the south-west by ditches 80243 and 80244 defining the droveway's south side; ditch 80245 may also have been an element of the droveway in the south-west. Gaps in the ditches provided access to the enclosure and to presumed fields to its north-east, south, and west. Although not as well-preserved, there may have been a droveway along the northern edge of the enclosure, where ditch 80073 ran parallel to, and 6 m outside, enclosure ditch 80078/80207.

Burials

Four substantially complete inhumation burials were identified, together with redeposited bone from an additional individual. Three of the graves (80299, 80406, and 80467) were recorded adjacent to each other in the northern terminal of ditch 80079 within the central division of the enclosure (Fig. 19). It was not established from what depth the graves had been cut, or what order they were dug in, although they are

Plate 22. Jeavons Lane: graves 80406 and 80467

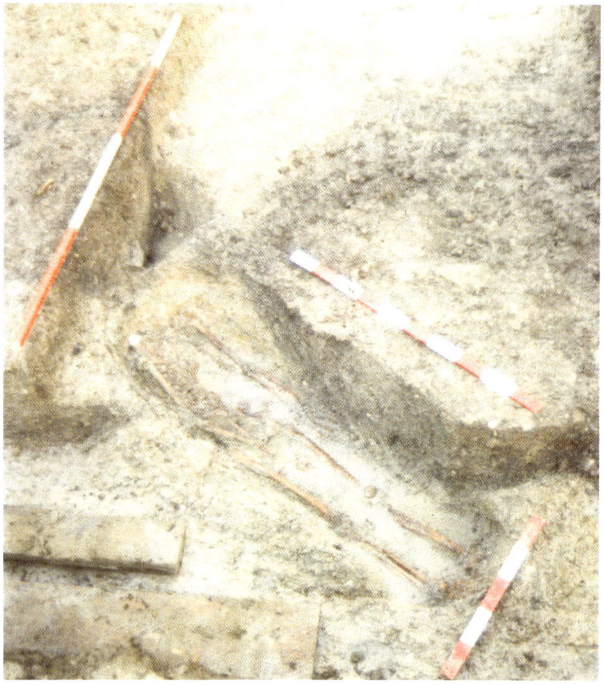

Plate 23. Jeavons Lane: grave 80423 ?decapitation burial

likely to have been broadly contemporary. Each body lay on its side in one of a variety of positions and orientations (Pls 21 and 22). Grave 80299, that of an adult female of *c.* 25–30 years, contained a small number of hobnails, fragments of two copper alloy finger rings (found near the left and right elbows) and 2nd–3rd century pottery. Grave 80406, containing an adult male of *c.* 35–45 years, had 62 hobnails near the feet. Grave 80467, that of another adult male of at least 55 years, contained 2nd–3rd century pottery, fragments of shell and fired clay, and a small fragment of unworked Blisworth Limestone from Northamptonshire (a fragment of the same type of stone was found 150 m to the north-west, near the fourth skeleton). Only the finger rings in grave 80299 and the hobnails (from boots) in grave 80406 are likely to have been buried with the individuals and these indicate a late Romano-British, possibly 4th century date; the other finds may all be residual.

The fourth grave (80423) was dug into the centre of partly silted-up Phase 2 waterhole 80004 at the northern end of the site (Pl. 23). It measured 1.5 m by 0.5 m and 0.4 m deep, orientated north–south. It contained the skeleton of an adult male aged *c.* 40–50 years, laid supine, although there was no trace of the skull and upper cervical vertebrae and this probably represents a decapitation burial. The grave cut two large pits (80418 and 80421). Pit 80421 contained a human femur from another adult, possible male, which had been gnawed by a dog showing that it had been exposed on the surface for at least a short time before burial. In turn, the grave was cut by pit 80458, and all these features were sealed by a layer of natural silting.

Broadway Farm

The site lay at *c.* 56 m aOD on the east side of a spur between two streams at the southernmost tip of the Development Area, centred on NGR 532195 258240 (Figs 1 and 2). It was only 50 m from a small stream to the east, the closest of any of the Cambourne sites to an existing watercourse. The site comprised a rectangular area 150 m by 80 m (*c.* 1.2 ha), and at the time of the excavation was set-aside land.

Its position on locally high ground may have made the site susceptible to erosion, as this was the only excavated site within the Development Area where virtually no medieval ridge and furrow was visible, presumably as it had been largely removed by post-medieval or modern ploughing. This could explain the lack of post-holes or drip-gullies, indicative of settlement, within the excavated enclosures.

All of the features investigated during the excavation were assigned to the later Iron Age, with no features or finds of Romano-British date. However, earlier evaluation produced a small amount of early Romano-British material from a gully just to the north of the site, within an area unavailable for subsequent excavation.

Phase 2B

All features dated to this period – three enclosures with no obviously contemporary internal features, a small number of isolated hearths, pits/post-holes, and two ditches – lay within the northern half of the site (Fig. 20). A single 10 m length of curvilinear ditch (50007) was cut at its eastern end by a ditch of the western enclosure, and so pre-dated it. It was 0.9 m wide and 0.3 m deep, and filled with redeposited natural, containing small amounts of Iron Age pottery, animal bone, and fired clay.

Part of a small, sub-square enclosure with a narrow entrance on the northern side lay in the north-eastern corner of the site. It was formed by ditches 50099 and 50100, measured 18 m by at least 10 m internally, and continued to the east beyond the limit of excavation. The ditches were 2 m wide and up to 0.8 m deep, their sequence of fills suggesting the possibility of an internal bank.

Immediately to its west was a second enclosure, formed by ditches 50101 and 50102. It measured approximately 28 m by 30 m, an area of *c.* 0.08 ha, the ditches being 1.9 m wide and 0.8 m deep. This enclosure had a narrow entrance on its western side, but appeared to be open at the east. If contemporary

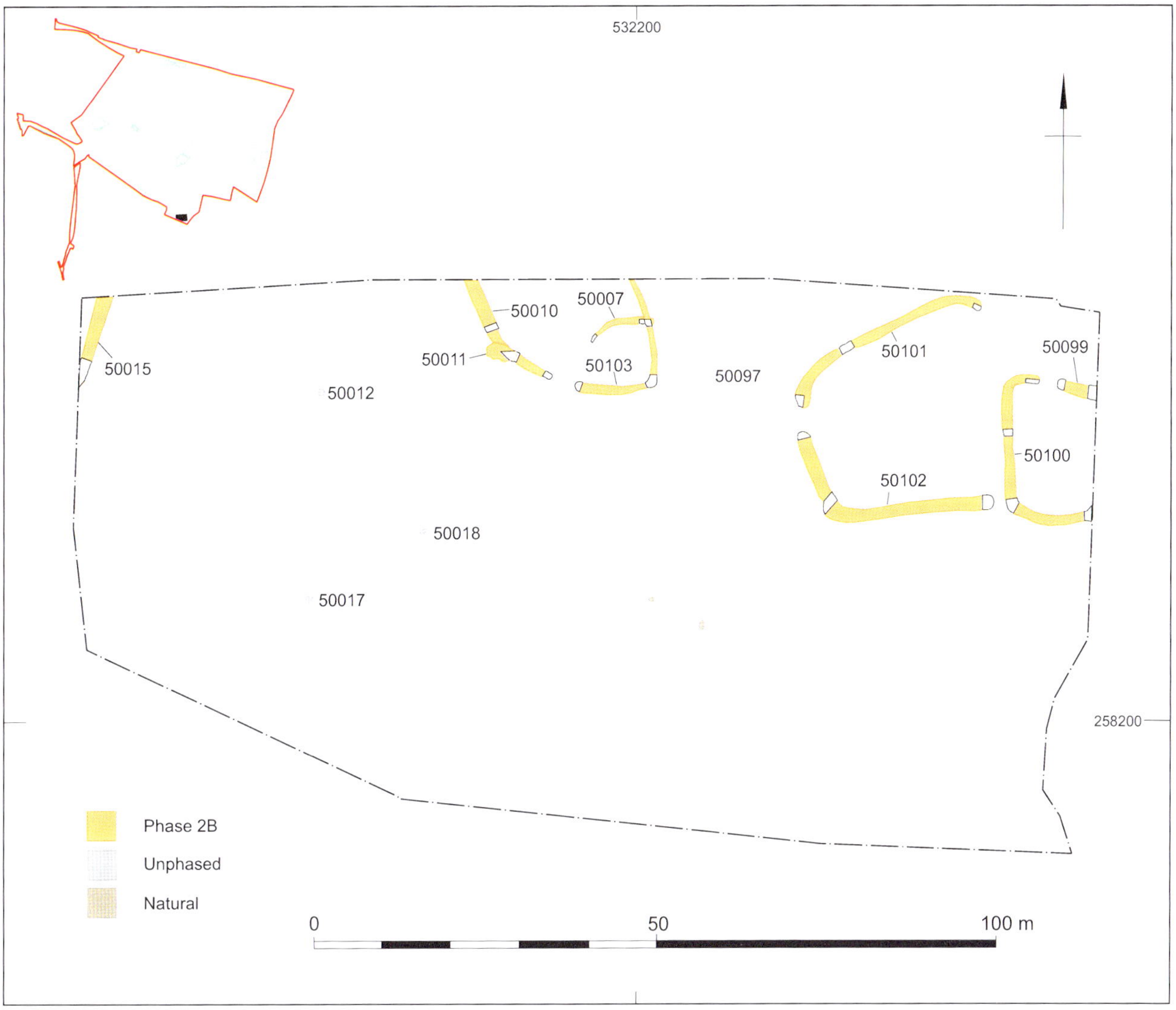

Figure 20 Broadway Farm; later Iron Age (Phase 2B) features

with, or slightly later than the enclosure to the east, its eastern side would have been partly closed by ditch 50100, with a narrow gap at the south-east and a wide gap at the north-east.

A third, possibly oval enclosure, formed by ditches 50010 and 50103, was identified 20 m further west, with a narrow entrance on its southern side. It measured at least 25 m by 17 m, extending beyond the limit of excavation, and occupied an area of at least 0.04ha. The ditches were 0.7m wide and at least 0.35m deep, the sequence of fills suggesting the presence of an external bank. A possible hammer stone of local Greensand was recovered from the eastern ditch terminal. Ditch 50010 was cut by irregular pit or probable tree-throw hole 50011.

Other features included a short section of ditch (50015), running north-east to south-west across the north-western corner of the site. It was 1.6 m wide and 0.65 m deep, and produced a small amount of Iron Age pottery.

Many of the features contained small amounts of fired clay, possibly the remains of daub and perhaps indicative of the former presence of structures, and heat-damaged stones were recovered from several of them.

Unphased

At least six further features, contained no dating material, were identified, mostly in the central and north-western areas of the site. Two heavily truncated hearths (50017 and 50018), both *c.* 0.8 m in diameter and 0.1–0.15 m deep, showed heavy burning of the natural clay and contained large quantities of fire-cracked stone. Pit 50012, 1.2 m in diameter and 0.3 m deep, to the west of the enclosures, and post-hole 50097 between them, also both contained burnt stone, the latter in addition containing animal bones.

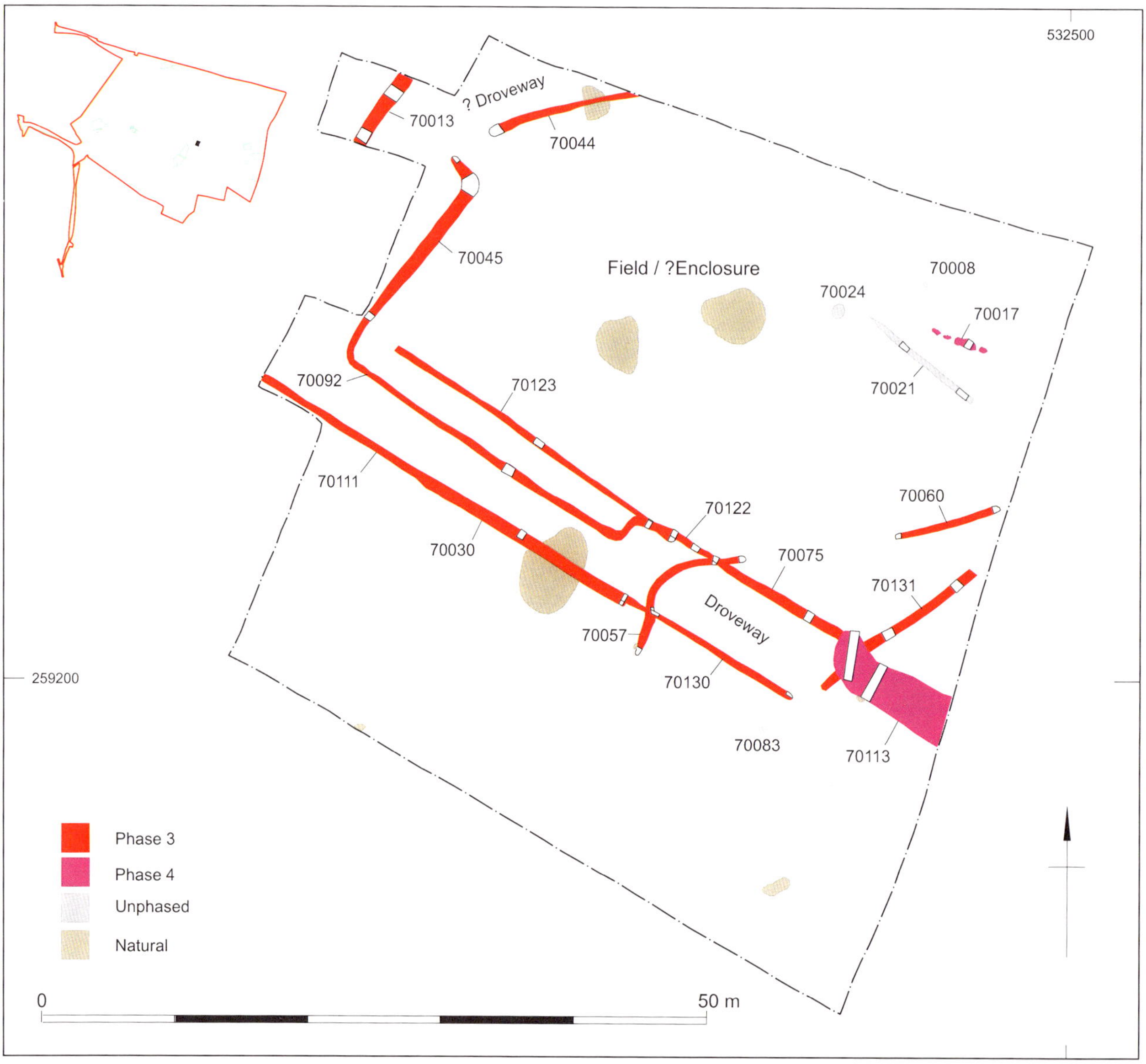

Figure 21. Monk Field Farm: Romano-British (Phase 3) and Saxon (Phase 4) features

Monk Field Farm

This site was near the centre of the Development Area, centred on NGR 532460 259220 (Fig. 1). It was situated on the north-west side of a stream valley, at *c.* 68 m aOD, only 200 m to the north-east of Jeavons Lane (Fig. 2). It comprised a roughly rectangular area 55 m by 55m (*c.* 0.3 ha) which was agricultural land at the time of the excavation.

The excavation produced structural evidence and a modest amount of artefactual evidence for Romano-British and very limited Saxon activity. Remains of medieval ridge and furrow were found over the entire area (Fig. 2). At least two tree-throw holes pre-dated the Romano-British ditches, two others are likely to be of similar, possibly pre-Romano-British date.

Phase 3 – Mid–late Romano-British

Almost all the archaeological features date to the Romano-British period, although not all were contemporaneous. The principal features identified were one or two droveways and a field or possible enclosure. A relatively small amount of datable material, mostly pottery, was recovered, including also a very small amount of Romano-British building material and two coins, as well as two pieces of prehistoric struck flint.

The earliest ditches appear to have been 70030 and 70123, lying parallel and *c.* 7 m apart, and averaging 0.45 m wide and 0.15 m deep. It is possible they were no more than 25 m long, although they may have formed a droveway extending to the north-west of the excavation, but stopping short of a curvilinear ditch (70057) to the south-east. Ditch 70057 may have continued to the north-east as 70060, but the function of this layout of ditches is unclear.

The possible droveway was subsequently remodelled – its western part was narrowed when ditch 70092 replaced ditch 70123, and ditch 70030 was recut as ditch 70111. Curvilinear ditch 70057 went out of use and the droveway was extended to the south-east by ditches 70122/70075 and 70130, extensions of ditches 70092 and 70111 respectively. Ditch 70122 was little more than a shallow gully and may have marked an entrance between the droveway and a field or enclosure to the north. Ditch 70131, almost blocking this end of the droveway, may also have been dug at this time.

At the north-west, ditch 70092 turned sharply to the north-east, as ditch 70045, and with ditch 70044 marked the curving western edge of the field or enclosure, with a 2.5 m wide gap between them creating an entrance. These ditches may also have formed the east side of another droveway leading off to the north-east. Ditch 70013, which may have marked the western side of this possible droveway, was slightly more substantial than most of the other ditches and may indicate more than just a droveway or field boundary.

It was noticeable that the upper fills in most of the ditches dug in the latter part of this phase – i.e. ditches 70044, 70045, 70092, 70075 and 70131 – were of slightly darker material than those of the earlier ditches.

Phase 4 – Saxon

A few sherds of Saxon pottery were recovered from a substantial ditch or waterhole (70113), a probable hedge line (70017, comprising a short line of irregular, shallow scoops), and the upper fill of Romano-British ditch 70045. Ditch or waterhole 70113 was at least 10 m long, 3 m wide and 1 m deep, with an irregular terminal at the north-west end and continuing beyond the limit of excavation to the south-east. It was on the same alignment as the Romano-British droveway defined by ditches 70075, 70130 etc, but it contained several sherds of Saxon pottery near its base. The pottery had an average weight of 4 g and the few fragments of animal bone and fired clay all weighed less than 6 g, suggesting that all of this material may have been residual, making it uncertain whether this feature was dug during the Saxon period, or later.

Unphased

Three undated features – a small ditch or gully (70021), a probable pit (70024), and an isolated sub-circular post-hole with stone post-packing (70008) lay within the possible Phase 3 field north of the droveway. To the south was a small, undated pit (70083).

Little Common Farm

The site lay on the eastern side of the Cambourne Development Area, centred on NGR 533140 259180 (Fig. 1). It was situated towards the head of a shallow valley, at *c.* 70 m aOD, and sloped gently to the north-west (Fig. 2). Approximately 60 m to the north-west, at the base of the valley, was a field boundary formed by a westerly flowing stream. The excavation area covered an approximately rectangular area of 110 m by 90 m (*c.* 1 ha) and was agricultural land at the time of the excavation (Pl. 24).

The excavation produced widespread structural evidence, and a relatively large amount of artefactual evidence, for Middle–Late Iron Age activity. This comprised settlement within a D-shaped enclosure of possibly two or three sub-phases, three roundhouses, a four-post structure, and several associated fields and small enclosures (Fig. 22).

The fills of the ditches within and immediately around the D-shaped enclosure were of dark brown clayey silt, whereas the outlying ditches generally had paler fills. Sections through them revealed many episodes of cleaning and recutting, and it was not possible to understand the full sequence represented. Many features produced Late Iron Age material from the lower fills overlain by charcoal-rich, domestic refuse also containing some Middle Iron Age pottery giving the impression that, after the site was abandoned, midden-like deposits containing earlier domestic material were spread over and filled slight hollows.

Phase 2A

A roundhouse (90240), surviving as discontinuous segments of a drip-gully with a diameter of *c.* 9 m, was sited just north of the D-shaped enclosure, and has therefore been assigned to the pre-enclosure phase (2A), although it could belong to Phase 2B; its backfill produced Late Iron Age pottery. Immediately to its north-east was a roughly circular pit (90354), 1.7 m in diameter, 0.38 m deep, with variable sides and a flat base, which produced over 0.5 kg of Late Iron Age pottery, smaller quantities of fired clay (some with vitrified surfaces), burnt flint, and animal bone.

Phase 2B

The general form of the settlement became established in this period with the laying out of the D-shaped enclosure (see Pl. 24) and associated ditches.

Plate 24. Little Common Farm: aerial view from the north, showing Iron Age D-shaped enclosure overlain by medieval ridge and furrow

Because of the difficulties in identifying the stratigraphical relationship within and between the ditches, the development of the D-shaped enclosure has been difficult to establish. Several sub-phases are represented and perhaps the most likely change was from a larger to a smaller enclosure.

D-shaped enclosure

The largest and probably the earliest form of the D-shaped enclosure was defined by ditch 90006 on the north-west and south-west sides and ditch 90037 to the east, enclosing an area with maximum dimensions of 65 m by 50 m. Ditch 90006, which was 2–6 m wide and 1.5–2 m deep, produced a mixture of Middle and Late Iron Age pottery, animal bone, stone, and a small amount of fired clay. There may have been a southern entrance into the enclosure, across a narrower, shallower part of ditch 90006 immediately east of field ditch 90526, where the fills appeared to have been consolidated. Ditch 90037, which was 0.7–3 m wide and 1–1.5 m deep, produced predominantly Late Iron Age pottery, although a small number of Middle Iron Age sherds were also present, often in the primary fills; other artefacts included *c.* 1 kg of fired clay and much animal bone.

The principal internal ditch (90075), which was 1–3 m wide and 0.7 m deep, divided the enclosure into two parts, leaving a 4 m wide entrance between them at its north-west end, possibly associated with a short length of ditch (90170). It produced mainly Middle Iron Age pottery and animal bone, but may be a slightly later development, rather than a primary feature of the D-shaped enclosure.

A series of short ditches projected into the enclosure at right-angles from its eastern side, their proximity to ditch 90037 suggesting that there was no internal bank at this time. Two appear to respect drip-gully 90145. They were typically 3–6 m long, 0.5 m wide and 0.25 m deep, and although only three, 90239 in the north, 90243 in the centre and 90259 in the south, produced datable material – Middle Iron Age pottery – their similarity suggests that they were contemporary.

Roundhouses and associated features

In the northern half of the enclosure were the remains of two roundhouses (90145 and 90237), with a later ditch (90038) between them. Drip-gully 90145, which was up to 0.36 m wide and 0.17 m deep, formed less than a quarter of a circle *c.* 11 m diameter, with no evidence for an entrance; it produced small quantities of Middle Iron Age pottery and animal bone.

Drip-gully 90237 was 0.3 m wide, 0.15 m deep and 8.5 m in diameter, with a 2 m wide gap in the east forming a probable entrance; it produced fragments of non-local Greensand quern-stone. Two post-holes set 1 m inside the entrance, lay 1.5 m apart. They

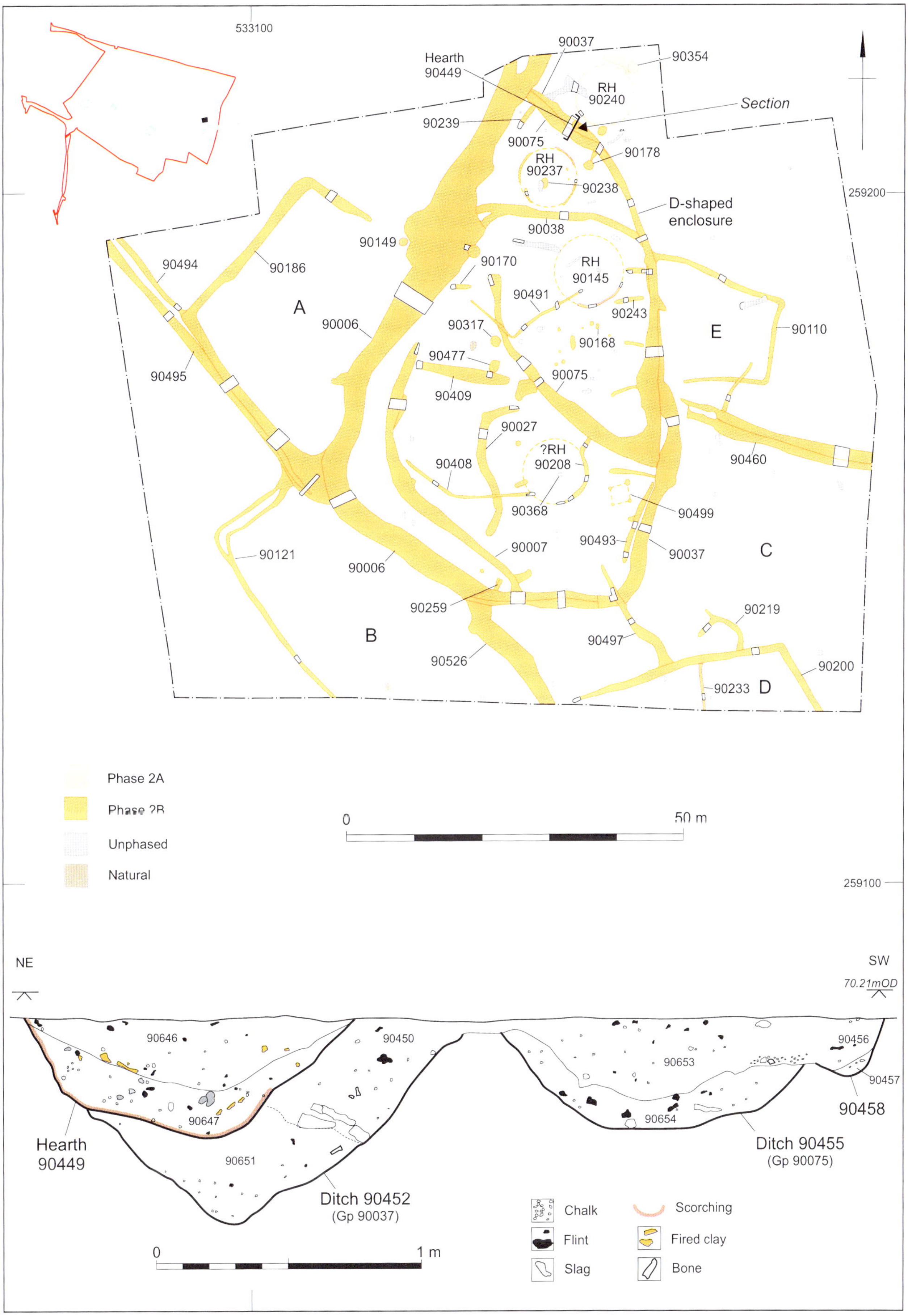

Figure 22. Little Common Farm: later Iron Age (Phases 2A and 2B) enclosures, roundhouses, and associated features

were *c.* 0.2 m deep. Slightly south-west of centre was an area of scorched natural (90238), 1.5 m by 0.7 m, probably the remains of a hearth.

Immediately to the east of roundhouse 90237 was sub-circular pit 90178, 1.4 m in diameter and 0.55 m deep with steep-sloping sides and a rather irregular base, which contained several Middle Iron Age pots (eg. Fig. 29, 6) and animal bone. North-west of roundhouse 90237, and possibly post-dating it, was a hearth (90449) cut into the top of silted up enclosure ditch 90037 (Fig. 22). It measured 1.25 m by 0.9 m and was 0.45 m deep, with a layer of heat-reddened clay at the base, and contained a circular fired clay plate with a central perforation, probably a piece of portable kiln furniture.

Near the centre of the enclosure and south of roundhouse 90145 was a group of at least 12 pits or post-holes and burnt patches. There are noticeably more of these features in this area than anywhere else on site. Only one, post-hole/pit 90168, contained any artefacts – Late Iron Age pottery, animal bone, and fired clay.

In the southern part of the enclosure, curvilinear ditch 90208 is probably that of a roundhouse drip-gully, having a diameter of *c.* 9 m. It was up to 0.78 m wide and 0.33 m deep with a flat base, becoming deeper and wider to the north to enable it to drain into ditch 90075. A patch of burnt clay (90368), 0.6 m in diameter and 0.12 m deep, may have been the remains of a central hearth.

To its east was a slightly irregular four-post structure (90499) measuring 2.6 m by 2.8 m. The post-holes were between 0.4 m and 0.8 m in diameter and 0.17 m and 0.28 m deep. None contained any dating evidence.

Immediately south-west of ditch 90075 was a circular pit (90317), 1.4 m diameter and 0.28 m deep. On its base were the base and body sherds of a Late Iron Age vessel – possibly a 'placed deposit'. A few metres to its south, pit 90477 also contained Late Iron Age pottery.

Other internal features

Various ditches within the D-shaped enclosure are likely to reflect a remodelling of its interior, or a reduction in its size. The east and west boundary ditches (90037 and 90006) were maintained throughout this period, although not always recut on exactly the same line. Recuts were identified in the north, north-east, and south of the enclosure, while a 12 m long ditch (90493), running parallel to and 0.4 m inside the southern part of ditch 90037, may also be a later addition.

Similarly, ditch 90007 parallel to and *c.* 4 m inside the south-western part of enclosure ditch 90006, may have redefined the enclosure boundary in this area. Ditches 90006 and 90007 both contained Late Iron Age pottery and may both have been open at the same time, although it is possible that the inner ditch replaced the outer, with its northern terminal forming an entrance to the west.

The main internal ditch (90075) may have silted up and been replaced by 90038 further to the north, slight kinks in the latter suggesting that the roundhouses 90145 and 90237 still stood when it was dug. It was 1.25 m wide and 0.33 m deep, its west end showing at least one recut, and it contained Late Iron Age pottery, animal bone, ceramic building material, and fired clay. The western enclosure ditch (90006) was unusually wide at this point; perhaps functioning there as a waterhole.

Internal ditch 90409 may have created a further division within the enclosure, perhaps separating domestic occupation to the north from stock and/or 'industrial' activity to the south. It was 14 m long, 1.3–2 m wide and 0.35 m deep, and contained Middle Iron Age pottery, animal bone, and fired clay. Curving ditch 90027, apparently respecting ditches 90007 and 90075, also appears to have been an internal division. It was 1.3 m wide, 0.6 m deep and contained relatively unabraded Middle Iron Age pottery, including a pygmy cup, animal bone, and fragments of fired clay.

Two later internal ditches (90408 and 90491), cutting ditches 90027 and 90075 respectively, were different in character, being straighter and narrower, up to 0.4 m wide and 0.57 m deep with very steep to vertical sides. They contained a mixture of Middle and Late Iron Age pottery, including a 1st century BC amphora handle.

External features

The D-shaped enclosure was surrounded by other, smaller, enclosures and possible fields. The low level of finds from their ditches and the absence of structural remains indicate that these were not settlement enclosures, and their phasing is tentative.

Ditch 90495, extending north-west from the western corner of the enclosure, was 1.4 m wide, 0.4 m deep and produced a few sherds of Middle Iron Age pottery and some animal bone. It was subsequently cut by ditch 90186, which turned north-east then south-east back towards the main enclosure, defining Enclosure A, covering an area *c.* 20 x 30 m, with an entrance at its north-east corner. The ditch was 1.5 m wide and 0.4 m deep with a U-shaped profile, and although it contained no artefacts it appeared to be contemporary with ditch 90494 which continued to the north-west, parallel to the line of ditch 90495. Ditch 90494 produced a small amount of Middle Iron Age pottery. On the south-east side of the entrance was a circular pit (90149), 1.25 m in diameter and 0.36 m deep, with large sherds of Late Iron Age pottery on its base, and an upturned cattle skull in the centre of the top fill; these may represent 'placed deposits'.

To the south-west of the main enclosure, ditch 90121 formed a rectangular field or enclosure (Enclosure B) probably broadly contemporary with Enclosure A. It was 1 m wide and 0.2 m deep and showed signs of recutting; it contained Middle Iron Age pottery.

South and east of the main enclosure, ditches 90460 and 90526, both of which continued beyond the excavation area, may define a field or a further, relatively large enclosure (Enclosure C), and were probably added at broadly the same time as Enclosures A and B. Neither ditch contained any artefacts. Between them was a series of smaller ditches (90200, 90219, 90233, and 90497), mostly up to 1 m wide and 0.5 m deep, and some forming a rectilinear layout of small fields or enclosures (Enclosure D). One (90497) cut ditch 90037 of the main enclosure indicating that this group was a later development (although how much later is not known).

East of the main enclosure, and a few metres to the north of recut ditch 90460, ditch 90110 formed a *c.* 15 m by 15 m sub-square enclosure (Enclosure E) with an entrance at its south-west corner. This ditch was 1 m wide, 0.25 m deep and contained Late Iron Age pottery, animal bone, and some fired clay.

There were, in addition, 28 probable tree-throw holes across the site. Although all undated, many contained burnt material.

The Fields

The Fields excavation lay midway between Little Common Farm and The Grange and close to Great Common Farm, at NGR 533140 258980 (Fig. 1). The site was located on flat ground between two streams at *c.* 71 m aOD (Fig. 2). A rectangular area measuring 50 m by 72 m (0.36 ha) was stripped.

The Site was excavated in order to recover a plan of two superimposed field systems of probable Romano-British date that were identified in evaluation. However, truncation by medieval ridge and furrow and the similarity in the nature of the fills, meant that it was not possible to demonstrate conclusively which system was the earliest. An unusually large number of tree-throw holes were present; where relationships could be established these pre-dated the field systems.

Phase 2 – Later Iron Age

Ditches 77054 and 77055, both aligned approximately ENE–WSW, were the earliest features (Fig. 23). Ditch 77054 was irregular in plan and had steep to gently sloping sides and a flat base. Ditch 77055 to the south was similar and perhaps an offshoot of 77054, but the relationship between the two had been obscured by medieval ridge and furrow. They were 0.63–0.92 m wide and 0.34–0.55 m deep, and both contained small quantities of abraded Middle Iron Age pottery. They may have been boundary ditches associated with Little Common Farm Phase 2 settlement to the north (see above).

Phase 3 – Mid–late Romano-British

Two rectilinear ditch systems were recorded, on slightly different alignments, both containing Late Iron Age/early Romano-British pottery (Fig. 23). A small number of investigations was undertaken on areas where the relationship between them might be observed, although, as noted above, the relationship was difficult to establish. However, the earlier of the two systems was probably that bounded to the west and south-west by ditch 77042, and divided by east–west aligned ditches 77044 (in the middle of site) and 77056 and 77053 (to the north). Parallel to ditch 77042 in the south-west was ditch 77046; these two ditches possibly defining a 7.8 m wide droveway running north-west to south-east.

Ditch 77042 was 0.66 m wide and 0.18 m deep with sloping sides and a concave base. Ditch 77044 was 0.56 m wide and 0.28 m deep with vertical sides and a flat base; Ditch 77053 was 0.86 m wide 0.21 m deep with sloping sides and a concave base. Ditch 77056 was not excavated. None produced any datable finds.

The later ditch system consisted of grid pattern of broadly parallel ditches, aligned WSW–ENE and NNW–SSE, which appeared to cut earlier ditches 77042 and 77044, although the shallowness of the ditches and similarity in their fills makes this uncertain. The ditches, which formed a series of rectangular 'compartments', approximately 9 m wide and 13 m to 17 m long, were of similar size and profile to those of the earlier system, and produced only occasional pottery, all of early Romano-British date. Gaps in ditch 77041, in the centre of the site, may mark entrances, although as no similar gaps were identified, they may simply represent variations in the depth of the ditch.

To investigate the possibility that the ditched 'compartments' formed animal pens, a magnetic susceptibility survey was undertaken with readings on a 5 m grid. The results are difficult to interpret, but there were peaks in the readings that may relate to the NNW–SSE aligned ditches. Particular peaks were identified along the eastern edge of the site and also on the possible entrance terminals along ditch 77041, possibly indicating areas of trampling.

The regularity in the layout of these ditches, particularly that of the second system, finds no

Figure 23. The Fields: later Iron Age (Phase 2) and Romano-British (Phase 3) features

parallel elsewhere at Cambourne. It could, therefore, be suggested they are not Romano-British in date, and that the few finds in them are residual. However, they post-date the Iron Age features and pre-date the medieval ridge and furrow, which is on a different alignment. A Romano-British date is, therefore, the most likely for both ditch systems, although whether they were for stock or were small arable fields remains unclear.

Great Common Farm

The site at Great Common Farm lay on a plateau, along the eastern limit of the Development Area, centred on NGR 533300 259050 (Figs 1 and 2). It comprised a rectangular plot of land of *c.* 0.87 ha, and at the time of the excavation was under a set-aside regime. The few archaeological features identified were principally of Romano-British date (Fig. 24).

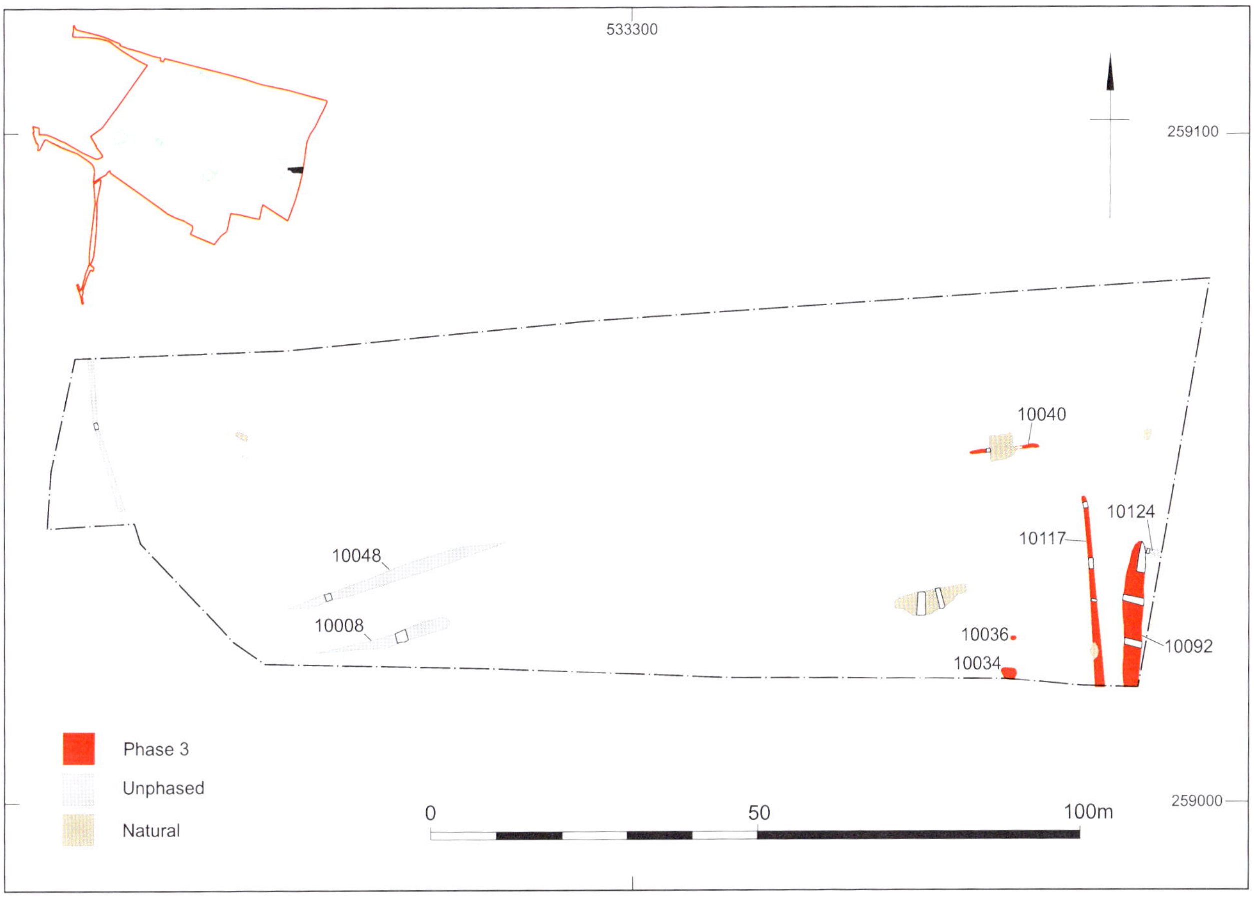

Figure 24. Great Common Farm: Romano-British (Phase 3) features

Phase 3 – Mid–late Romano-British

Romano-British features were concentrated in the south-eastern corner of the Site. Ditch 10092, which ran north for 22.5 m from the southern edge of the site, was 2.5–3 m wide and 1.2 m deep with steep sides. Romano-British pottery of 1st–3rd century date and animal bones were recovered, and the primary fill contained relatively large amounts of cereal processing waste. Four metres to the west, on a slightly diverging alignment, was ditch 10117, which was at least 35 m long, 0.8 m wide, and 0.3 m deep. Some 2nd century pottery and a small quantity of fired clay were the only finds recovered.

Approximately 10 m north-west of the terminal of ditch 10117, was a very badly truncated east–west gully 10040, 10.9 m long, 0.52 m wide and 0.07 m deep, cut by a large tree-throw hole. It produced four sherds of Romano-British pottery.

There were two pits (10034 and 10036) 12 m west of ditch 10117. Sub-rectangular pit 10034, which measuring 2.4 m by at least 1.6 m and 0.42 m deep and extended south of the site, contained 1st to mid-3rd century Romano-British pottery. To its north, a small oval pit (10036), 0.85 m long and 0.65 m wide, contained two iron nails of probable Romano-British date.

Unphased

Three undated, shallow ditches, with maximum depths of 0.2 m, were identified in the western part of the Site, all of them predating the medieval ridge and furrow. Two (10008 and 10048) were parallel, and the third ditch lay at a right angle to them.

The Grange

The site was on the eastern edge of the Development Area, centred on NGR 533270 258800 (Fig. 1). It lay at *c.* 70 m aOD on the edge of the east facing side of a broad stream valley that drained south to the Bourn (Fig. 2). At the time of excavation the area was set-aside land.

A significant proportion of the site was affected by modern disturbances, probably associated with Bourn Aerodrome that once extended into the eastern parts of the Development Area. Large sub-rectangular features, the remains of 20th century buildings, dominated the north-eastern corner of the site, and within the interior of the Romano-British enclosure, an area of 555 m^2 was disturbed by a modern intrusion. A trench containing a ceramic water pipe

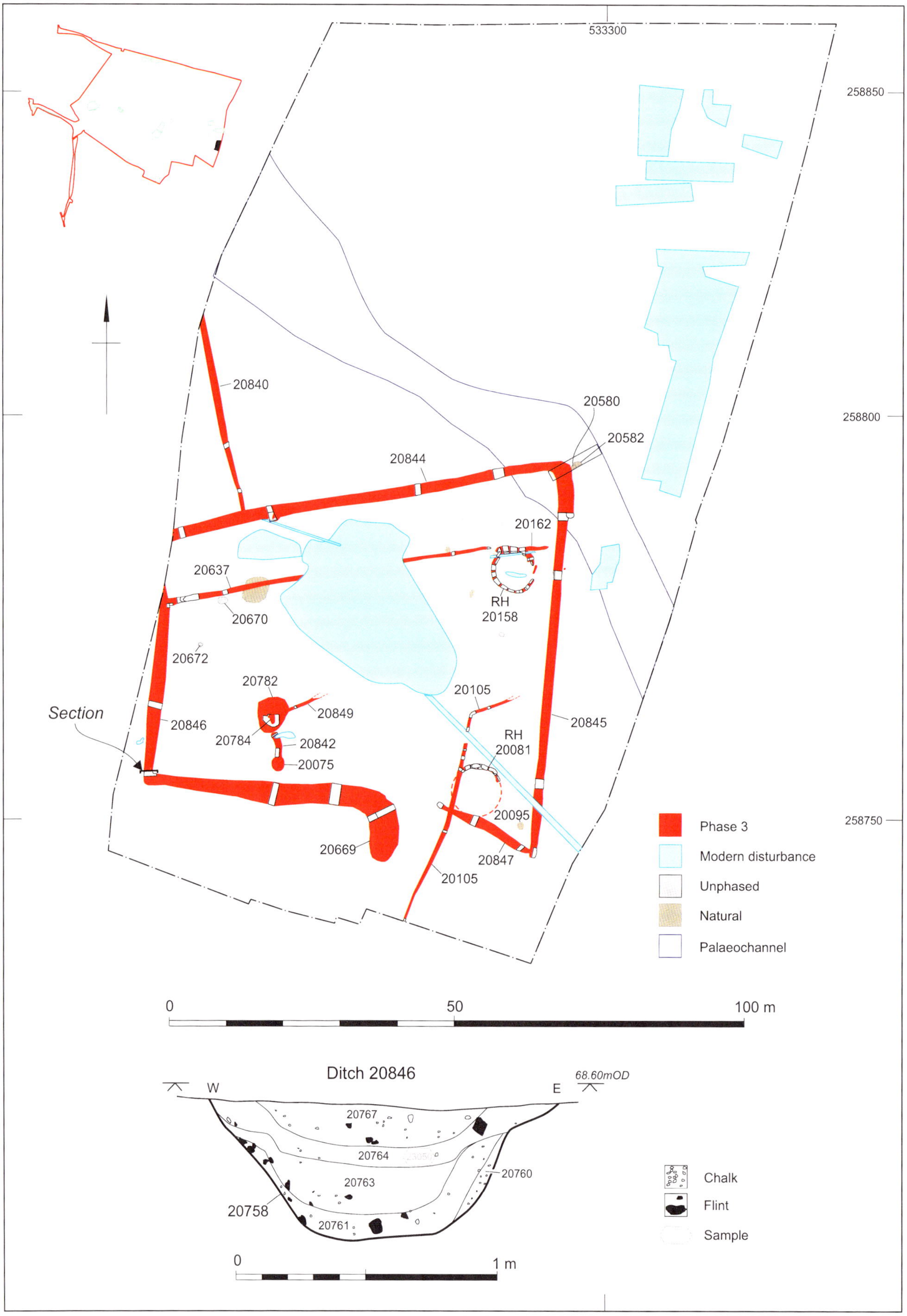

Figure 25. The Grange: Romano-British (Phase 3) features

extended from this disturbance, running south-west to the edge of site.

Activity was principally of the 1st–3rd centuries (Phase 3) and, although a small but significant proportion of the pottery was Early Saxon, no features could be dated to this period. Medieval ridge and furrow was observed across much of the site.

Phase 0 – Undated and natural features

The site was crossed by an undated palaeochannel, 6–22 m wide (Fig. 25). Where sectioned, it was 8.6 m wide and 1.3 m deep, with a shallow sloping side to the south-east, a steeper north-west side, and a 3 m wide flat base. The fills were broadly horizontal, comprising reddish-brown or grey, sandy silt loams.

Two pit-like features (20580 and 20582) in the upper fill of the palaeochannel are assumed to be natural, formed during the final stages of palaeochannel development; they were cut by the Romano-British enclosure ditch.

Phase 3 – Mid–late Romano-British

Enclosure

The principal feature was a trapezoidal enclosure measuring 70 m east–west and 45–65 m north–south, with a *c.* 6.5 m wide entrance towards the south-east corner (Fig. 25). It enclosed an area of *c.* 0.35 ha that contained at least two roundhouses, represented by drip-gullies.

The enclosure was defined by ditches 20669, 20844, 20845, and 20846, and a further ditch (20847) narrowing the entrance. The ditches were recut at least once, during which the largest ditch, ditch 20669 on the west side of the entrance, was slightly remodelled, the recut reducing its width from 5 m to 3.5 m but deepening it from 1.2 m to 1.4 m. No closely datable material was recovered from the original cuts, but dating evidence from the recuts comprised principally 1st to mid-3rd century pottery, although 1.4 kg of 4th century sherds were recovered from the recut of ditch 20845. In addition, small quantities of Saxon pottery came from the upper fills in three sections of the recuts of ditches 20844 and 20846.

Excavated section 20758 of ditch 20846 (see Fig. 25) is typical of the sequence of infilling of the enclosure ditches. There were three components of the primary fill: 20760 was a reddish-brown sand eroded from a geological band in the east of the cut; 20761 was a reddish-brown sandy clay containing some animal bone; and fill 20763 was a greyish-brown silty clay. Secondary fill 20764 was very dark greyish-brown silty clay with very few inclusions. The tertiary fill, 20767, was a dark greyish-brown silty clay.

Pottery was the principal find from the enclosure ditches, but other finds included copper alloy objects, a puddingstone quern fragment, and a small quantity of animal bone. Cereal processing waste was recovered from three locations, all close to the roundhouses. Charcoal appeared to be most common in the central parts of both the northern and western enclosure ditches.

Ditch 20637, parallel to the northern side of the enclosure, created a 10 m wide internal division, with a *c.* 11 m wide gap between its eastern end and the enclosure ditch. The gap was subsequently blocked by a shallow gully (20162), 9 m long, 0.8 m wide and 0.25 m deep, which produced no finds and which cut roundhouse gully 20158 (below). Ditch 20637 was recut twice, the first time leaving a 2 m wide gap at its western end; the second increasing this gap to 2.5 m. Pottery from it was of 1st to mid-3rd century date and, as with the main ditches, Saxon material was present in its latest fill.

Extending at least 35 m NNW from the enclosure was a probable field ditch (20840), measuring 0.7–1.05 m wide and 0.1–0.2 m deep, with a fairly shallow U-shaped profile; it produced no artefacts.

Roundhouses

A roundhouse drip-gully of two phases was identified in the north-east corner of the enclosure, south of the gap at the east end of internal ditch 20637 (Pl. 25). The earliest element comprised a 6.6 m long curved gully, averaging 0.38 m wide and 0.12 m deep, with a U-shaped profile. This was succeeded by a penannular gully (20158), *c.* 6.5 m in diameter with an east facing entrance marked by well-defined rounded terminals. This gully was 0.35–0.8 m wide and 0.15–0.3 m deep with a U-shaped profile and several post-holes or post-impressions in the base. It contained 1st to mid-3rd century pottery, fired clay, animal bone, a small amount of shell, and a stone rubber. Considerable quantities of cereal processing waste came from either side of the entrance. Within the entrance was a slightly off-centre gully, measuring 1.4 m by 0.15 m and 0.17 m deep, probably part of the entrance arrangements.

In the south-eastern corner of the enclosure was curvilinear gully (20081), averaging 0.6 m wide and 0.2 m deep, which formed the northern quarter of a circle of *c.* 8.5 m diameter, the rest probably truncated by ridge and furrow. Like penannular gully 20158, it had several poorly defined post-holes in its base. It contained predominantly 1st to mid-3rd century pottery, along with small quantities of fired clay, animal bone, and two iron nails.

Plate 25. The Grange: roundhouse 20158

Plate 26. The Grange: Anglo-Saxon copper alloy girdle hanger (length = 117 mm)

Other internal features

To the north-west and south of drip-gully 20158 were several possible post-holes, ranging from 0.2 m to 0.8 m in diameter and 0.1–0.4 m deep. Few contained artefacts and there was no patterning to their distribution.

Several features were recorded in the south-west part of the enclosure. These included an irregular, shallow hollow (20782), *c.* 6 m in diameter and 0.22 m deep, containing 1st to mid-3rd century pottery, a small number of iron objects, animal bone, fired clay, and shell. The hollow (and gully 20849, below) was cut by pit 20784, measuring 0.63 m by 0.3 m and 0.15 m deep, which contained possibly 1st–2nd century pottery and animal bone.

Pit 20075, 4 m south of the hollow, was 2.33 m in diameter and 0.36 m deep, both its fills producing 1st to mid-3rd century pottery; its upper fill had many sherds from a single whiteware flagon, a quern fragment, and a hammer stone. Between pit 20075 and the hollow was curvilinear gully 20842 containing Romano-British pottery. Another gully (20849), running north-east from the hollow for 5 m before being truncated by ridge and furrow, also contained Romano-British pottery as well as some burnt stone.

A few other features within the enclosure may have been contemporary with it but contained no datable finds. They include, at the west, a possible sub-circular pit (20672), *c.* 0.7 m in diameter and 0.2 m deep, containing *c.* 10 kg of burnt stone. A nearby, possible pit (20670) had a sterile fill. Close to the enclosure entrance was tree-throw hole 20095.

Later features

A later phase of activity is represented by gully 20105 which cut enclosure ditch 20847 and the western side of drip-gully 20081. It was at least 41 m long and aligned SSW–NNE, turning ENE near its northern end where it was truncated by ridge and furrow. Gully 20162 (see above), which cut the northern side of drip-gully 20158, may be a contemporary feature.

Phase 4 – Saxon

Early Saxon material was present in the upper fills of several features, but no Saxon features were identified. A total of 300g of Saxon pottery was recovered from the upper fills of enclosure ditches 20844, 20846, and the latest recut of internal ditch 20637, and a Saxon copper alloy girdle hanger (Pl. 26) came from the surface of ditch 20846.

3. Evidence of Earlier Prehistoric Activity

The local and wider Neolithic and Bronze Age landscape

by Chris J. Stevens

Rising waters

Cambourne lies just beyond the fen-edge, between the Great Ouse valley and the Cam valley. The period spanning the 4th millennium BC to the beginning of 1st millennium BC saw several changes within the fens immediately to the north as the existing hydrological systems readjusted to the rising sea-level.

In the millennium prior to the Neolithic there is evidence to suggest that silts were being laid in the lowest parts of the fens as a result of the increased sea-level. The onset of peat formation is also seen in the tributaries and main channels of both the Great Ouse and the Cam in response (Hall and Coles 1994, 28). In the southern fen there was occupation of the edges of the drier islands and the fen-margin during the Neolithic, many sites becoming buried by subsequent alluviation and peat formation. The beginning of the 3rd millennium BC saw a rapid growth of marine influence in the fen area, with Whittlesey becoming an island. By the mid–late 3rd millennium the marine influence had spread much closer to the southern fen-edge, depositing marine silts over much of the basin between Whittlesey and March, and on the northern side of the Isle of Ely. The 2nd millennium saw a reversion to freshwater influence, particularly in the south-east fen edge from the Ouse to the Cam Valley. By the end of the millennium several of the slightly elevated areas of land lying within the fen had become isolated, forming small 'islands', for instance the area encompassing Stonea, Chatteris, March, and Manea, and eventually most of Ely.

Settlement of Neolithic–Late Bronze Age date is well documented for much of the area to the north of Cambourne, along the lower reaches of the Ouse Valley, for example in the area around Barleycroft, Willingham, and Over (Evans and Knight 2000; 2001). However, settlement of this date around Cambourne itself, as seen at the excavated sites, is much rarer. This, combined with the generally lower potential for the preservation of environmental evidence in the area, means that by comparison with the fen the environment of Cambourne at this date is much less well known.

The clearing of forest

Palynological studies have demonstrated a transition in the general region from the Early Mesolithic to the beginning of the Neolithic, from forest dominated by pine and hazel to one dominated by oak and elm woodland, a pattern mirrored across parts of southern and eastern England (Godwin 1984). Work conducted during the fenland dyke project indicated not only a Late Mesolithic/Early Neolithic climax woodland dominated by oak, elm, ash, and hazel, but probably also with a substantial lime component (Scaife 1992; 1993; 2001; Hall and Coles 1994, 39; French 2003, 102). It is likely that alder and willow carr dominated the river floodplains throughout most of the later Mesolithic and Neolithic (Martin and Murphy 1988; Scaife 1992; 2001)

Pollen evidence hints at patches of localised forest clearance during the Early and Middle Neolithic, at Haddenham (Simms 2006) and Etton, Maxey (Scaife 1998), with some indication of arable and probably pasture at both these sites. In many places this might be seen to relate to occupation on the drier gravel terraces and stands in marked contrast to other sites in the area where there is little evidence for clearance during this period of the Neolithic (Hall and Coles 1994, 23).

In the later Neolithic and Early Bronze Age the landscape appears to have still been largely wooded. Forest regeneration can be seen at sites such as Haddenham (*ibid.*) and several other locales in this part of East Anglia (Scaife 1988; Waller 1994), although it is suggested that the area around Eynesbury, near St Neots, to the west of Cambourne, remained largely deforested during the Late Neolithic (French and Wait 1988).

The earliest large-scale clearances appear to have occurred in the first half of the 2nd millennium (Martin and Murphy 1988). Certainly, evidence from Godmanchester to the north-west of Cambourne indicates that the wooded landscape there had largely been cleared by the middle of the millennium (Brown and Murphy 1997). However, it is within the Middle–Late Bronze Age (*c.* 1600–800/700 BC) that wider-scale forest clearance can be seen to occur across the region in general.

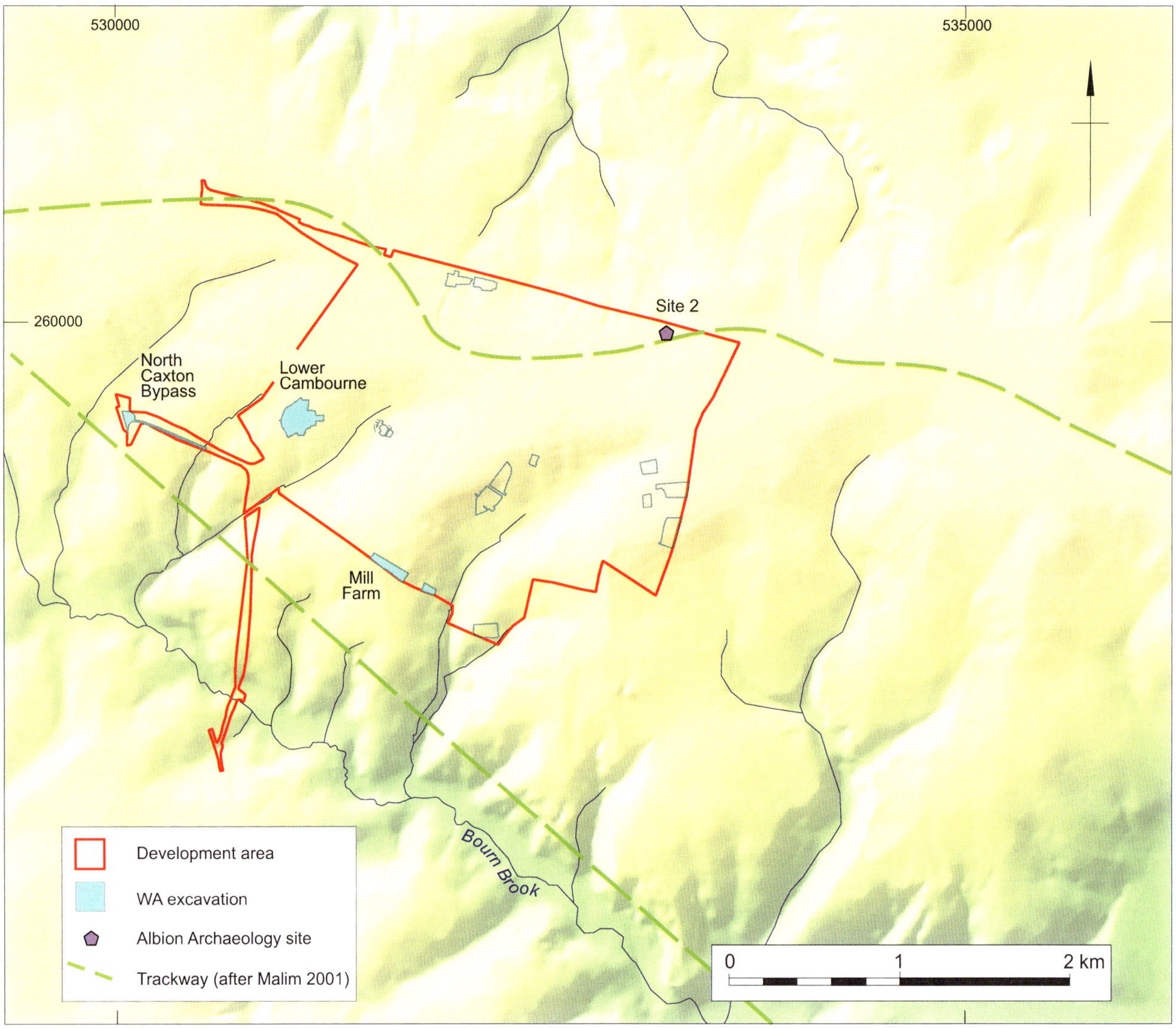

Figure 26. Terrain model of Cambourne: sites with Bronze Age (Phase 1) features

Environmental evidence from Cambourne

Neolithic and earlier Bronze Age settlement evidence within the general area encompassed by the Ouse and Cam valleys is fairly sparse, and with it environmental information that might pertain to the nature of the pre-Iron Age landscape within this part of Cambridgeshire (Fig. 26). Very little indication of Neolithic or Early Bronze Age activity was recorded during the excavations at Cambourne or the A428 improvement scheme (Abrams and Ingham 2008) immediately to the north, and no environmental evidence for these periods was recovered.

Environmental data associated with later Bronze Age activity were, however, obtained from three of the sites at Cambourne: North Caxton Bypass, Mill Farm, and Lower Cambourne. Most of this information pertains to charcoal and charred plant remains, although mollusc samples were obtained from Lower Cambourne.

From the small amount of environmental data associated with this period it seems likely that much of the Mesolithic and Neolithic forest had been cleared by the Middle–Late Bronze Age. The only evidence of local conditions around the settlement areas themselves came from a single mollusc sample from the roundhouse at Lower Cambourne, and this indicated relatively open conditions (Allen, Volume 2, 190–3).

Charcoal from Bronze Age features provided evidence for the collection of oak, hazel, ash, field-maple, and willow/blackthorn, along with elements of scrub such as blackthorn and hawthorn/*Sorbus* group (Gale, Volume 2, 135–6, 136–42, 144–6). It is probable that the material was collected from remnants of mixed, open woodland in the local area, and there was also some evidence, from Mill Farm, for the collection of hazelnuts (Stevens, Volume 2, 165–6) no doubt from such stands of open woodland.

It is notable even at this early, Bronze Age, date that elements of riverine carr, such as alder, are generally not present, although Mill Farm did produce willow charcoal (Gale, Volume 2, 154–6). Whether this absence is due to the clearance of woodland along the river edges, or whether it is that such areas were not exploited, cannot be established from this data alone. A palaeochannel at Mill Farm has been assigned to this period, but there was little to no preservation of pollen or other environmental remains (Barnett, Volume 2, 221–3). The channel appears to have become infilled by the end of the Bronze Age, possibly through increased sedimentation associated with localised agriculture and clearance and/or through general hydrological changes.

North of Cambourne, Bronze Age field systems are a common feature of the landscape (eg, French and Pryor 1992). These were laid out adjacent to the fen edge with droveways providing access into the fens themselves, and it may be that much of the region was clear of woodland by this date (French *et al.* 1992). The pollen evidence suggests that by the later Bronze Age much of this area of north Cambridgeshire was open with floodplain 'meadows' giving way to drier pasture beyond the fen-edge (French *et al.* 1992). There may have been seasonal use of wetter fen-edge pastures through much of the year with enclosed winter pastures located inland.

Early settlement at Cambourne

by James Wright

Natural palaeochannels and some tree-throw hollows were the earliest excavated features at Cambourne. Four palaeochannels were exposed. Two probably survived into the Romano-British period, either seasonally or at least as boggy areas, and another still flows periodically, although it is now canalised in a field ditch. Some tree hollows contained dating evidence, usually Iron Age or Romano-British pottery. The undated ones could belong to any period up to the medieval period. Some of these hollows were identified as tree-throws, created as a result of the tree falling over. In others the remains of a root system survived, but with no evidence of the fate of the tree. The term 'hollow' has been used to encompass both examples.

Not all of the palaeochannels appeared to be in predictable locations, with two being only a few metres below the local high point. However, it is likely that there were more, and larger, streams in prehistory than now, and springs were known in the parish of Bourne in the 18th and 19th centuries (*VCH* Cambridgeshire V, 5); also, as the example above shows, it is likely that some former streams are now canalised in field boundary ditches. Unfortunately none of the palaeochannels preserved any environmental data and, as noted above, we have virtually no evidence for vegetation for the early period within the Cambourne site as a whole.

A single Mesolithic bladelet core recovered from the crest of a ridge between two streams during fieldwalking, to the west of the Mill Farm site, may reflect the low intensity exploitation of the resources of a wooded area – game, nuts, and seeds, as well as possibly flint, wood, and other material necessary for maintaining equipment. West Cambridgeshire is relatively sparse in Mesolithic material, with few entries in Wymer's Mesolithic gazetteer (Wymer 1977). The nearest spot find for material of this period is a perforated macehead from Kingston 4 km to the south-east (*ibid.*, 27), although dense scatters of Mesolithic/Early Neolithic worked flints are recorded 14 km to the west on the banks of the Great Ouse (Ellis 2004, 6). Hunting was probably undertaken during the Early Neolithic, with leaf-shaped arrowheads being found at Lower Cambourne and Knapwell Plantation. It is possible that Early Neolithic activity in western Cambridgeshire was concentrated in the Great Ouse valley, where various monuments of this date are known (McAvoy 2000; Malim 2000; Ellis 2004). The Ouse and Cam or Granta would have formed corridors linking the fens with the Chalk uplands and the Icknield Way.

Some form of Late Neolithic/Early Bronze Age activity is indicated by a plano-convex knife and a flint flake with scraper-like retouch, both from Lower Cambourne; some of the flint debitage from the same site could also have been of this period, left by people taking advantage of a south-east facing slope and nearby source of water.

During the Bronze Age trackways were established linking the Cam and route of the later Icknield Way to the east with the Great Ouse to the west. One track is mapped close to the route now taken by the A428, approximately following the plateau forming the watershed between the Great Ouse and the Bourn Brook (Malim 2001, fig. 2.2). Two trackways near the eastern end of the Bourn converged and passed to the south of the Development Area on the north side of the brook (see Fig. 26).

The exact path of the plateau track is not known. The Development Area extends across the plateau but no remains of a trackway were encountered during excavation or evaluation. This is not surprising considering that it was probably not laid as a metalled surface and did not comprise a narrowly defined route. The plateau does not follow a straight line and occasional detours across the tops of stream valleys were probably taken as short cuts. Temporary detours to avoid waterlogging or trampled areas can also be imagined, creating a wide and meandering route that would leave little or no archaeological evidence.

Bronze Age activity in the Development Area was confined to the south, in two valleys and on a ridge (Fig. 26). At Mill Farm there was no clear evidence of settlement in terms of actual structures, but pottery and worked flint were recovered. Small quantities of abraded Middle–Late Bronze Age pottery, worked and some burnt flint, and a few tiny fragments of animal bone were retrieved from several shallow features in or close to the palaeochannel.

At North Caxton Bypass and Lower Cambourne single examples of what may be Middle or Late Bronze Age roundhouses were recorded. Both comprised post-holes forming circles of *c.* 5 m diameter. No dating evidence was recovered from either, but they differed from the Iron Age and Romano-British roundhouses which all had drip-gullies, few post-holes, and were *c.* 10 m or more in diameter. On typological grounds these two are considered to be Bronze Age. The only artefacts recovered were burnt stones, from all the post-holes at Lower Cambourne and from an adjacent pit, all of this material probably representing potboilers. No worked flint was present at North Caxton, although worked flint was collected at Lower Cambourne, but usually it was residual in later features. While a Bronze Age date is likely for much of the flint, most was undiagnostic waste, and later Neolithic or Iron Age dates are also possible.

The North Caxton roundhouse may have had a pen appended to its north, though the evidence is equivocal. At neither site was there evidence of field systems or droveways and the small amount of evidence points to a settlement lasting perhaps for a single generation, probably farming in fields next to the settlement which, if demarcated, had hedges or possibly fences around them (see below). To the north-east, along the route of the A428, the only Bronze Age features were two apparently isolated pits at Ash Plantation (site 2), close to the postulated prehistoric trackway (Abrams and Ingham 2008, 17).

The limited evidence is in agreement with Brown and Murphy's suggestion (2000, 20) that settlement was shifting or semi-permanent, which goes some way to explaining the difficulty of finding such ephemeral structural features in an area subjected to later agriculture or development.

Earlier prehistoric material culture

by Matt Leivers

Early prehistoric material is limited to a small amount of struck flint and less pottery. The early element of the lithic assemblage is predominantly of value as an indicator of human activity around the tributary streams draining off the plateau into the Bourn to the south and Great Ouse to the north. Although residual and of limited quantity, the material pre-dating the establishment of agricultural settlements on the plateau, and especially that dating to the Mesolithic and Neolithic periods, is indicative of activity predominantly concerned with transient and episodic resource acquisition.

Lithic raw materials were collected locally: the highly varied nature of the material (in terms of quality, colour, cortex thickness, and condition) reflecting the Chalk and flint erratics in the local Boulder Clay drift. The assemblages are dominated by flake debitage which is not susceptible to close dating, but which indicates tool creation, use, and maintenance: much of this element could belong anywhere between the Late Neolithic and Middle Bronze Age. Tools are predominantly scrapers which, with a few notable examples, are similarly difficult to date, but which suggest tasks associated with processing rather than acquisition, and which may date to the Bronze Age.

From a chronological perspective, the earliest activities attested by the lithics are almost impossible to reconstruct: a small Mesolithic bladelet core from near Mill Farm does nothing but indicate a human presence in the area, and demonstrably Early Neolithic activity is scarcely better-represented. Single leaf-shaped arrowheads (Fig. 27, 1 and 2) from Lower Cambourne and Knapwell Plantation perhaps indicate small-scale, sporadic hunting episodes, with the arrowheads representing chance losses during these.

Recognisable Early Bronze Age evidence is very slight, but the range of implements is rather different. A single plano-convex knife (Fig. 27, 3) and a combined knife and scraper (Fig. 27, 4) from Lower Cambourne indicate processing rather than hunting tasks. The same kind of small-scale, low impact settlement may be visible around the palaeochannel at Mill Farm. Here, small quantities of Middle or Late Bronze Age ceramics and struck flint (including a flake with marginal retouch, and an irregular end scraper) were recovered in association with heat-cracked flint and a few unidentifiable fragments of animal bone, perhaps marking the location of a cooking-place.

The ceramic record suggests that agricultural settlements did not begin to appear on the plateau until the Late Bronze or Early Iron Age. The difficulties of separating material of this date from the bulk of the Middle Iron Age pottery means that only in the very few instances where diagnostic forms are present is it possible to identify early settlement with any certainty.

A very small number of vessels have features suggesting that they may be Early Iron Age rather than

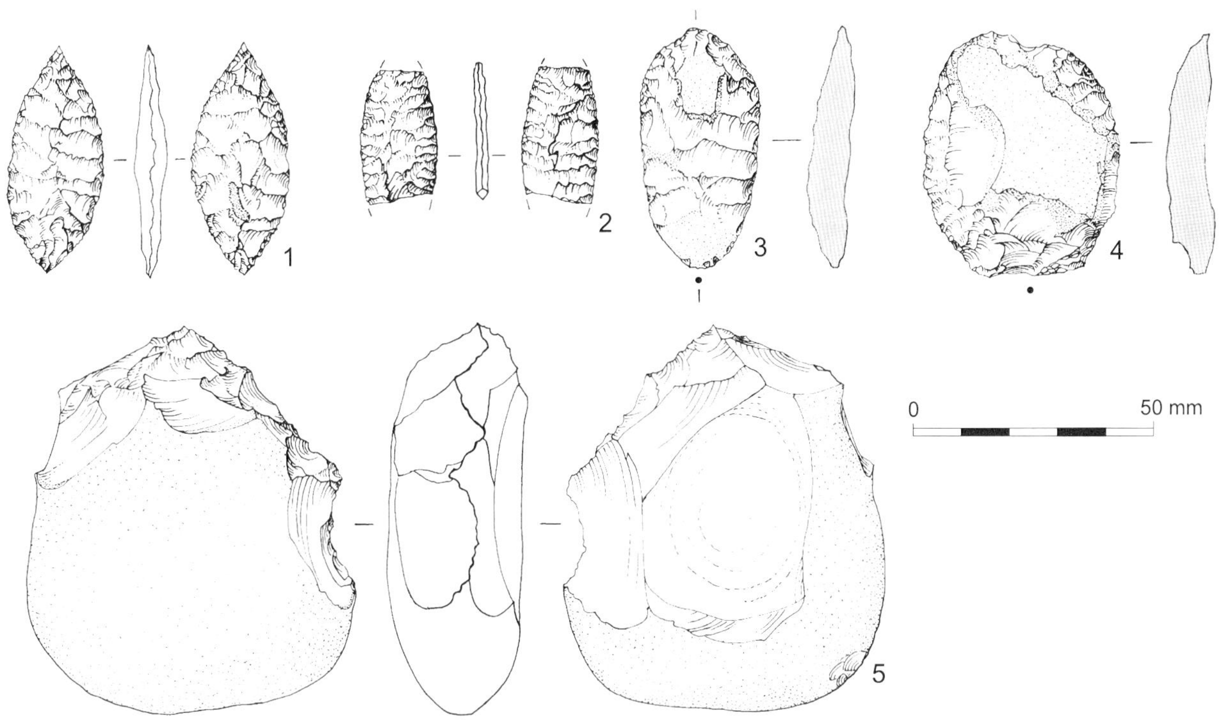

Figure 27. Struck flint: 1. Sf 86; leaf-shaped arrowhead, Lower Cambourne, 45978, ditch group 1321; 2. Sf 61003; leaf-shaped arrowhead, Knapwell Plantation, 45972, (60168) pit 60264; 3. Sf 126; plano-convex knife, Lower Cambourne, 45978, unstratified; 4. Sf 531; Lower Cambourne, knife/scraper, 45978, (2170) pit 2139; 5. Chopper, Jeavons Lane, 50068, (80415) waterhole 80004

Middle Iron Age in date. These came from Knapwell Plantation (Fig. 30, 27), Little Common Farm, and from Lower Cambourne. The latter site also produced a quantity of struck flint, mostly unretouched debitage, with a very few core fragments, preparation flakes, and rejuvenation tablets. Hard hammers had been used in every instance where technology was identifiable and tended to result in crude debitage that may not all have been produced during the creation of tool blanks. However, end and end-and-side scrapers were present, mostly crude and thick, and typical of the later Bronze Age or even Iron Age.

The Bronze Age agricultural economy

by Chris J. Stevens

Environmental evidence from features associated with the two probable Bronze Age roundhouses was scant, but charred cereal remains showed the cultivation of both spelt and emmer with a slight indication that hulled barley was also grown.

While emmer is considered the dominant crop in the Bronze Age, spelt can be seen as a Middle Bronze Age introduction. Spelt is recorded from around the mid-2nd millennium at Godmanchester (Brown and Murphy 1997) and Barleycroft Farm, while by the Late Bronze Age it had become the principal crop at Lofts Farm, Essex (Murphy 1991b). However, despite spelt becoming the dominant crop for large parts of southern England, emmer appears to have had a continued important role in the economy until at least the Romano-British period in large parts of East Anglia. In terms of weed seeds the samples from Cambourne yielded little information other than occasional seeds of dock.

While the evidence for crops is only slight it might be a reflection of short-lived, low intensity occupation rather than of a low reliance on cultivated cereals. Such evidence, it might be noted, is generally poor for other Middle–Late Bronze Age sites in Cambridgeshire (cf. Stevens 1997c; Stevens in press b), and in southern England in general (eg, Campbell 1992; Carruthers 1989). No evidence for storage structures associated with the Bronze Age roundhouses was seen, although four-post structures have been recorded from later Bronze Age fenland sites (cf. Evans and Knight 2000; 2001).

While no useful information was obtained from the tiny assemblages of poorly-preserved animal bone from the Cambourne sites (or from those along the A428 improvement; Rielly 2008), larger and better-preserved animal bone assemblages have been recovered from other Middle–Late Bronze Age sites in Cambridgeshire.

At West Fen Road, Ely, for example, cattle and sheep/goat with smaller amounts of pig and horse were recorded (Brown and Murphy 1997). There is some suggestion from this site that during this period cattle were used mainly for draught while sheep and goats were kept for milk (Olsen 1994). The fenland in general is often seen as supporting a more pastoral economy (Hall and Coles 1994, 90), centred on cattle and sheep/ goat, and this may also have been the case at Cambourne. No Bronze Age field systems were identified and the possible pen at North Caxton Bypass may have been associated with the keeping of animals.

4. The Later Prehistoric Period

The local and wider Iron Age landscape

by Chris J. Stevens

Island and floodplain settlements

In the earliest part of the Iron Age there is evidence that the wetland encroached further, with marine incursion and the formation of freshwater peats limiting many settlements to the fen-edge and drier islands, as seen in the south of the fen at Coveney, Ely, and Stonea (Dawson 2000; Hall and Coles 1994; Evans 2003). There is also evidence to suggest that such inundation extended into the lower reaches of at least the Great Ouse valley (French 2003, 112). It is during the Iron Age that there was a general increase in settlement activity along the fen-edge itself (Evans 1992a; 1992b), to which Cambourne, some 10 km from the fen-edge, can be added.

During the later Iron Age, for both the Ouse and Nene, some settlement appears on the floodplain, but increasing alluviation and flooding are apparent, as they are for southern England as a whole (eg, Thames Valley; Lambrick 1992a; 1992b; Allen and Robinson 1993). In many cases this flooding can be seen to have led to the abandonment of settlements in the Ouse/Nene region by the 1st century AD (Dawson 2000; Tebbutt 1957; Tilson 1973; 1975).

In the previous chapter it was suggested that the main deforestation of the region began in the Middle–Late Bronze Age. It is probable that many surviving, uncleared areas of the local landscape were opened up by at least the beginning of the Early Iron Age (cf. Brown and Murphy 1997), with the continued clearance of smaller woodland stands through the later Iron Age (Murphy 1997). At Willington, south-east of Cambourne, deforestation has been dated to the Late Bronze Age–Early Iron Age transition *c.* 800 BC (French and Wait 1988, 55), while at Scole, near Diss in Suffolk, major woodland clearance does not seem to have taken place until the Late Iron Age or early Romano-British period (Wiltshire cited by Murphy 1997).

It is notable that many of the earlier, Bronze Age, field systems seem to have been abandoned during the Iron Age, with the ditches becoming infilled (see French 2003). Yet while there is a noticeable decline in the evidence for a formalised laying-out of the agricultural landscape there is no shortage of evidence for either arable or animal husbandry in the Iron Age, as is also the case at Cambourne. However, as noted below and by French (2003), there are indications for the existence of well-established hedgerows by the later Bronze Age (cf. Wilson 1984). It is therefore feasible that existing field divisions, represented by hedgerows, continued in use from the Bronze Age through the Iron Age, and it is only in the Late Iron Age and early Romano-British periods when this landscape was replanned that evidence for field ditches re-appears.

In the following discussion, and elsewhere in this publication, the term 'later Iron Age' is often used for Phase 2 features, rather than specifically 'Middle Iron Age' and/or 'Late Iron Age', following Hill and Braddock (2006, 190; Bryant 1997), and refers to the period 300 BC–AD 43–50.

Environmental evidence and the local environment at Cambourne

Six of the excavated sites yielded features that contained useful and varied environmental evidence. Pollen data for the Iron Age was present at Knapwell Plantation and Jeavons Lane and it might be noted that pollen preservation at both these sites, and those along the A428, was often poor (Scaife 2008; cf. Volume 2, 215–6). A pollen sequence for the later Iron Age/early Romano-British period was also present at Lower Cambourne.

Six of the seven sites with Iron Age features: Lower Cambourne, Knapwell Plantation, Poplar Plantation, Little Common Farm, Broadway Farm, and Jeavons Lane, produced charcoal, charred plant remains and, in all but one case, molluscs. A waterlogged deposit dated to the Iron Age also came from an enclosure ditch at Little Common Farm.

The earliest pollen evidence came from a waterhole and a pit at Knapwell Plantation and a field ditch and a pond at Jeavons Lane, all of later Iron Age date. At both sites it indicates largely open grassland or pasture, with some evidence of cereal agriculture (Scaife, Volume 2, 215–6). The nature of the features from which the pollen was recovered, while providing only a restricted view of the environment, still indicates localised stands of oak within mixed

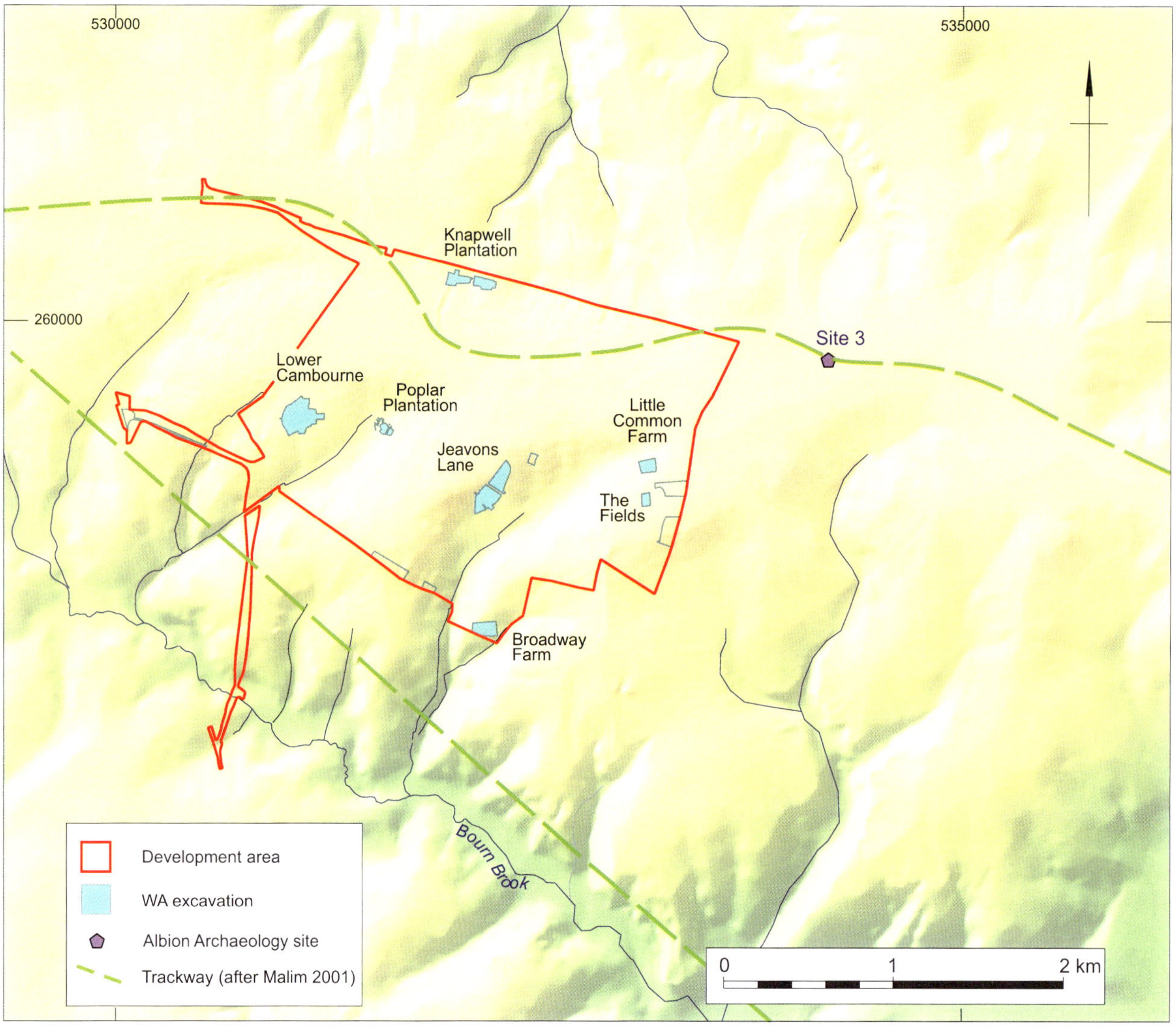

Figure 28. Terrain model of Cambourne: later Iron Age (Phase 2) sites

woodland on drier soils, and perhaps alder within lower-lying wetter areas. However, the broader picture implies that the area had probably become largely deforested at least by the Early–Middle Iron Age, and quite possibly earlier. Combined with the evidence for an absence of woodland, the low number of pigs might further be taken as an indicator of low-availability of woodland pannage and a generally open landscape (Hamilton-Dyer, Volume 2, 94). The samples also indicated quite high amounts of bracken and other ferns, but relatively few sedge and other characteristic wetland elements were present (see below).

The charcoal assemblages from the later Iron Age occupation of Cambourne, as with the earlier samples from North Caxton Bypass, also reflect this open landscape. They are dominated by narrow roundwood and twiggy material, mainly from species of scrubland, such as the hawthorn group, buckthorn/sloe (*Prunus spinosa*), *Viburnum*, and possibly *Sorbus*, as opposed to oak and other species of mature forest (Gale, Volume 2, 152–3). The charred plant assemblages also included frequent thorns and occasional fruit stones of hawthorn (*Crataegus monogyna*) and buckthorn/sloe, confirming the collection and use of these specific species for fuel (Gale, Volume 2, 143–4; Stevens, Volume 2, 175–6). In addition, a single fruit stone of dogwood (*Cornus sanguinea*), a common element of woodland edge, points to the presence of this scrub species.

While always a minor component in the charcoal samples there is at least some indication of the use of heartwood or slow-grown large-wood, in particular from oak (*Quercus* sp.). This might be taken to confirm the continued existence of small, but well-established stands of old naturalised forest within the general Cambourne area, perhaps on the lower, more sheltered slopes (Gale, Volume 2, 143–4, 151–2). There was little evidence from the charcoal analysis to suggest that woodland was managed during the Iron Age. Charcoal from one enclosure ditch may relate to coppicing, although it could come from immature trees or twig and branch wood. This same context also indicated probable heather (Gale, Volume 2, 146–8).

From the relatively wide range of species, such surviving woodland as there was is likely to have been relatively mixed, with oak, field-maple (*Acer campestre*), ash (*Fraxinus excelsior*), and hazel (*Corylus avellana*) all present. Charcoal of wild cherry (*Prunus avium*) and/or bird cherry (*P. padus*) recovered from Poplar Plantation might also indicate this species growing within such woodland environments (Gale, Volume 2, 143–4).

From the pollen evidence there appears to have been at least some stands of alder surviving along the fringes of the floodplains, but alder was absent from the wood charcoal assemblages from all the Cambourne sites (Gale 2008). This may be because it provides poor firewood (cf. Gale, Volume 2, 146–8), but equally given the high quantities of airborne pollen that alder produces it may be that such stands were located at some distance from the Cambourne sites (cf. Scaife, Volume 2, 215–6). It might be noted, however, that even further into the fens, where such stands would be expected, there was only limited evidence for alder pollen from both Haddenham and Wardy Hill (Simms 2006; Wiltshire 2003).

Willow and/or poplar, also indicative of riverine, wetter environments, appear to have been occasionally collected for fuel at Cambourne. These species are poor pollen producers and, therefore, small stands and isolated trees could have been locally present, as proven at Haddenham by the presence of leaves within the ditches (Hunt 2006).

A number of the Iron Age features also yielded remains of hazelnut, for instance at Knapwell Plantation (Stevens, Volume 2, 159–62, 163–4, 167–9, 175–6). While fragments of hazelnut are not uncommon on British Iron Age sites, their frequency on the sites around Cambourne suggests that there was still some effort put in to their collection, presumably from remaining stands of open woodland and long established hedgerows.

Pollen analyses from other later Iron Age sites in the region have also indicated a largely deforested landscape. At Wardy Hill those trees represented by small amounts of pollen included oak, alder, birch, lime, and elm, all seen for the Cambourne sites, as well as beech (Wiltshire 2003). Lime (*Tilia*) is usually seen as being in decline over much of England within the Late Bronze Age (Scaife, Volume 2, 217–8) although, as with Wardy Hill, it is possible that its presence at Jeavons Lane indicates its survival into the Iron Age. Certainly no lime pollen was found in later deposits and it appears to have disappeared entirely from the landscape by the early Romano-British period (see next chapter). As seen at Cambourne and Wardy Hill, Haddenham also demonstrated an open, unwooded landscape, although this may to some extent reflect the site's proximity to the fen itself (Simms 2006).

Cereal-type pollen from Knapwell Plantation might provide evidence that arable fields existed in close proximity to the settlement, although such pollen might equally be released if crops were brought back and processed on the site after harvest. That ard marks were recorded near to the settlement in the earliest occupation at Haddenham (Evans and Hodder 2006, 129–34) might, nevertheless, suggest that it was normal to have some arable fields situated adjacent to the settlements.

It seems clear that the Cambourne sites were located in a seasonally wet environment, particularly in the later Iron Age when several features were noted to contain alluvium, for example the Iron Age well at Knapwell Plantation (Barnett, Volume 2, 219–29). Such events also account for the frequent occurrence of aquatic molluscs in a number of the Iron Age features (Allen, Volume 2, 199–200, 203–4, 205–6, 211–12; see also Pipe 2008).

It is likely that during much of this period flooding became an increasing problem and that the enclosing of the sites may, in part, have been a direct response to issues of water management (see Chapter 2). In particular, at Broadway Farm, a difference was seen between the aquatic molluscan assemblage in the roundhouse drip or ring-gully that contained standing water and that in the enclosure ditch that seemed to indicate that flood waters had entered it (Allen, Volume 2, 203–4). This might indicate that such enclosures helped to channel flood water around and away from the interior of the settlement (cf. Evans 1997).

In terms of the immediately surrounding vegetated environment, the molluscs indicate a relatively open, wet grassland, while occasional shade components may reflect localised habitats found in ditches, hedges, long grassland, or over-grown patches allowed to grow in the shade of roundhouses (Allen, Volume 2, 194–5). Similar patterns were seen at the nearby sites to the east on the A428 (Pipe 2008), although the assemblages from Scotland Farm showed generally more shaded conditions within the enclosure ditches, with wet grassland beyond.

Where features were dug below the water-table there is a chance, provided the water-table does not drop substantially, that waterlogged plant material may be preserved. Such material can provide a picture of the local environment within the settlement itself. Waterlogged deposits of Iron Age date were only recovered from one feature at Cambourne, an enclosure ditch at Little Common Farm. The deposit yielded seeds of bramble (*Rubus* sp.) and thorns of hawthorn or buckthorn/sloe, indicative of woody thorny scrub within close proximity to the ditch, probably in the form of a hedge.

Such hedges may have been deliberately 'planted' or layered material, especially since hawthorn is self-rooting from cuttings and hence very suitable for such purposes. At Wardy Hill and Haddenham it was suggested that the material dug from the ditches was piled up to form adjacent banks which, at least in the former case, may also have been hedged (Wiltshire 2003; Evans 2003; Evans and Hodder 2006). It is of interest that several Iron Age sites further afield have produced generally similar evidence from waterlogged deposits. Evidence for thorny shrub and possible hedgerows growing along the edge of ditches is seen at Fisherwick, Staffordshire (Williams 1979), Mingies Ditch, Oxfordshire (Allen and Robinson 1993), St Ives, Cambridgeshire (Taylor 1996), and Rectory Farm, West Deeping, near Peterborough (Murphy and Fryer, cited in Brown and Murphy 1997).

On the other hand it might be noted that waterlogged samples from the enclosure ditches at both Earith and Haddenham to the north of Cambourne provided little such evidence (Stevens in press a; 2005; Hunt 2006), although possibly some elder shrub may have been present.

There are many further species represented in the waterlogged deposit from Little Common Farm that indicate what might be considered today a typical 'farmyard assemblage' with species characteristic of trampled, nitrogen-rich, churned soils that are often associated with animals (Stevens, Volume 2, 200–2). Seeds of several species such as buttercup, thistle, and docks were also common and can be seen as indicative of rough, grassland pasture, both thistles and buttercup becoming prevalent by virtue of being avoided by grazing animals. Seeds of several species associated with standing, well-vegetated and slightly stagnant water within the ditches were also recorded, such as pondweed, (*Potomogeton* sp.) and duckweed (*Lemna* sp.), along with ephippium (egg cases) of the water-flea (*Daphnia* sp.) and shells of the aquatic mollusc *Anisus leucostoma*.

Seeds and pollen of sedges (Cyperaceae including *Eleocharis,* etc.) were abundant at both Haddenham and Wardy Hill (Simms 2006; Hunt 2006; Murphy 2003; Wiltshire 2003), but generally absent from the deposits at Cambourne. This may reflect the greater proximity of the former sites to the fen-edge, but also suggests that while the sites at Cambourne were subject to flooding, during summer many of the ditches dried out.

Bones of wild animals are relatively rare on Iron Age sites (Grant 1984a), suggesting that hunting of wild animals was seldom practised. Most of the remains of red and roe deer were represented by antler fragments, and were found at all the sites except Knapwell Plantation. However, a single radius of roe deer from Little Common Farm may represent some evidence for hunting (Hamilton-Dyer, Volume 2, 96). Deer were absent from Scotland Farm on the A428 (Rielly 2008), while at Wardy Hill, also in Cambridgeshire, deer (probably red deer) was represented by just a few fragments of antler (Davies 2003).

A number of bones of water-vole were noticed in the assemblages (Hamilton-Dyer, Volume 2, 96), a species that commonly inhabits not only riverbanks, but also ponds and ditches and so a potential part of the local fauna of the settlement itself.

Other than deer, water-vole, and single finds of swan from Lower Cambourne and a raven from Little Common Farm, few wild animal bones were recovered from the Cambourne sites. However, other sites in the region do provide a more complete picture of the wildlife in this part of East Anglia during the Iron Age. At Wardy Hill (Davies 2003) otters can no doubt be associated with the fen itself, while hare would have inhabited long, open grassland. Both badger and fox would have been found in woodland and hedge environments, and are likely to have been in the Cambourne area at this time. The site at Haddenham is well known for its unique and varied faunal remains (Serjeantson 2006) that include, in addition to the above-mentioned species, remains of beaver, polecat, and squirrel, as well as many water birds including swan, pelican, ducks, crane, coot, and sea eagle.

Later Iron Age settlement at Cambourne

by James Wright

Landscape organisation

In common with the rest of Britain, the number of settlement sites in eastern England increased through the Iron Age. During the Late Bronze Age/Early Iron Age transition settlement had tended to cluster where the major rivers entered the fens (Bryant 1997). By the Late Iron Age sites were still principally in the river valleys, as at Little Paxton Quarry *c.* 15 km to the west near the Ouse (Jones 2001), Barrington to the south-west (Malim 1997), and Trumpington to the east (Fox 1923), both in the Cam valley. Hillforts are also known at Wandlebury and Cherry Hinton (Fox 1923) on the eastern side of the Cam.

There was, however, also expansion onto the boulder clay, as at Caldecote Highfields (Kenney 2007) and Madingley to the east (Tipper 1994) and Foxton to the south-east (Bryant 1997, 28). In addition, recent work has revealed Iron Age sites with enclosures, roundhouses, and pits at Scotland Farm (sites 7 and 8), occupied between the 4th and 1st centuries BC, and an enclosure at Bourn Airfield (site 3) on the boulder clay along the route of the A428 immediately north of Cambourne (Abrams and Ingham 2008).

With the increase in population it is likely that the earlier, Bronze Age, trackways continued in use, but there appears to have been a hiatus in settlement within the Development Area, and it was not occupied at the start of the Iron Age. The earliest, Middle Iron Age, settlement is likely to have been at Lower Cambourne, Knapwell Plantation, and Little Common Farm where it seems that unenclosed roundhouses were built and where possibly Early Iron Age pottery forms were still in use. Unenclosed settlement would be in keeping with other sites in the region during the earlier part of the Iron Age (Champion 1994, 131), where such settlement is considered to be a continuation of the pattern of Late Bronze Age open sites. This is in contrast to Wessex, for example, where enclosure was the norm.

At Knapwell Plantation the unenclosed phase may have lasted two generations or more as there were at least two roundhouses, one or possibly both of which were rebuilt after an indeterminable period. The enclosure ditch cut through one of these structures and new roundhouses were constructed within the enclosure, possibly following a period of abandonment. At Lower Cambourne the enclosure may have been created relatively soon after the original settlement was established as the enclosure ditch respected an earlier roundhouse showing that it was still standing. At Little Common Farm there is no indication of the length of time that elapsed between the beginnings of the unenclosed and enclosed phases, although it is likely that there was no hiatus in the sequence.

Each of these three unenclosed sites lay near the upper end of one of the three main stream valleys in the Development Area (the two presently existing streams in the south of Cambourne and the north-flowing stream mapped as starting immediately north of the A428). While it has been shown that there were more streams, with some surviving to the Romano-British period, the present streams probably represent the principal ones existing during the prehistoric period. It is suggested that each valley had one site, apparently a farmstead, which survived for perhaps two or more generations after its establishment. Each would have had access to land within their respective valleys and the adjoining interfluves and plateaux, providing the widest range of environments available, with the slopes of the valleys providing the most easily cultivable land.

It is not possible to say how far down the valleys the land associated with these settlements extended beyond the Development Area, although it is likely that settlement was denser further down the valleys towards their confluence with the Bourn Brook to the south, and that, as in the medieval and modern periods, the Bourn valley itself was more intensely occupied (Oosthuizen 2005).

Other sites were established within the Development Area but their remains are less complex and it seems they were very short-lived. Poplar Plantation, Jeavons Lane, and Broadway Farm are the principal short-lived, 'satellite' sites, as well as, possibly, Bourn Airfield (site 3) on the A428 (Abrams and Ingham 2008, 34–5) beyond the north-east corner of the Development Area.

Topographic features aside, very few features lay between the above-mentioned sites. Only at Lower Cambourne and Poplar Plantation were droveways present that may have led between sites and, as with the trackway along the Ouse/Bourn watershed, it must be assumed that away from the settlements a degree of flexibility was needed to cross the area in bad weather conditions. In contrast, in the north Chilterns and Hertfordshire to the south-west and near Stansted to the south-east, many of the settlements were separated by ditches or linked by trackways (Bryant and Niblett 1997; Cooke pers. comm.).

The limited evidence for fields around the farmsteads shows them to have probably extended between 50 m and 150 m away from the enclosures. Little Common Farm had a field system around it that possibly extended as far as the Iron Age ditch at The Fields *c.* 160 m to the south. At Jeavons Lane approximately half of a probably domestic enclosure was exposed, beyond which were two parallel ditches that may have been field boundaries. At Lower Cambourne one or two ditches could have been field boundaries, and possibly two field ditches radiated to the west of the Poplar Plantation enclosure. No field ditches were present at either Knapwell Plantation or at Broadway Farm, though both lay on the edge of the Development Area and associated field ditches could have extended beyond the area investigated.

The enclosures and settlements

There is a question as to whether the enclosure of settlements was some form of status symbol in response to social change, or a purely practical reaction to the environmental conditions. It appears that at Cambourne there was a definite element of practicality to the creation of enclosure ditches, as flooding and drainage were certainly problems on the clay soils. Although the slight Bronze Age remains and the earliest Phase 2 buildings were not enclosed, it seems that after a settlement became established it was necessary to protect it from flooding by surrounding it with a ditch. Even at Lower Cambourne, the northern side of which had a substantial double ditch and bank, the outer enclosure ditch functioned to drain water into a small pond or waterhole at its eastern end. However, the double ditch at Lower Cambourne echoes that of the enclosure at Haddenham (Evans and Hodder 2006), and it is difficult to discount the influence of social status or regional tradition in its construction. The large enclosure ditches (and banks) at Scotland Farm (site 7) on the A428 may also be related to conspicuous display (Abrams and Ingham 2008, 31).

The environmental evidence shows that by the time the enclosures and their ditches were abandoned the ditches would have contained standing water, with weeds growing in and adjacent to the water. The presence of nitrogen-rich, soil-loving species may reflect an animal as well as human presence. Brambles, hawthorn, or blackthorn and possibly elder could have formed continuous hedges or intermittent clumps which supplemented any barriers formed by associated banks. Only at Lower Cambourne, however, was evidence for a bank identified and that was between two ditches.

The enclosures are comparable in shape and layout to others in the region, generally defined by curving ditches and sometimes with other enclosures added to them (Jones 2001; Malim 1997). The arrangement at Knapwell Plantation shows some similarities to that at Scotland Farm (site 7) on the A428 (Abrams and Ingham 2008, fig. 1.11) where a linear series of enclosures represents an unusual Iron Age layout, perhaps a reflection of increasing settlement nucleation seen in eastern England from the 3rd century BC (Bradley 1984, 139). There were also sub-rectangular enclosures at Knapwell Plantation and Little Common Farm, although these did not contain buildings. Some enclosures were sub-divided with, in some cases, an area possibly used for stock. These putative stock divisions were usually close to a droveway, as at Lower Cambourne and Poplar Plantation. Entrances into the enclosures varied, and although at Poplar Plantation there was no causeway through the enclosure, some form of bridge opposite the droveway may have been used.

At Knapwell Plantation and Lower Cambourne there were what may have been C-shaped shelters or small, fenced enclosures. The only four-post structures were at Lower Cambourne and Little Common Farm. Pits, some substantial, were present at Lower Cambourne, Poplar Plantation, and Knapwell Plantation. However, the number of pits compared with other sites of this period is quite small, and the absence of grain storage pits can very likely be attributed to the ground conditions and general wetness of the area, particularly in the winter months.

While there were various differences between enclosures, in many of them the roundhouses appeared to be 'paired', with one larger than the other. This has been noted elsewhere and the larger building assumed to be domestic, and the smaller an ancillary structure (Evans 2003, 223). At Lower Cambourne this arrangement may have been more complex, comprising a 15 m diameter ring-gully centrally located in an otherwise virtually empty enclosure, with an adjacent enclosure containing probably a single, smaller (but replaced) roundhouse, a possible shelter, and a four-post structure, a situation more in line with the 'satellite' inter-relationship model of Evans (2003, fig. 115). The 'satellite' roundhouses were too badly truncated to make any comparisons between, for example, their associated artefacts, but it is possible that this was an area for food processing and perhaps craft industries.

Three of the Iron Age sites, Poplar Plantation, Broadway Farm, and Little Common Farm, had virtually no Romano-British pottery and must have been abandoned permanently before the Conquest. The farmstead at Little Common Farm was the only one excavated in the Development Area that produced a significant amount of Late Iron Age pottery, and its abandonment is slightly surprising given that imported, pre-Conquest pottery had been used there, showing perhaps a taste for wine and suggesting at least some level of economic success. Only at Lower Cambourne, and possibly also Knapwell Plantation, did later Iron Age settlement continue unbroken into the Romano-British period.

Later prehistoric material culture

by Matt Leivers

Later prehistoric material culture is, for the most part, indicative of the same kinds of agricultural settlement suggested by the archaeological features.

The pottery described here comprises those fabric types and vessel forms attributed to the Middle Iron Age (possibly continuing to the Late Iron Age but excluding those that remained current into the Romano-British period, see Seager Smith, Chapter 5). The ceramics attributed to this period are hand-made, of materials that could have been obtained locally from the local drift geology, although the variety of inclusions suggests that a number of different clay sources were being used. Grog, however, was present in only very small quantities. The predominance of sand-tempered rather than shelly fabrics indicates closer links with the ceramic traditions of the Ely and Cambridge areas rather than those closer at hand at Hinchingbrooke and St Neots (Sarah Percival pers. comm.), although the presence of both demonstrates that these traditions were not exclusive. No individual sites have exclusively shelly or sand-tempered wares, although there are individual deposits with distinct differences: at Lower Cambourne, for example, pottery was concentrated in two adjacent features, one of which had pre-dominantly sandy wares, the other shelly wares.

Forms are predominantly jars and bowls, the former probably for storage, the latter for processing and cooking. The majority of identifiable vessels are round or slack-shouldered bipartite jars with short upright or slightly everted rims, found at Broadway Farm, Knapwell Plantation, Little Common Farm and Lower Cambourne (Fig. 29, 1, 2, 4, 6–9). Bulbous-bodied or tub-shaped jars with inturned rims form a minor component at Knapwell Plantation, Little Common Farm, Poplar Plantation, and Lower Cambourne (Fig. 29, 3, 10; Fig. 30, 11–12), as do proto-bead-rimmed jars at Little Common Farm, Lower Cambourne, and Poplar Plantation (Fig. 30, 13). The predominant bowl form is the short-necked shouldered bowl, examples of which come from Broadway Farm and Knapwell Plantation (Fig. 30, 14–16); while at Knapwell Plantation and Lower Cambourne slightly closed bowls were also present (Fig. 30, 17).

Other forms suggested by a very few sherds include a thick-walled vessel with a large, flat, everted rim (Fig. 30, 18) and a very small, round-bodied vessel from Little Common Farm. Rims tend to be simple and plain, upright or everted, with rounded, pointed or flat tops, although a few internally bevelled (Fig. 30, 19), externally rolled (Fig. 30, 20), hooked (Fig. 30, 21), 'T'-shaped (Fig. 30, 22), expanded (Fig. 30, 23), and out-turned (Fig. 30, 24) examples are present. Two large handles are likely to derive from jars (Fig. 30, 25); one is clearly plugged into the wall of the vessel. A sub-conical piece may be an applied boss (Fig. 30, 26).

A single vessel of uncertain form from Lower Camborne was elaborately decorated with an all-over pattern of complex incised designs (Fig. 31, 28). Although the fabric of this vessel matches the rest of the assemblage, the form suggests that it may be significantly earlier, perhaps related to the Beaker tradition. Apart from some surface smoothing, other decoration and surface treatments are limited to finger-impressed or incised rims and shoulders (Fig. 31, 33–36), burnishing of some or all of interior or exterior surfaces, and a technique which ranges from light wiping to deep deliberate scoring (Fig. 29, 5; Fig. 31, 29–32, 37).

The finer element is likely to derive from tablewares. In terms of individual site assemblages, only jar forms were recognisable at Lower Cambourne and Little Common Farm, while jars and bowls were present at Poplar Plantation, Knapwell Plantation, and Broadway Farm. These differences are unlikely to be significant however, and will derive from the very fragmentary nature of the assemblages and the consequent difficulty of assigning sherds to forms.

It may be the case that there was a change in the ways in which rubbish was disposed of over time. At Lower Cambourne, Knapwell Plantation, and Little Common Farm (the three sites proposed as the earliest settlements) sherds appear to have been disposed of in pits or ditches as primary waste. At Poplar Plantation and Broadway Farm however, sherds tend to be smaller, more worn, and to occur more widely spread across the sites in later features, suggesting that the material was middened and/or manured into fields.

Other, more cultural activities are represented by a worked goose bone that might have been intended for use as a flute, found associated with Middle Iron Age pottery in a ditch at Lower Cambourne. Craft activities include weaving and textile working. Loomweights were recovered from Knapwell Plantation, Lower Cambourne, and possibly Little Common Farm, while a bone needle from Lower Cambourne and an awl from Knapwell Plantation were both associated with Middle Iron Age ceramics. Briquetage was recovered from Little Common Farm and Lower Cambourne, possibly from vessels used to transport salt (and consequently brought into the settlement from elsewhere). Salt production has been well-documented in the fens (Lane and Morris 2001; Hall and Coles 1994) and it is likely that this material represents evidence for trade in this commodity. The briquetage at Little Common Farm was also in forms suggesting kiln or oven furniture which may be attributable to some form of manufacturing process on the site.

Possible 'industrial processes' are demonstrated by fuel-ash slag from Lower Cambourne, Little Common Farm, and Knapwell Plantation. This material has no clear association with metalworking, but appears rather to derive from some process involving the exposure of clay to high temperature. This process does not appear to be pottery manufacture.

The remaining classes of material culture are limited to various stone tools. The most numerous are rotary and saddle querns (Fig. 32, 1–4), the former in a wider range of stone types, including foreign ones, the latter in fine greensands derived from the local glacial till. The pattern of deposition of querns suggests a generally low level of disposal of broken pieces, probably as normal rubbish (although one more structured deposit is typical of such items known in both the Iron Age and Romano-British periods). Most likely to have been used in domestic contexts, it appears that querns were generally removed from those areas and disposed of away from houses, in enclosure and field system ditches. Three rotary quern-stones and one saddle quern were recovered from the junction of enclosure ditch 1365 and ditch 1001 (to the south of Enclosure H) at Lower Cambourne. As many as four whetstones (including Fig. 32, 9) may be of Iron Age date and were recovered primarily from pits associated with

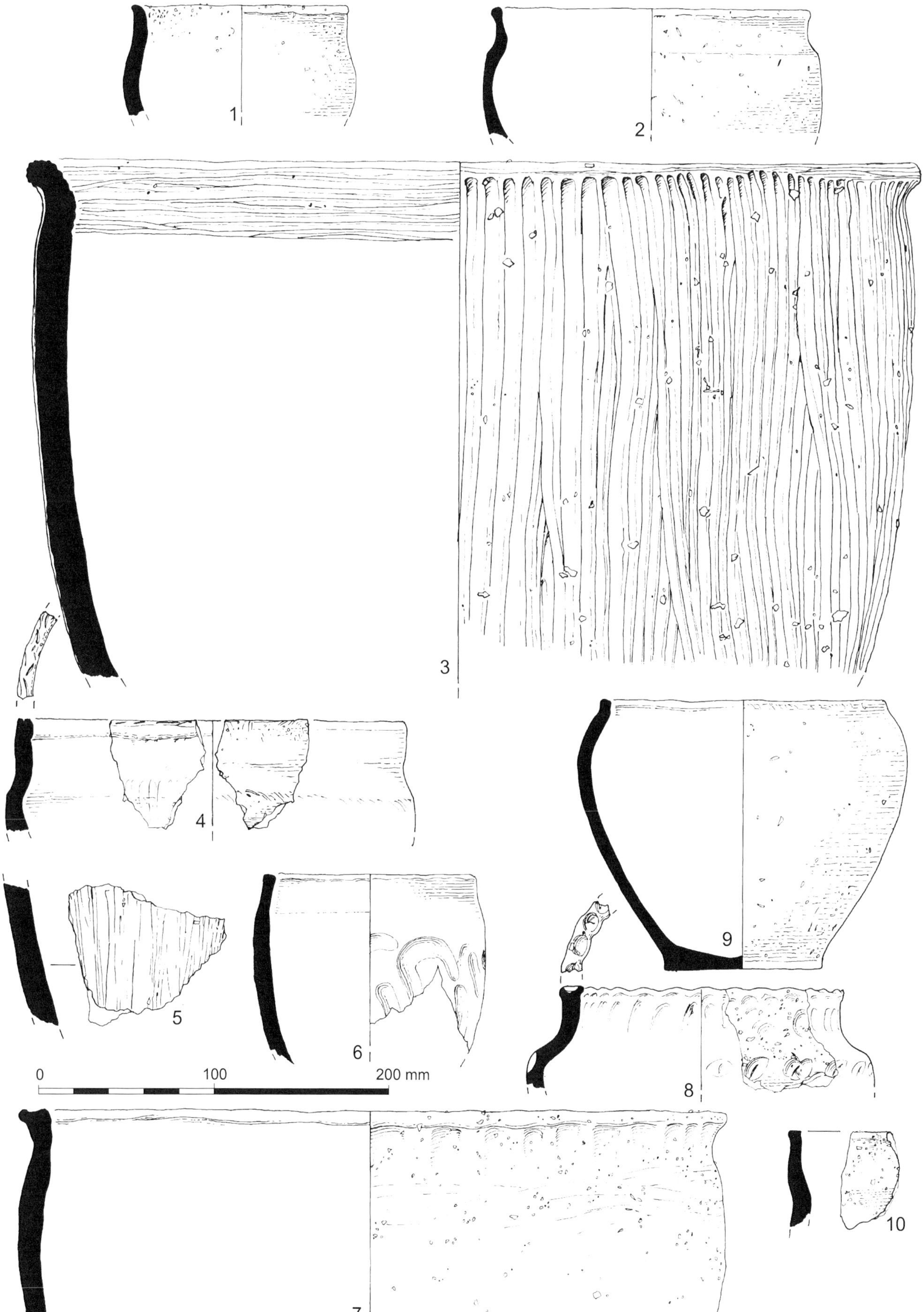
1
2
3
4
5
6
7
8
9
10
0
100
200 mm

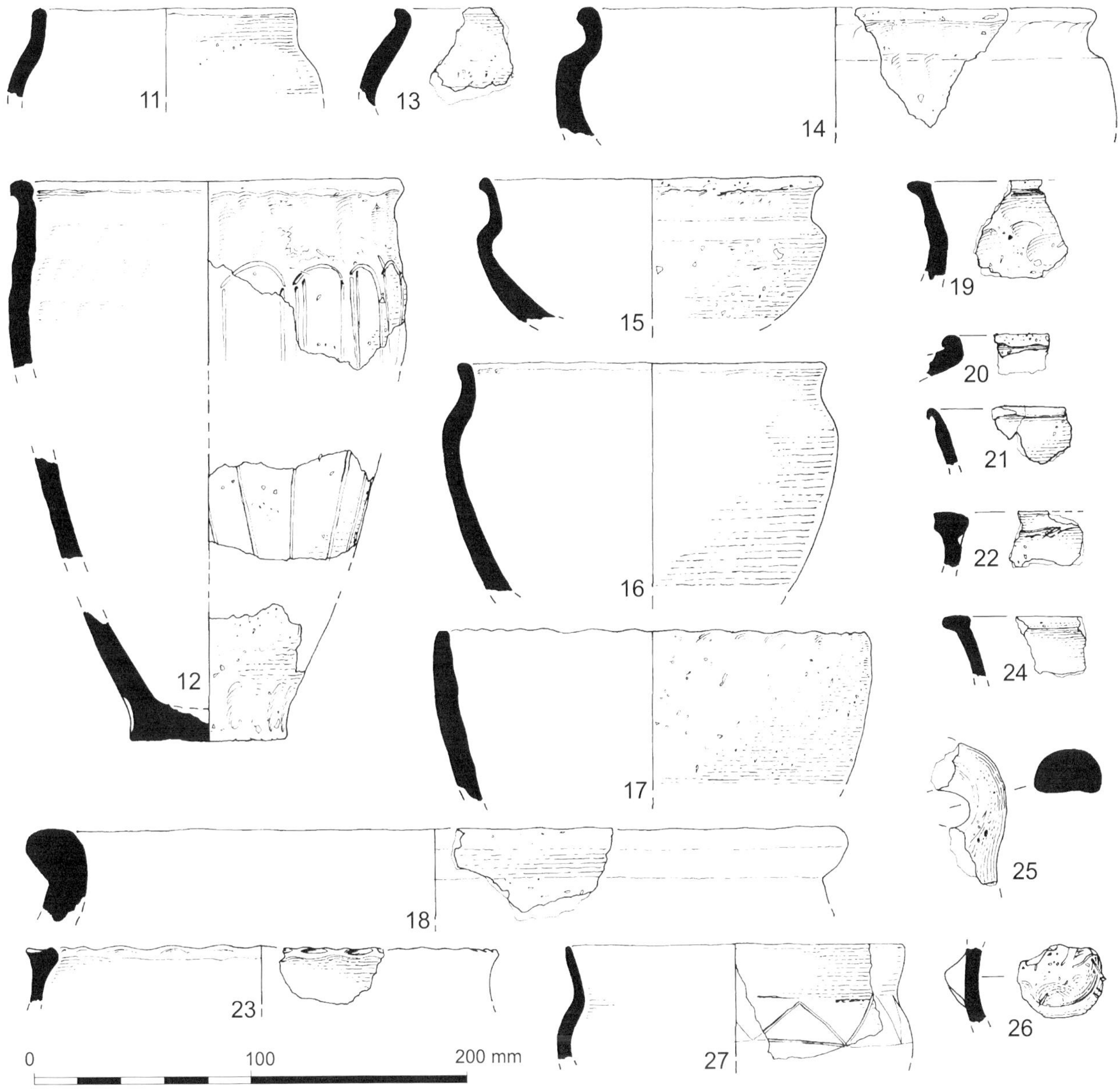

Figure 29 (opposite) and Figure 30 (above) Prehistoric pottery (see text for details)

roundhouses, possibly indicating areas of task specialisation.

The chronology of quern-stones is not well understood. The saddle querns are most likely to be of Iron Age date, but so too may be the beehive rotary querns. The variety of rock types present among the querns indicates that imports (either of raw materials or finished products) came from a wide area, not limited to Britain. The pattern of presence and absence is similar to other sites in the general area, and is perhaps significant. There also appears to be an emerging relationship in the occurrence of querns of imported lava and those of local Puddingstone. For example, at *Verulamium* King Harry Lane, Puddingstone was entirely absent, while lava formed approximately half of the total; at Baldock, Puddingstone was present, and lava formed only one-sixth of the assemblage (Stead and Rigby 1989, 51–2). This last ratio holds good for Cambourne, and also for Braughing, Hertfordshire, while the former is true at Colchester (Buckley and Major 1983, 75). Stead argues that this occurrence is unlikely to be due to physical differences of access to Puddingstone (or by extension lava) and suggests instead that the reason may be chronological, with those sites occupied earlier (Baldock, Cambourne) having Puddingstone querns of typical beehive form.

The Colchester evidence suggests an alternative explanation, with lava querns predominating on Romano-British settlements, and traded separately from the native Puddingstone. Rudge's (1968) distribution of Puddingstone querns demonstrates a predominantly East Anglian distribution opposed to the widespread occurrence of lava. That there need

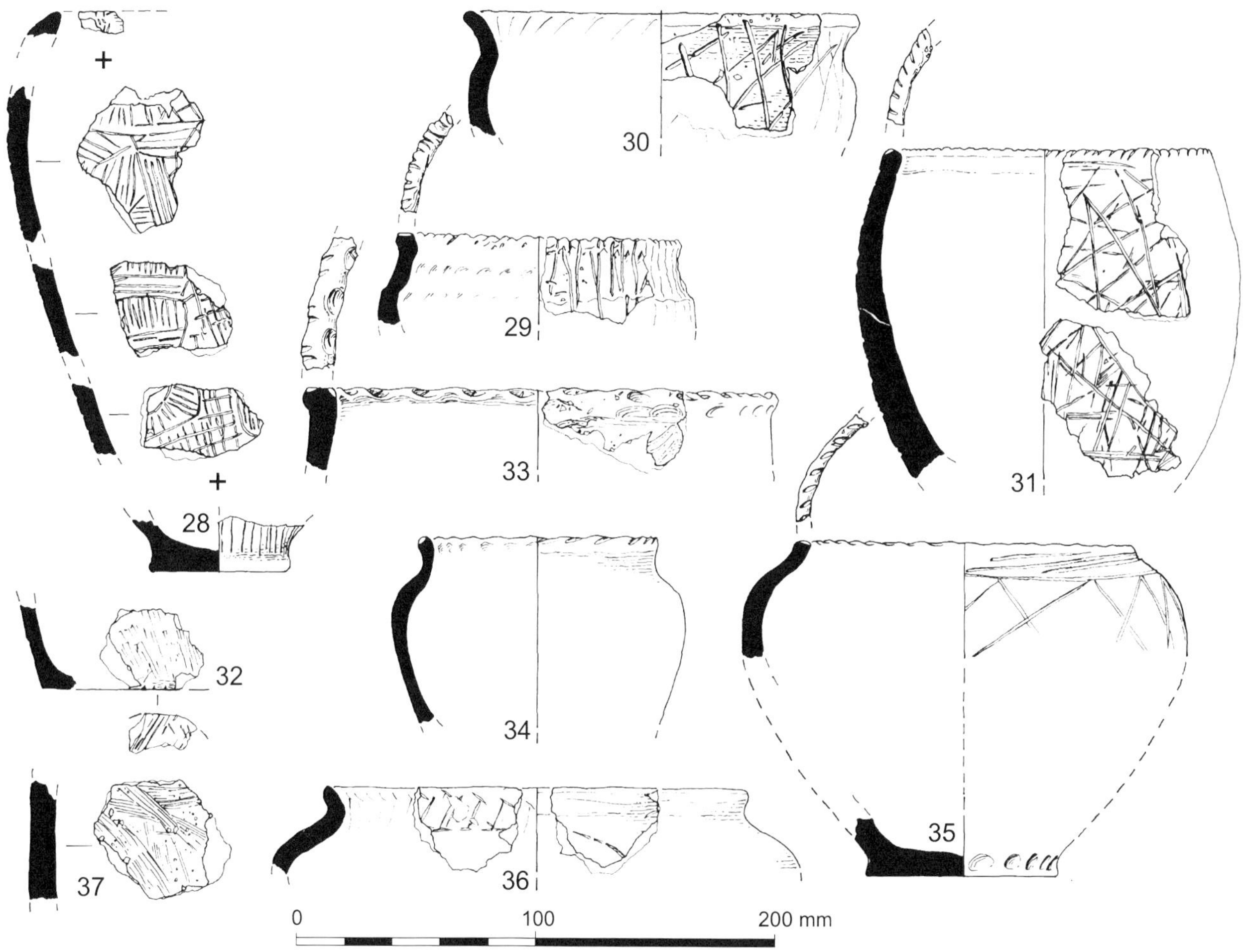

Figure 31 Prehistoric pottery (see text for details)

not be a straightforward replacement of one type by the other is highlighted by Welfare (1986) who points out the economic desirability of a flourishing local manufacture.

The only other tool is a crude pebble chopper from Jeavons Lane (Fig. 27, 5), typical of Iron Age lithics, in which flint tends to be used expediently for very crude implements (cf. Young and Humphrey 1999), mostly associated with crushing or pounding, perhaps in food processing tasks.

The Iron Age agricultural economy

by Chris J. Stevens

Charred cereal remains were recovered from six of the sites. Good assemblages were only available from Knapwell Planation and Little Common Farm, while the assemblages from Lower Cambourne, Poplar Plantation, Broadway Farm, and Jeavons Lane contained relatively few remains.

Despite the ample evidence for cereals in charred form, the lack of such remains, especially glume bases, in the single waterlogged deposit appears to be a common characteristic of Iron Age sites in the region. Comparative waterlogged deposits from Wardy Hill (Murphy 2003) and Earith (Stevens 1998; in press a) also failed to produce such evidence. It may be that the activities that generated such waste were confined to the household, away from enclosure ditches, and that much of the waste was discarded into the domestic hearth.

Animal bones were recovered from Iron Age features on only four of the sites, Lower Cambourne, Knapwell Plantation, Jeavons Lane, and Little Common Farm. Preservation at both Little Common Farm and Lower Cambourne was quite good, and preservation generally within the Iron Age features was better than for the Romano-British ones (Hamilton-Dyer, Volume 2, 85).

Cereal crops and other food remains

Cereal remains comprised predominately spelt (*Triticum spelta*) and emmer wheat (*T. dicoccum*). Most of the remains were glume bases rather than grains, and these were recovered from all the Iron Age

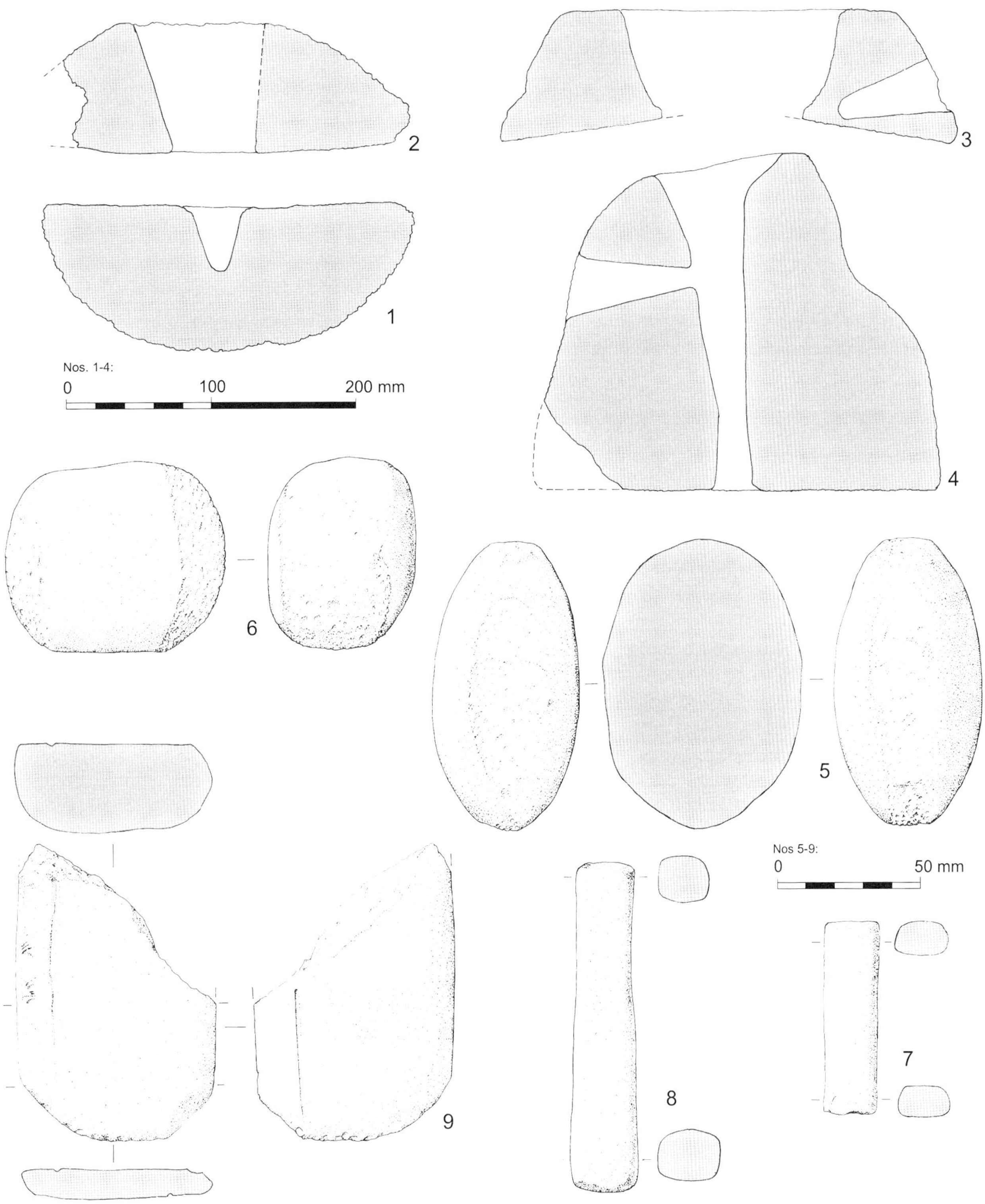

Figure 32 Worked stone: 1–4. quern-stone fragments; 5–6. hammers/grinders; 7–9. whetstones

phases. Generally many glume bases were unidentifiable and none from Broadway Farm or Poplar Plantation could be identified to species. At Knapwell Plantation and Little Common Farm, where identification was possible, emmer appeared to be as well-represented as spelt (Stevens, Volume 2, 167–8, 175–6). At Lower Cambourne spelt wheat glumes were more numerous in a few features, although, given the concentration of later Romano-British occupation and the presence of intrusive Romano-British pottery in some of these features, some glumes may be intrusive.

Spelt wheat dominates Iron Age charred assemblages across much of central and southern England, as it does in parts of the north-east, and seems to be the preferred crop over emmer (Jones 1981; Campbell 2000; Robinson and Wilson 1987). It is notable, however, that several Iron Age sites in East Anglia have produced evidence for similar quantities of both wheats; for example, Coln Fen, Earith (Stevens 1998; in press a), Wardy Hill (Murphy 2003), Haddenham (Jones 2006), and Wandlebury (Ballantyne 2004b), although at Maxey Murphy (1997) notes a shift towards spelt. To the south, a similar pattern is also seen at Asheldham, Essex (Murphy 1991a) and also for many sites in Kent (Giorgi 2006; Stevens 2006). Further, it is also notable that emmer persists in parts of north-east England (van der Veen 1992).

Such explanations for the continued preference for emmer wheat may be historical, cultural, and/or ecological in nature. Most modern strains of emmer wheat are noted to do better on lighter, drier soils that often fail to produce a good crop of spelt (Percival 1921). It is also noted that many strains of emmer are less tolerant of colder winters (cf. van der Veen and O'Connor 1998), a reason for its possible association with spring sowing (Percival 1921; cf. Jones 1981). However, the possibility that strains existed in the past that were different in nature must be considered; for instance, some modern strains are capable of producing good yields on flooded soils (Davies and Hillman 1988). Furthermore, Reynolds (1981) notes that autumn sown emmer generally produced better yields than spelt in experiments at Butser, with the exception of a single year where there was heavy frost. The presence of both species in a pit at Wandlebury, Cambridgeshire (Ballantyne 2004b) might indicate they were commonly sown as a maslin (a mixed emmer-spelt crop), as it would seem probable the pit was filled in one event from a single harvest. The growing of maslins would then compensate for such unforeseen events as flooding or heavy frosts, although it is also possible that Iron Age farmers in the region did not greatly distinguish one crop from the other.

While barley was present there were generally fewer identifiable grains than those of wheat. It should be noted, however, that generally cereal grains were poorly represented within the Iron Age phases, with the possible exception of Little Common Farm. No barley rachises were recovered, and no remains of any crops other than cereals were present within the Iron Age samples.

One aspect of the samples that is notable and discussed above is the number of fragments of hazelnut shell and stones of sloe. Remains of potential wild food resources are usually more common than cereal remains on Neolithic sites, but generally rarer on Late Bronze Age, Iron Age, and rural Romano-British settlements. While such finds may be residual, in the general absence of earlier activity it seems probable that such remains are indeed of Iron Age date. Remains of potential wild foods were most notable from Poplar Plantation, Lower Cambourne, Little Common Farm, Mill Farm (from which only hazelnut fragments were recovered), and Knapwell Plantation, which also contained a possible pip of crab apple (*Malus sylvestris*).

Crop husbandry

It seems probable that most if not all the inhabitants of Iron Age Cambourne were directly engaged in agriculture and that at least some fields were located close to the settlements. While the charred cereal remains demonstrate the growing of spelt, emmer, and barley, the weed seeds provide an insight into how these crops were cultivated. The poor representation of weed flora at all sites other than Little Common Farm means that most of the interpretations concerning the cultivation of crops during the Iron Age are based on the data from this one site.

Those weed seeds present were predominately of larger seeded species, brome grass (*Bromus* sp.), oats (*Avena* sp.), buttercup (*Ranunculus acris/repens/ bulbosus*), cleavers (*Galium aparine*), docks (*Rumex* sp.), ribwort plantain (*Plantago lanceolata*), and perennial rye-grass (*Lolium perenne*). Smaller seeded species included red bartsia (*Odontites vernus*) and orache (*Atriplex* sp.), while Little Common Farm also yielded finds of small seeded grasses, clover (*Trifolium* sp.), and fat-hen (*Chenopodium album*).

As seen above, there is evidence to suggest that many of the sites were prone to flooding during the later Iron Age, and so it might be expected that such conditions are reflected in the range of weed species whose seeds were recovered from the sites. The majority were ecologically unspecific, although several are more commonly associated with drier, slightly calcareous to calcareous soils. These included black medick (*Medicago lupulina*), red bartsia, ribwort plantain, and self-heal (*Prunella vulgaris*). Nevertheless, frequent seeds of buttercup indicate the cultivation of at least some damp to wetter soils. However, while seeds of sedge (*Carex* sp.) and blinks (*Montia fontana ssp. chondrosperma*) were present in the samples, these along with other indicators of the cultivation of wet or seasonally flooded soils, such as spikerush (*Eleocharis palustris*), were generally rare or, in the latter case, absent. Similar results were also seen on the A428 at Bourn Airfield (site 3) and Scotland Farm (sites 7 and 8) to the east (Giorgi 2008). This may indicate that the inhabitants located arable fields in relatively well-drained parts of the landscape, and/or that flooding events were relatively rare with soils substantially drying out in summer.

It is likely that soils at this time would be tilled by ard, an indication of which is usually seen through the high numbers of perennial species on such soils (cf. Behre 1981; Hillman 1981; 1984; Wilkinson and Stevens 2003, 187–9). Perennial species were generally poorly represented, although this is more likely a product of crop-processing. Many perennial species have smaller seeds that may have been removed by fine-sieving before the crop was brought to the settlement and/or stored. However, the presence of perennial and possible perennial species, such as perennial rye-grass, clover, buttercup, and cat's-tail (*Phleum* sp.) can be taken to indicate the relatively minimal soil disturbance associated with ard cultivation.

The time at which crops were sown is difficult to establish from the weed flora alone. Cleavers has been seen as an indicator of autumn sowing (Jones 1981; 1988a; 1988b; Reynolds 1981) and is present within several samples. Likewise the ratio of seeds of Chenopodiaceae to Leguminosae may be taken as an indicator of soil fertility (Jones 1981; 1988a; 1988b) or time of sowing (Stevens 1996; Wilkinson and Stevens 2003, 191). While seeds of the Chenopodiaceae were poorly represented it is probable that, as with the under-representation of perennial species, this is a product of crop-processing (cf. Jones 1992). The presence of both emmer and spelt might indicate a dual sowing regime, the former associated with spring sowing, the latter with autumn sowing, although as noted above these crops may have been sown together as a maslin (cf. Jones and Halstead 1995).

Harvesting, as seems to be the case for many British Iron Age sites, appears to be by sickle and at least in some instances the cereal plant was cut close to the ground (cf. Hillman 1981; 1984; Wilkinson and Stevens 2003, 193). Such harvesting would explain the presence of low growing species, such as clover and cinquefoil (*Potentilla* sp.).

Crop processing and storage

The relatively high proportion of seeds of larger seeded species indicates that crops were probably stored relatively well-processed. Weed seeds are removed through the various stages of processing, with smaller-headed and lighter seeds removed within the earlier stages leaving mainly larger 'grain-sized' weed seeds to be removed during the final stages of processing (Wilkinson and Stevens 2003; Hillman 1981; 1984; Jones, G. 1984; 1987). Charred remains, in that they are often glume-rich, can be seen to be the product of the dehusking and processing of crops taken from storage as and when required (Stevens 2003a). The waste from this processing is often discarded straight onto the fire (Hillman 1981) and as such can be used to identify which processing stages were conducted shortly after harvest, potentially in the field, and which were conducted after storage in the settlement (Stevens 2003a).

Most of the assemblages were richer in glumes than grain, characteristic of the waste from dehusking, and indicating the storage of emmer and spelt wheat within the spikelet. The presence of few, but mainly larger seeded weed species would further indicate that crops were most probably threshed, winnowed, and sieved in the field or perhaps on a specially prepared threshing floor prior to their storage. These crops then would have been taken from storage, possibly within four-post granaries (seen at Lower Cambourne and Little Common Farm; Chapter 2), then processed to produce clean grain as and when required. Such processing would have involved the dehusking of the grains, probably in wooden mortars, followed by sieving and winnowing to remove glumes, lighter chaff, and remaining weed seeds from the grain. Finally, larger weed seeds and other remaining contaminants would be removed by hand. At least in some cases this waste would have been thrown into and become charred in the hearth, after which it became incorporated into archaeological features, perhaps via surface middens into which hearth waste was discarded.

Much of the dehusked grain is likely to have been ground into flour upon the saddle querns of types similar to those recovered from Lower Cambourne and Knapwell Plantation. A rotary quern was recovered from later Iron Age deposits at Little Common Farm (Haywood, Volume 2, 59). Saddle querns usually dominate Iron Age sites in East Anglia and only saddle querns were found at Scotland Farm (Duncan 2008), Wardy Hill, and Haddenham, although some less identifiable pieces from Wardy Hill may be from rotary querns (Lucas 2003, 189; 2006, 204). Some of the grain may have been fermented and used for beer but, unlike the Romano-British phases at Cambourne, there is no evidence that malted grain was used in the Iron Age.

The sites at Cambourne compare well with each other and little variation occurs between, at least, those with the richest charred plant assemblages. In terms of other Iron Age sites in the county, there are published assemblages from Bourn Airfield (site 3) and Scotland Farm (sites 7 and 8) to the east on the A428 (Giorgi 2008), from Trumpington (Wilson 1973) and Wandlebury (Ballantyne 2004b) to the south-east, and from Wardy Hill (Murphy 2003) and Haddenham (Jones, G. 2006) to the north. Unpublished material is also available from sites in north Cambridge (Stevens 1997a), on the fen-edge at Earith (Stevens 1998; 2005; in press a; Ballantyne 2004a; Bower 2000), as well as to the east of Cambridge at Greenhouse Farm (Stevens 1997b). To the west, several Iron Age assemblages were also examined from Broom, Bedfordshire (Stevens in press b).

Some differences do emerge, however, in the ways crops were stored and processed. While the Cambourne sites, as seen above, and probably also those from Bourn Airfield (site 3) and Scotland Farm (sites 7 and 8) on the A428, contained only a few larger weed seeds (Giorgi 2008), suggesting crops were stored in a relatively clean state, for many other sites in the region (eg. Wardy Hill, Hurst Lane near Ely, Earith, Greenhouse Farm, and North Cambridge) samples are dominated by small weed seeds indicating crops were stored in a relatively unprocessed state (Stevens 1997a; 1997b; 2003b; 2005).

The degree of processing conducted prior to storage has been associated with the size of the crop and the availability of labour to perform what are quite time-consuming operations. For some larger settlements, including hillforts, for example Wandlebury, crops appear to have been stored almost clean as 'semi-clean' spikelets (Stevens 2003a). The interpretation of this pattern is that, on some sites, labour was pooled to perform harvesting and processing, allowing crops to be more fully processed prior to storage. Such concentration of labour may reflect larger, extended households or the organisation of agricultural work through family ties. While no one site at Cambourne appears to represent a settlement or large farmstead comprising several families, it may be that, given the proximity of the settlements, some degree of agricultural communal labour existed. This was perhaps established through kinship ties and allowed crops to be harvested and stored in a relatively processed state. It is interesting to note that while the settlements to the east and north-east of Cambourne appear to have stored crops in a less processed state, patterns were seen from sites around Broom, Bedfordshire, where similar assemblages with respect to crop processing were recovered (Stevens in press b).

In comparing cultivation practices it is notable that seeds of both the Chenopodiaceae and wetland species are better represented on many of the other Iron Age sites in Cambridgeshire than at Cambourne or the A428 sites to the east (Giorgi 2008). As noted above, many of these other sites, because they have a larger number of processing stages present, have a larger range of weed flora represented. For this reason, comparisons are difficult to make, although several of these sites, for example Haddenham, Earith, and Wardy Hill, are located on the fen-edge and so might be expected to produce a more characteristic wetland flora.

Unlike the sites at Cambourne, hazelnuts and sloe are either absent, or at least poorly represented, on many other Iron Age sites in the county, for example Earith, Greenhouse Farm, Huntington Road, and at Wardy Hill where a single feature produced hazelnut, hawthorn, and sloe (Murphy 2003, table12: pit 102). Such differences may reflect a genuinely greater reliance or utilisation of wild resources by the inhabitants of Cambourne, although it might be noted that hazelnut was not recorded at either Bourn Airfield (site 3) or Scotland Farm (sites 7 and 8) less than 5 km to the east (Giorgi 2008).

Animal husbandry

The animal bone assemblages were dominated, as might be expected, by bones of cattle, sheep/goat, and pig. On most of the sites, apart from the later Iron Age phase at Jeavons Lane, bones of cattle and sheep/goat were fairly equally represented. At Jeavons Lane cattle bones predominated to a large degree, while on most other sites they were only slightly better represented than sheep/goat; at Knapwell Plantation the reverse was the case (Hamilton-Dyer, Volume 2, 98). Pig, while consistently present, was usually a minor component, perhaps reflecting low levels of woodland pannage in the general area. Fish bone was entirely absent.

As at Cambourne, Scotland Farm, on the A428, was dominated by bones of cattle and sheep/goat, with cattle generally better represented (Rielly 2008). Similar patterns were also noted for a Late Iron Age site at Tort Hill East on Ermine Street (Albarella 1998). At Wardy Hill and Barrington bones of sheep/goat were generally more common (Davies 2003), and at Haddenham sheep bones far outnumbered those of cattle, with also fairly low levels of pig (Serjeantson 2006). The sites at Great Barford were also dominated by sheep/goat during the Iron Age (Holmes 2007).

There was some indication that cattle may have been somewhat smaller during the Iron Age than during the Romano-British period (Hamilton-Dyer, Volume 2, 88). Similarly, there was a slight indication of smaller cattle at Scotland Farm (Reilly 2008), while it is also noted that the cattle from Wardy Hill and Barrington were 'fairly small' (Davies 2003).

Where sheep and goat could be distinguished, the identification of sheep appeared more common, although goat was identified from Jeavons Lane and Little Common Farm (Hamilton-Dyer, Volume 2, 92–3). At Wardy Hill only sheep were identified, (Davies 2003) and they also formed the major part of the sheep/goat assemblage from Haddenham (Serjeantson 2006).

Horse bones were consistently represented, although often in low numbers. Many were still articulated, with less evidence of butchery, and some may relate to whole burials or specially placed deposits (Hamilton-Dyer, Volume 2, 95). Horse bones are present in similarly low frequencies on sites in the area, with the exception of Scotland Farm where they were quite well represented (Rielly 2008). On the latter site bones are also mainly articulated with little sign of butchery. Horse bones in placed deposits are a common feature on Iron Age sites in southern England as a whole, particularly in the Wessex region (Gibson and Knight 2007), although it might be noted that at Haddenham many horse bones were disarticulated with some indication of butchery (Serjeantson 2006).

The ditches defining the enclosures on the various sites seem to have been predominately associated with drainage, although the presence of probable hedges and droveways, at least at Little Common Farm (Chapter 2), suggests that animals may have occasionally been herded within the enclosures.

For many of the Cambourne sites it is noticeable that shells of dwarf pond snail (*Lymnaea truncatula*) were common (Allen, Volume 2, 187–210). The species today has significance for modern farmers as it is the intermediate host for the liver-fluke, *Fasciola hepatica*, which can affect both cattle and sheep which graze upon the same marshy grassland that the snail inhabits. Whether the association between snail and parasite was well-established in Iron Age Britain cannot be ascertained. Severe infection may result in death of both sheep and young calves and, while adult cattle are more resistant to infection, it can affect both breeding and milk production. On the basis of the greater resistance in cattle it has been suggested that ancient farmers in wetter areas may have favoured cattle (Robinson in prep.; Allen, Volume 2, 196–8). While it is possible that sheep were not grazed in wetter areas, given the high numbers of sheep bones seen on the Cambourne sites, and in many of the wetland sites listed above, it is questionable to what extent this association affected herd composition in Iron Age England. If liver fluke infection was widespread it may be that no connection was made by Iron Age farmers with grazing sheep on wetlands; alternatively it is possible that farmers persisted in grazing sheep in marshy areas, as they did in medieval Cambridgeshire even when the connection had been well-established (see Trow-Smith 1957, 249).

Infection in humans from this source is rare today and, while consumption of infested livers is unlikely to result in complications, the consumption of unwashed native aquatic plants which *Lymnaea truncatula* inhabits, such as water-cress (*Rorippa nasturtium-aquaticum*), could well have resulted in human infections in Iron Age Britain.

There is at least some indication on cattle bones from Little Common Farm that the animals in question were either used for pulling a cart or plough (Hamilton-Dyer, Volume 2, 88). A few fragments of loomweights came from Knapwell Plantation, Lower Cambourne, and possibly Little Common Farm, and indicate textile working, possibly using wool from locally raised sheep.

Butchery and age distributions

Most of the cattle bones probably came from adults (aged 3–4 years plus), with few younger and no young calves represented. Only a single, elderly, individual was recorded (Hamilton-Dyer, Volume 2, 87). This compares well with the data from Scotland Farm, Haddenham, and Great Barford where the assemblages comprised mainly adults (Rielly 2008; Serjeantson 2006; Holmes 2007).

The sheep bones showed a similar pattern in that few young lambs were recorded and many of the bones appear to have come from sub-adults and adult individuals aged between 9 months and 3–4 years (Hamilton-Dyer, Volume 2, 93). This pattern is similar to Scotland Farm (Rielly 2008) and Wardy Hill (Davies 1999) where animals are likely to have been killed within the first 3 years, with few individuals of less than 6 months of age recorded. It contrasts quite strongly, however, with the sheep-dominated assemblages from Haddenham where a high proportion of juvenile animals is seen (Serjeantson 2006) and that from Great Barford where sheep were slaughtered at 2–3 years (Holmes 2007).

In terms of butchery during the Iron Age, there is evidence for knife marks on cattle bones related to skinning and the removal of meat – and, in one case, the animal's tongue (Hamilton-Dyer, Volume 2, 86–7). Very few butchery marks were noticed on the sheep/goat bones. Cleaver marks were recorded on one horse bone from Little Common Farm; these were of an unusual nature in which the bone was chopped axially, ie, longitudinally along the bone (Hamilton-Dyer, Volume 2, 95). Such butchery practices have also been recorded on Late Iron Age cattle bones from Tort Hill East, possibly for marrow extraction, though it is noted that such practices are usually typically Romano-British (Albarella 1998).

5. The Romano-British Period

The local and wider Romano-British landscape

by Chris J. Stevens

The landscape in the 1st–5th centuries AD

Beginning in the 1st century BC, and during the early Romano-British period, water-levels receded in the region, and the 2nd century AD saw some drying out of the previously inundated areas (French 2003, 122). The retreating fen-edge allowed some expansion of settlements on to the Flandrian silts (Dawson 2000; Hall and Coles 1994, fig. 68). In the middle of the 3rd century, however, it appears that extensive flooding took hold, especially in the southern fens (French 2003, 111). While there is evidence to suggest some reoccupation in the 100 years following the late 3rd century, this appears short-lived and by the end of the Romano-British occupation, settlement of the fens was in noticeable decline (Potter 1981, 132). Flooding within the general region appears much more extensive during the later Romano-British period and continues well into the medieval period (French 2003). It is also during this period that extensive alluviation occurred, burying many of the earlier, prehistoric sites.

The Romano-British period also marks the appearance of several major routeways and roads in the region. The sites at Cambourne fall in between two relatively major Roman roads converging to the north at Godmanchester (*Durovigutum*). The nearest is Ermine Street immediately to the south-west bringing traffic from *Londinium*, while *c.* 7 km to the north-east is the *Via Devana* running from Cambridge (*Durolipons*) to the north-west. Additionally there is a smaller, less formalised, localised route, Roman Road 231 (Margary 1993), that may even be pre-Roman, running along the northern edge of the site on the line of the A421 (Abrams and Ingham 2008). Within the fens themselves the drier phase, in the 1st century AD, sees the Fen Causeway being laid across former peats (Pryor 1984; 2001). The digging of some major waterways across the fens probably took place sometime during the Romano-British period, including construction of the Car Dyke.

Accompanying these changes there is evidence for a general replanning of the landscape during this period, with enclosure taking place on a larger scale as well as the appearance of rectilinear field systems.

The local environment at Cambourne

Evidence for the local environment at Cambourne is better represented for the 1st–4th centuries AD than for the other periods, pollen data being available from Lower Cambourne, Mill Farm, Jeavons Lane, and The Grange (Fig. 33). These sites, along with North Caxton Bypass, also provided environmental evidence from charcoal and, apart from The Grange, from molluscan analysis; molluscs were also analysed from ditch deposits at Great Common Farm. Sedimentary analysis accompanied the pollen sequences and provides some history of localised alluviation for each of the sites.

As in the Iron Age, the landscape appears to be relatively open during the Romano-British period. The earliest evidence for the later Iron Age–Romano-British transition comes from pollen sequences obtained from the pond/waterhole at Jeavons Lane. This provides only slight evidence for a few tree species, including oak, and grasses predominate.

The later 2nd–4th century pollen sequences continue to demonstrate little evidence for woodland. At The Grange, Mill Farm, and Lower Cambourne there is some evidence for oak and hazel in the local landscape while, in addition to these species, small amounts of pine and birch were also recorded at Jeavons Lane (Scaife, Volume 2, 211–2, 213–6, 217–8).

The charcoal indicates a similar range of species to that seen in the Iron Age. The assemblages are dominated by shrubs, including blackthorn (*Prunus spinosa*), hawthorn/*Sorbus* group (Pomoidae), hazel (*Corylus avellana*), and Guelder rose/Wayfaring tree (*Viburnum* sp.), along with more woodland elements, such as oak (*Quercus* sp.), ash (*Fraxinus excelsior*), field maple (*Acer campestre*), and elm (*Ulmus* sp.) (Gale, Volume 2, 136–42, 149–51; 2008). Of some interest was the possible use of heather, from North Caxton Bypass (Gale, Volume 2, 135–6).

Three of the sites, Lower Cambourne, The Grange, and Jeavons Lane produced evidence for fast-grown oak, coppiced on fairly short cycles, an activity that would have led to more limited pollen production of this species (Gale, Volume 2, 136–42, 149–51). Similar evidence for oak coppicing was also seen at Childerley Gate (site 5) on the A428 to the east (Gale 2008). The association of coppiced wood with iron working might further indicate that managed woodland was selectively used for fuel (including charcoal burning) for such industrial activities (Gale, Volume 2, 149–51; 2008).

Further evidence for shrub came in the form of charred thorns of blackthorn and/or hawthorn (*Crataegus monogyna*) from several of the sites (Stevens, Volume 2, 159–62, 170–2, 175–8) where there was some hint of continued exploitation of wild resources, indicated by fragments of hazelnut and fruit stones of sloe in several of the samples, although some of these may be reworked from earlier phases of activity. The combined pollen and charcoal evidence suggests a relatively open landscape with limited stands of managed mixed deciduous woodland and a fairly high degree of woody scrubland, some or much of which may relate to hedges.

The waterlogged evidence from the late Romano-British enclosure ditch (5267) at Lower Cambourne indicates a substantial amount of shrub in close proximity to the ditch, comprising hawthorn, sloe, and elder. Such shrubs may have belonged to a formalised hedge, although the possibility that the ditch had become substantially overgrown in places cannot be ruled out. A waterlogged deposit from an earlier, Late Iron Age/early Romano-British pit (3070) at this site also contains thorns, stones, and seeds of shrub species, suggesting that shrub may have been quick to colonise more neglected areas of the settlement.

It is questionable whether the evidence from Lower Cambourne is entirely representative of the environment, of the enclosure ditches and possible hedges, at the other Cambourne sites. It might be noted, however, that another enclosure ditch (3080) there does have a high proportion of molluscan species of shaded environments suggesting possible hedges or local scrub. This, along with a sample from The Grange, differs from many of the other samples examined from Cambourne where open country species predominate (Allen, Volume 2, 190–3), perhaps suggesting that not all the enclosures had such hedging. Mollusc samples from several sites on the A428, specifically Ash Plantation (site 2), Bourn Airfield (site 3), and Childerley Chapel (site 4), also had quite high proportions of molluscan species of shaded environments (Pipe 2008), perhaps suggesting the existence of hedges at these sites.

As with the Iron Age ditches it is probable that the Romano-British enclosure ditches functioned as much for drainage, channelling water away from the settlement and living areas, as they did for controlling livestock. The waterlogged evidence at Lower Cambourne, especially from ditch 5267, indicates standing, probably stagnant water throughout much of the year including duckweed (*Lemna* sp.), horned-pondweed (*Zannichellia palustris*), water-crowfoot (*Ranunculus* subg. *Batrachium*), and water-plantain (*Alisma plantago-aquatica*), as well as ephippium (egg-cases) of the water-flea. Water-pepper (*Persicaria hydropiper*), tasteless water-pepper (*P. mitis*), gypsywort (*Lycopus europaeus*), bur-marigold (*Bidens tripartita*), and meadowsweet (*Glyceria maximum*) would have grown on the sides of wet ditches.

At several of the sites the remains of aquatic molluscs also indicate a high water table and probably standing water for much of the year (Allen, Volume 2, 201–2, 207–8, 209–210), although some of the waterholes may have contained only periodic standing water (Allen, Volume 2, 188–9, 190–3, 196–8).

As seen for the Iron Age at Little Common Farm, the waterlogged material from Lower Cambourne provides evidence for a general 'farmyard' environment. In other words, a flora that indicates nitrogen-rich, disturbed, trampled soils supporting plants such as many-seeded goosefoot (*Chenopodium polyspermum*), fig-leaved goosefoot (*C. ficifolium*), henbane (*Hyoscyamus niger*), swine-cress (*Coronopus squamatus*), and chickweed (*Stellaria media*).

Plants of common nettle (*Urtica dioica*), thistle (*Cirsium*/*Carduus* sp.), and buttercup (*Ranunculus acris*/*repens*/*bulbosus*) along with docks (*Rumex* sp.) can be associated with patches of rough pasture around the enclosures and probably also survived trampling and grazing on the edges of ditches. Along with these it is interesting to note seeds of hemlock (*Conium maculatum*) in the samples, a species of wet wasteland that is absent from Iron Age deposits at Little Common Farm and is largely thought to be a Roman introduction (Godwin 1984).

Molluscan remains at several sites indicates that, while the ditches seemed to contain water, probably in some cases for much of the year, there was a relatively dry, well-established, short grazed grassland environment, with possibly some indication of arable, beyond them (Allen, Volume 2, 201–2, 207–8). Several of the Romano-British sites on the A428 also indicated relatively dry, well-grazed, short turf grassland, at least in the earlier part of the Romano-British period (Pipe 2008). In contrast, both Mill Farm and North Caxton Bypass demonstrate, from the molluscan evidence, wet grassland with probable flooding from nearby channels and watercourses.

While sedges are generally poorly represented at Cambourne in comparison with the fen, a pollen sample from a ditch at Mill Farm, as well as another from The Grange, did produce a fair amount of sedge pollen along with that of bur reed/greater reed mace (*Typha angustifolia*/*Sparganium*).

It is interesting to note that even at Knapwell Plantation, the most elevated of the sites excavated, not only is there evidence for long periods of standing water in the ditches, but a lightly grazed, damp grassland existed beyond (Allen, Volume 2, 199–200). The A428 sites are, like Knapwell Plantation, also on the higher, drier ridge to the north of Cambourne. At

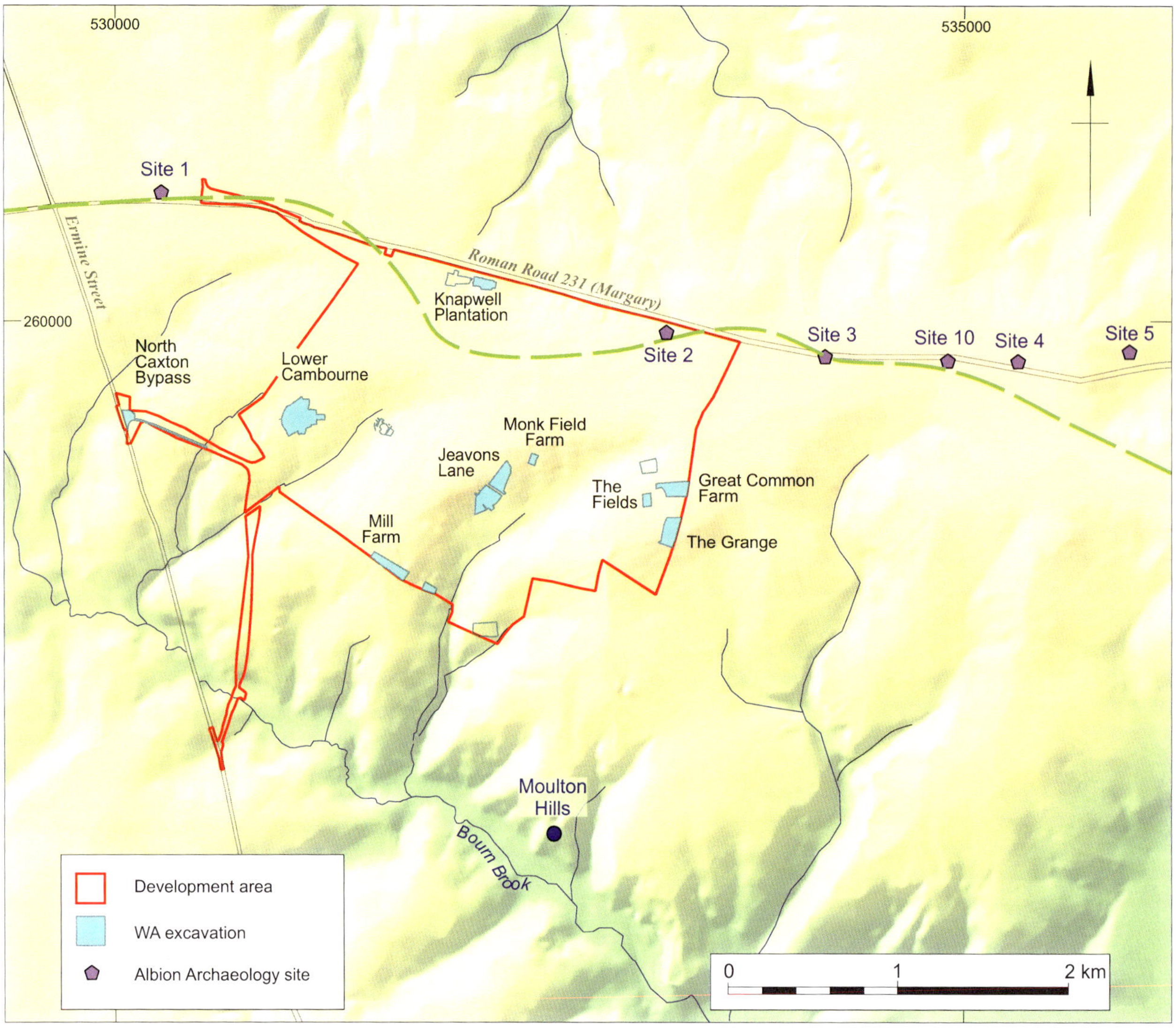

Figure 33. Terrain model of Cambourne: Romano-British (Phase 3) sites

Bourn Airfield (site 3) there was evidence for an expansion of more marshy grassland in the 4th century, while broadly contemporaneous ditches at Childerley Gate (site 5) contained a high proportion of aquatic species, generally increasing from the Iron Age to the Romano-British period (Pipe 2008). The ditch examined at Knapwell Plantation was also likely to be of 3rd–4th century date and, given the extensive flooding occurring in the fens in the mid-3rd and 4th centuries, it is possible that even areas marginal to the fen may have been affected by these events. Evidence for flooding is also seen in the later sedimentary infills of features at Lower Cambourne and The Grange (Barnett, Volume 2, 219–21, 229).

Most of the remains of wild fauna recovered can be associated with open woodland, shrub, and/or hedgerows, but others belong to more open arable landscapes, providing that some degree of cover is available. The range of species includes badger, hedgehog, field vole, raven, long or short eared owl, and corncrake (Hamilton-Dyer, Volume 2, 96–7), the last a species closely related to moorhens but favouring drier marshland and meadows rather than riverine environments. Some remains of duck were also encountered in Romano-British deposits, including possible mallard and smaller, unidentified ducks, and possibly plover or widgeon. Of a more unusual nature was a find of pine-martin, a species more commonly associated with woodland, but one that can be found in scrubland.

Small numbers of deer remains, both roe and red, were recovered, comprising mainly antler fragments, although other skeletal elements were recorded from Jeavons Lane and Lower Cambourne (Hamilton-Dyer, Volume 2, 96). As in the Iron Age, finds of wild game animals are relatively rare on Romano-British sites (Albarella 1998).

Romano-British settlement at Cambourne
by James Wright

Excavations at Cambourne and along the adjacent A428 (Abrams and Ingham 2008) have added substantially to the picture that is emerging of Romano-British settlement on the claylands of west Cambridgeshire. Ten of the 12 sites at Cambourne revealed Romano-British features, with the other two (Little Common Farm and Broadway Farm) providing evidence for later Iron Age settlement only (Fig. 33). Of the nine Romano-British sites, four (Lower Cambourne, Knapwell Plantation, Jeavons Lane, and The Fields) also had later Iron Age features, although in only one (Lower Cambourne) or possibly two (Jeavons Lane) cases is there reasonably clear evidence for continuity of settlement. On the A428, no sites covering this transitional period were identified (*ibid.*).

Roads and field systems

Cambourne lies very close to Ermine Street, the Roman road between London (*Londinium*), Lincoln (*Lindum*), and York (*Eboracum*), with the northern edge of the Development Area adjacent to Roman Road 231 (Margary 1973), a minor road which broadly followed the route of a prehistoric trackway and is itself partly followed today by the A428 (*ibid.*, fig. 1.7). This minor route met Ermine Street at Caxton Gibbet and continued west to Bosmead Manor and Bolnhurst. An area of cobbling with an adjacent ditch recorded during evaluation at the southern end of the Caxton Bypass may have been the remains of Ermine Street. No trace of Road 231 was identified at Knapwell Plantation, in any of the evaluation trenches, or at Ash Plantation (site 2) on the A428. This may indicate that Road 231 was unmetalled and perhaps, in places at least, not clearly defined.

To the north of Cambourne, along Ermine Street, a fort at Godmanchester was succeeded by the town of *Durovigutum*; to the south, also on Ermine Street, was a minor settlement at Wimpole Lodge (Ordnance Survey 1978). Approximately 12 km to the east was the small town of *Durolipons* (Cambridge), just west of which was the1st–4th century possible estate centre at Vicar's Farm (*Current Archaeology* 2002). Apart from Roman Road 231, other roads ran west from Cambridge to Godmanchester (the *Via Devena*) and to Wimpole Lodge, and Fox (1923, map iv) implies the presence of a further minor Roman road in the lower Bourn valley.

Ermine Street cut obliquely across the Bourn valley and several of the small tributaries and dry valleys which lay at 90° to it, whereas Roman Road 231 ran along the plateau between the watersheds of the Bourn Brook to the south and the Great Ouse to the north. However, neither of these routes appears to have been the most significant factor in the organisation of the Romano-British landscape in large parts of this area, particularly away from the flatter ground of the plateau. Instead, within the Development Area in particular, it was the location and the north-west to south-east alignment of the valleys and winterbournes which were the main influences on both the pattern and layout of the settlements. At North Caxton Bypass, adjacent to Ermine Street, the field boundaries closest to the road took their alignments from it, but further away they followed the north-east to south-west line of the valley to the east.

In contrast, at Caxton Gibbet on the A428, just over 1 km to the north, the field boundaries were parallel to Ermine Street (Abrams and Ingham 2008, fig. 1.6) and it appears that the presence of this road may have influenced the alignments of field boundaries, droveways, and enclosures on the featureless ground of the plateau to the east. This was seen at Ash Plantation (site 2), Childerley Chapel (site 4), and Childerley Gate (site 5) on the A428, up to 6 km to the east of Ermine Street (*ibid.*), although not at Bourn Airfield (site 3), Camford Way (site 10), or Knapwell Plantation where the north–south alignments presumably relate to the course of Road 231.

What remains uncertain is the extent of these field systems and their chronology. For example, several different systems, rather than one intermittent expanse, may be represented, and not all may have been contemporaneous. Some variations in their form suggest different complexes of fields, and there is no evidence that they extended continuously over several kilometres. Furthermore, although those on sites along the A428 have been assigned to the 1st century AD, this is based on very little evidence (Abrams and Ingham 2008, 39), and a probable 2nd century or later date is suggested for the ditches at North Caxton Bypass. Thus the possibility that these presumably arable fields were established to provide food for the army and were possibly part of a large, perhaps imperial, estate, as has been suggested elsewhere (*ibid.*, 42), cannot be further substantiated.

Topography and settlement

Topographic changes are gentle rather than dramatic on the claylands, but in general the plateau remained sparsely settled in comparison with the valleys. At Cambourne only one site (Knapwell Plantation) lay on the plateau, in addition to Ash plantation (site 2) on the A428, whereas the remainder were all within or close to the shallow valleys which dissected the south-western half of the Development Area. The plateau was used for pasture during most periods and only brought in to arable use when population pressure led to increased demands that could not be provided for by cultivation only of the better quality land in the lower parts of the valleys. This has been alluded to above, in the suggestion that some of this marginal land may have been utilised for arable cultivation early in the Romano-British period, perhaps to supply the army with food.

Various settlements might be anticipated within the Bourn valley, less than a kilometre to the south-west of Cambourne, and this was also the location of several villas. These are likely to have varied in size, and in their dates of establishment and decline, but unfortunately those investigations that have been undertaken all took place in the 19th or early 20th centuries and subject generally to only cursory recording (Scott 1993). At Comberton (NGR 5382 2555), painted plaster, glass, and pottery were recovered from a stone-built structure which included a hexagonal room. Coins from the site spanned the second half of 1st to the second half of the 4th century. Three villas may have existed near Grantchester at the confluence of the Bourn and Cam, but none is closely dated. One (NGR 543 255) is described only as a 'substantial building' by the Ordnance Survey; another (NGR 543 251) had at least one Doric column, bricks, and tiles, but may have been destroyed during World War I; and a third (NGR 543 254), noted during World War I, comprised stone and timber buildings with roof tiles, painted plaster, and *opus signinum*. A villa is also recorded at Harlton (NGR 537 252), on the southern side of the Bourn valley, with 2nd–4th century tile, but there are few details.

Romano-British barrows constructed in the Bourn valley include three on its north side at Moulton Hills, 2 km to the south of Cambourne (Fox 1923). One covered a cremation burial that included pottery, pins, brooches, and a coin of Marcus Aurelius (AD 161–180) (*ibid.*, 195; Philpott 1991, 290), possibly representing an occupant of one of the villas in the area.

The Romano-British settlements excavated at Cambourne all appear to represent farmsteads, and this was also the case Ash Plantation (site 2), Bourn Airfield (site 3), and Childerley Gate (site 4) on the A428 (Abrams and Ingham 2008), and also at Caldecote Highfields (Kenney 2007) 3.5 km to the east of Cambourne. These farmsteads were not all contemporaneous and they were dispersed across the Development Area, with the preferred locations being close to a stream or watercourse, in a slightly sheltered position (see Fig. 33). This might be on what was considered peripheral land, between the arable land in the lower part of the valleys and the pasture provided in the upper valleys and on the plateau above.

The evidence discussed further below indicates that the farmsteads were engaged in mixed agriculture, though pastoral farming dominated. This is reflected in the number of droveways, some of which may have had their origin in the Late Iron Age, but which appear to increase in number in the Romano-British period. This is likely to indicate a greater level of movement of both people and animals around the landscape than had been seen earlier, though whether this was because there was a lower density of settlement, or over-grazing, in the Romano-British period is unclear. A density of *c.* 1.3 settlements per square kilometre was suggested for the area of the southern Cam and its tributary valleys (Williamson 1984), but at Cambourne the density seems to be slightly less. It is likely that much of the Bourn valley was divided and organised as estates or farms, centrally managed from villas, although how such organisation related to the Cambourne sites is not clear.

All of the farmsteads, with the possible exception of Lower Cambourne, were small and of low status, apparently occupied for a relatively short period or at least not intensively, and of only one phase with little evidence for expansion or nucleation. Lower Cambourne was unusual in several ways, including the greater range of finds perhaps indicating a settlement of higher status, in the unusual group of 'placed deposits', and in the evidence for continuity of settlement.

Settlement morphology

Lower Cambourne is the only site where there appears to have been uninterrupted occupation from the Iron Age. This demonstrates that at this site at least, the Roman Conquest led to no significant changes in the morphology of the enclosures or the nature of the buildings (ie, roundhouses continued in use), although the nature of the finds assemblage did change (see below). In appearance, the new or still-occupied farmsteads would not have differed from their Iron Age predecessors. What is also evident is that major changes in the layout and appearance of the farmstead did not take place until the later 2nd century or possibly early 3rd century. It was at this time that new, sub-rectangular enclosures made their appearance at four sites apparently without roundhouses (Mill Farm, Knapwell Plantation, Jeavons Lane, and Monk Field Farm) and two where roundhouses were present (Lower Cambourne, and The Grange). The presence of roundhouses on these sites in the 2nd century or even later has been noted elsewhere, for example within the partially exposed, sub-square enclosure at Ash Plantation (site 2) on the A428 (within the Development Area) (Abrams and Ingham 2008, 51). This demonstrates a continuation of native Iron Age building traditions and serves to further highlight the failure of Romanisation to affect some aspects of settlement and culture in this area, a century and a half after the Conquest. In addition to roundhouses, a small number of four-post structures may have served as granaries or feed stores for animals.

The enclosures and associated droveways indicate a clear association with animal husbandry, and the presence of a number of waterholes (at Lower Cambourne, Mill Farm, and Jeavons Lane) confirms this. However, the enclosure ditches seem also to have served as drainage features as flooding appears to have been a recurring problem on these clayland sites. Beyond the enclosures on several sites (Lower Cambourne, Mill Farm, and probably Jeavons Lane) were fields, perhaps in some cases extending between sites, as might some of the droveways. The most unusual group of features was the network of very small fields or pens at The Fields whose function, and indeed date, remain uncertain. Fieldwalking undertaken in the valleys of the Cam, and its tributaries, in north-west Essex suggested that Romano-British settlements were surrounded by an often asymmetric area of up to 100 m radius which had been intensively manured, and which was interpreted as small plots or gardens (Williamson 1984).

The layout of the rectangular enclosure at Jeavons Lane, with its regular internal divisions, shows some similarities to the late 2nd century ladder system settlement at Childerley Gate (site 5) on the A428 (Abrams and Ingham 2008, 52, fig. 3.13). The latter appears to have been a planned layout, rather than resulting from organic development, perhaps undertaken in a single operation and possibly linked to one of the villas in the Bourn valley. The development at Jeavons Lane, unlike that at Childerley Gate, was on a site that had been occupied in the later Iron Age, but, with the exception of a possible droveway to the south, there is little evidence that the earlier enclosure and associated features had any effect on the Romano-British layout. The Childerley Gate ladder settlement was substantially remodelled in the early 4th century, but nothing of this nature was undertaken at Jeavons Lane. At Lower Cambourne, however, the Phase 2C, early Romano-British, enclosures were swept away and replaced by the Phase 3A and Phase 3B sub-rectangular enclosures, in the 3rd and 4th centuries respectively. A similar complexity of development is seen at the same time in the sequence at Childerley Gate (*ibid.*, fig. 3.23).

At Lower Cambourne and Jeavons Lane the establishment of sub-rectangular enclosures also saw the appearance of sub-rectangular buildings, at Lower Cambourne alongside at least one roundhouse; elsewhere, such as The Grange, there is evidence for roundhouses only. The exact form of these buildings is difficult to establish from what survives – a shallow, in some cases irregular hollow (indicating a sunken floor), some with cobbling, but all with few post-holes or other structural features. Although the alignments of the hollows appear to be at variance to those of the enclosures, the excavated remains are consistent with timber buildings resting either on cobbles or shallowly-founded timber sills, with cob or wattle and daub walls and a thatched roof. Such structures appear to have been present in the 3rd century at Godmanchester (Green 1982), and similar hollows or spreads of late 2nd–4th century date set within rectangular enclosures were suggested to be the remains of buildings near Peterborough (Coates *al.* 2001).

At Jeavons Lane a pair of adjacent sub-rectangular buildings is indicated, one perhaps an ancillary structure, while at Lower Cambourne there are two single buildings one each in the Phase 3A and Phase 3B enclosures, that in the earlier enclosure adjacent to a roundhouse. It is possible that the periods of use of the two buildings at Lower Cambourne overlapped, as it is suggested that the Phase 3B enclosure was added to the Phase 3A enclosure in the later 3rd or 4th century. The later of the two buildings is of particular interest due to the presence in its vicinity of three 'placed deposits' (see below) which might have been deposited in the 4th century while the building was still in use. The presence of a possibly contemporary, substantial, free-standing post next to this building may also be significant, although its function, and those of the internal divisions in the Phase 3B and Phase 3A enclosures, remain unknown.

At Lower Cambourne the coin evidence shows that the site continued in use until the late 4th or perhaps the early 5th century, with 12 coins minted AD 388–402 being found, the only site where there is such clear evidence for late activity. However, identifying 5th century settlements generally is extremely difficult, and other sites at Cambourne, and also at Childerley Gate (site 5) on the A428 (Abrams and Ingham 2008, 101), may have seen sub-Roman occupation (see below).

The burials

by Rachael Seager Smith

Glimpses of the actual people living at Lower Cambourne, Knapwell Plantation, and Jeavons Lane during the late Romano-British period can be gained from the few inhumation burials, located on, or close to, the margins of these sites (McKinley, Volume 2,

71–81). The seven graves each contained the remains of one adult, while undated infant remains, probably from a very shallow grave at the western end of Lower Cambourne, represented the only individual of this age. This apparent dearth of immature individuals is common in archaeological assemblages, especially those comprising small grave groups or singletons. In rural areas, burial in small groups such as these, associated with farmsteads or villas and often located close to boundaries (Esmonde Cleary 2000, 132–3, 137–8), continued throughout the Romano-British period, and in this area represent a direct continuation of the most common Iron Age inhumation rite (Whimster 1981, 5, 18, 25, and 227–35).

The adult burials comprise four males and three females. Objects, however, were more likely to be included with the women than the men, although all but one of these were worn at the time of burial, rather than being 'grave offerings'. Two of the women wore copper alloy finger-rings; one woman aged between 45 and 55, buried at Lower Cambourne (grave 1018), had a plain ring on her right index finger, while a younger woman (25–30 years old; grave 80299) from Jeavons Lane wore a plain ring with a D-shaped cross-section and another with a pale blue glass intaglio (see Fig. 41, 16) on the 4th and 5th fingers of her left hand. The third female, 40–50 years old, was buried in a nailed coffin, probably of oak, accompanied by a miniature greyware jar (Fig. 37, 40). One of the adult men from Jeavons Lane (grave 80406) was also buried wearing a pair of nailed boots or shoes, but only stray finds occurred in the other three male graves (grave 60300 at Knapwell Plantation, and graves 80423 and 80467 at Jeavons Lane).

Two of the skeletons survived in a sufficiently complete state for stature estimates to be made; the decapitated male from grave 80423 had an estimated height of 1.78 m (5' 10½") while the woman buried with the two finger rings was 1.51 m (4' 11½") tall. Compared with the 68 Romano-British males from the Baldock Area 15 cemetery, Hertfordshire (McKinley 1993a), the man was of above average height (1.69 m), falling within the upper part of the range represented there (1.51–1.81 m), while the female was shorter than the average of 1.58 m for the 43 females, falling towards the bottom of the recorded range (1.50–1.69 m). Strong muscle attachments noted on the man from grave 80467 suggest the extensive use of his upper body for heavy work; he also had an old, well-healed injury to his upper left arm/shoulder, possibly a fracture and/or soft tissue injury, but is unlikely to have suffered any lasting effects. This individual died after the age of 55, making him the oldest in the group.

Other evidence for trauma was limited to a broken finger, muscle tear, and one case of spondylolysis, an often symptomless condition but which sometimes causes deep lumbar back pain. Four individuals had suffered various dental problems (such as calculus, caries, abscesses, impacted and unerrupted teeth, and *ante mortem* tooth loss), some of which must have caused great discomfort. This small population had also suffered from conditions such as osteoarthritis and possibly rheumatoid arthritis, ruptured intervertebral discs, and degenerative disc disease, probably reflecting hard, physical work and age-related wear-and-tear.

The mature male buried in grave 80423 was distinguished from the other individuals buried at Jeavons Lane. Not only was his grave located away from the others, who were buried together in the southern half of the site, but he had been decapitated; the skull and four upper cervical vertebrae were not included in the grave. Decapitation is a well-recognised tradition in the Romano-British period, sometimes apparently *peri mortem* and under coercion, but more frequently 'ritual' and probably *post mortem* – with the subsequent placement of the head in the grave either in its normal anatomical position or between, or to one side, of the legs (Harman *et al.* 1981; Philpott 1991, 77–83; McKinley 1993a; 1993b; Boylston 2000, 367–8). Philpott (1991, 77–83) records five Romano-British sites in Cambridgeshire with decapitations, including one from King's Dyke, Whittlesey where, as here, no skull was recovered (*ibid.*, fig. 23). The remains of a probable five decapitated burials (2.7% of the cemetery population) were recorded in the Baldock Area 15 cemetery, but in each instance the skull had been placed in the grave (McKinley 1993a; 1993b).

The absence of the skull may suggest that this man was a victim of an execution or violent death (Philpott, 1991, 77, category 1), but there was no evidence of *peri mortem* trauma to the skeleton. His burial away from the others may indicate a deliberate 'distancing' of this individual from his contemporaries. Whether this reflects his position as an executed outcast from his community or an individual for some other reason deserving, or needing, to be ritually separated both geographically and by having his head removed, is a matter of conjecture. Late Romano-British rural burials often consist of lone individuals and, therefore, his position may have no particular significance.

Late Iron Age and Romano-British material culture

by Rachael Seager Smith

Evidence of Middle–Late Iron Age and/or Romano-British activity was recognised at all of the excavated sites within the Development Area. The pottery and other finds considered here include not only those of Romano-British date but also some later Iron Age pottery. This is for two reasons. First: 'a general conservatism in pottery manufacture and use during the later Iron Age' (Bryant 1997, 26) resulted in the same fabric types and vessel forms remaining current from around 400–300 BC into the Romano-British period, while other datable artefacts are also rare on sites in this area until the 1st century AD (*ibid.*; Bryant 2000, 14). In common with many other parts of rural Britain, this conservatism continued into the Romano-British period, the Conquest having little immediate impact on the native traditions of this area. It is unlikely, therefore, that the inhabitants experienced any significant degree of cultural change until at least the Flavian period (AD 69–96) (Ellis *et al.* 1998, 79), perhaps even into the 2nd century. Secondly, the nature of the excavated features themselves, and the resulting problems of intrusion and residuality, has limited the extent to which it is possible, or appropriate, to examine the artefacts recovered by phase. Few features contained discretely dated groups; most were chronologically mixed, and the artefacts often in poor condition, reflecting the frequent and extensive reworking of deposits, especially within ditches as they were cleaned and/or recut to facilitate drainage on the heavy soils of the area. Where possible, then, the more chronologically diagnostic items have been discussed within the periods in which they were made and used (but not necessarily deposited), while a range of other evidence could only be assigned a more general, Romano-British date.

Late Iron Age

The Late Iron Age ceramics discussed here were somewhat arbitrarily divided from those of the Middle Iron Age described previously (see Leivers, Chapter 4), reflecting the increased use of grog as a tempering material. Very little grog was present amongst the diagnostically Middle Iron Age groups, while a much higher proportion occurred among the Late Iron Age and Early Romano-British forms (Jones, Volume 2, 11–13; Seager Smith, Volume 2, 14–32). Vessels in the sandy, shell-tempered, and organic-tempered fabrics characteristic of the Middle Iron Age continued to be used but in much smaller quantities. The Late Iron Age forms, consisting of bead-rimmed jars (Fig. 34, 3), necked cordoned bowls/jars (Fig. 34, 1, 4, 7), bowls (Fig. 34, 2, 6, 8), large jars (Fig. 34, 5 and 9), and a few local copies of Gallo-Belgic platter forms dating to the latter part of the period, indicate that ceramics were being used in a wide variety of food preparation, serving, and storage roles. Although some of these forms continued to be made until the end of the 1st century AD (Farrar *et al.* 1999, 117), there is little in this assemblage to suggest that its date range extended far, if at all, into the 1st century AD. A Dressel 1 handle stump found at Little Common Farm, in ditch 90491 (Phase 2B), raises the possibility that the settlement's inhabitants had access to the Italian wine transported in these vessels during the 2nd and 1st centuries BC, although the flourishing trade in amphorae as empty containers (Callender 1965, 23–41) may be a more realistic explanation of its presence.

Few other finds are datable to this period. The two Iron Age copper alloy coins from Lower Cambourne are not unusual finds on Late Iron Age settlements and are sometimes seen as an indication that a market economy was functioning in the area prior to the Roman invasion. However, this need not be so and it has been argued that their economic use was part of social rather than market transactions (Haselgrove 1979, 206). Their use may also have continued for a generation after the Conquest (Haselgrove 1996, 82).

1st–early 2nd centuries AD (early Romano-British)

Although the economy and material culture of the area continued in the native traditions, evidence from the Development Area suggests an intensification of land-use and a marked increase in the population during the 1st century AD. With the exception of Broadway Farm and Little Common Farm, all the sites produced material of Romano-British date (*c.* AD 43–410), although only at Lower Cambourne, the largest and most complex site excavated, does the occupation appear to have been anything like continuous.

During the 1st and early 2nd centuries pottery continued to be the most common artefact type, with local sources providing a range of utilitarian food preparation, serving, and storage vessels in a variety of grog-tempered and, to a lesser extent, sandy fabrics. Shell-gritted wares were also common, obtained from a number of different, more distant centres (Gurney 1986, 200), probably including Harrold in Bedfordshire (Brown 1994) and the Nene Valley (Perrin and Webster 1990, 37; Perrin 1999, 118; Wessex Archaeology 2006). The introduction of wheel-thrown pottery was a complex process in Cambridgeshire (eg, Bryant 1997, 26) and at this time, hand-made and wheel-thrown vessels appeared together. Forms were limited to 'Belgic' style jars and bowls (Fig. 35, 13, 15, 17; Fig. 36, 27, 30–32; Fig. 37, 44–5), lid-seated (Fig. 35, 21; Fig. 37, 37–9; Fig. 38, 51) and bead rimmed (Fig. 38, 54) jars, bead-rimmed bowls (Fig. 38, 49), and a few carinated bowls (Fig. 39, 60, 61, 65) and large jars (Fig. 38, 55).

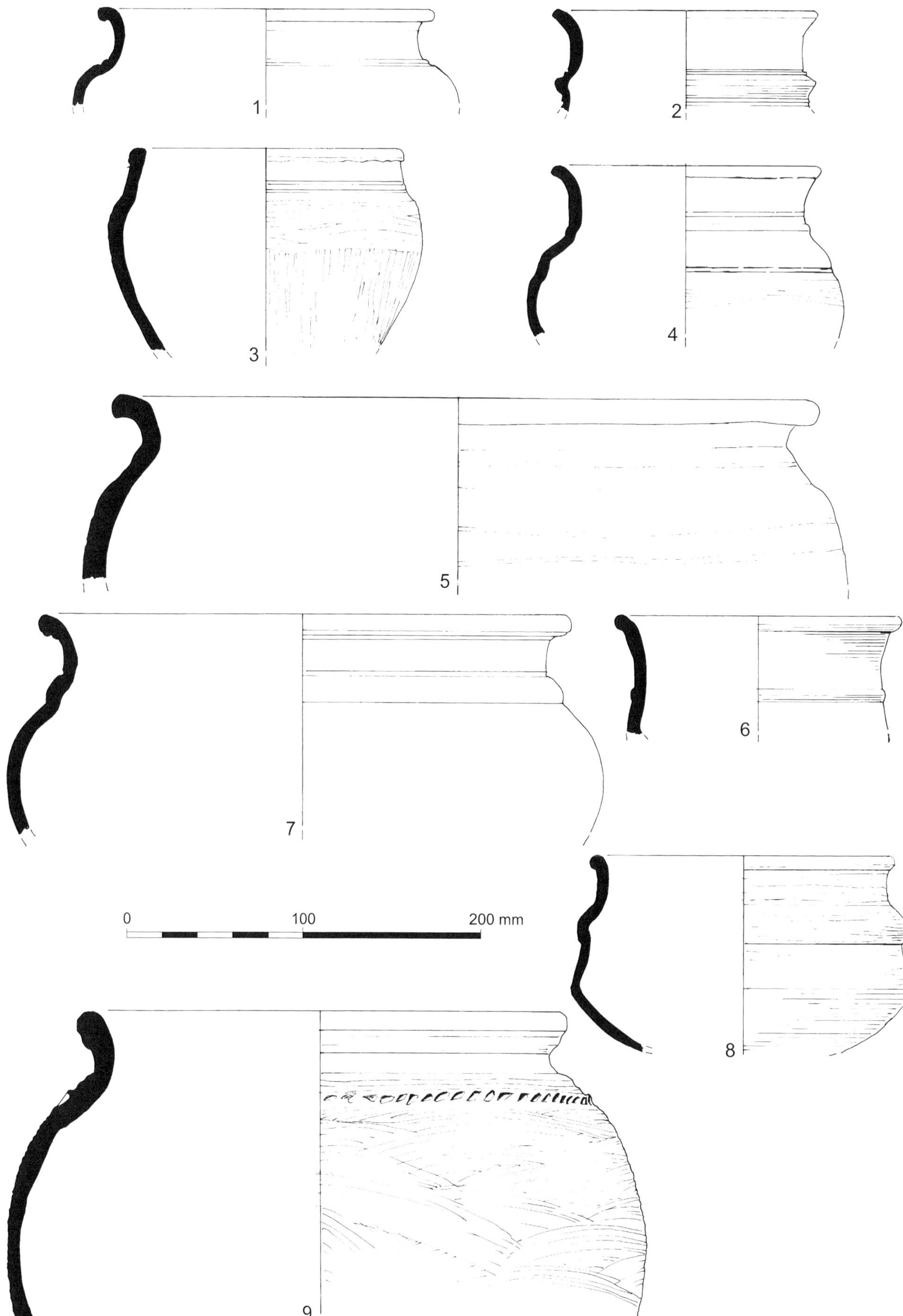

Figure 34. Late Iron Age pottery (see text for details)

Coins, however, were rare; only 16 date from the 1st century AD to the end of the *denarius* coinage in the early 3rd century (Wells, Volume 2, 48), and were found at Lower Cambourne and Jeavons Lane only. Although coins of this period are often poorly represented on multi-period sites, evidence from the ceramics also highlights the possibility that only a small proportion of the native, rural population was ever in direct contact with a market or actively participating in the Romanised economy during the 1st and early 2nd centuries (Condron 1995, 103).

Certainly, the distribution networks of imported tablewares and other specialist vessels, such as amphorae and mortaria, were barely reaching the more remote, small-scale communities like those at Cambourne. Fine tablewares were limited to Southern Gaulish samian and a few white butt beakers which find parallels among the 1st century AD groups in Cambridge (Pullinger *et al.*, 1999, pl. l, 188 and 191, pl. lvii, 239, pl. lxii, 306, pl. lxiv, 332) while two pieces of the distinctive 'black sand' Campanian amphora fabric, probably from the Dressel 2–4 form (Peacock and Williams 1986, class 10), may indicate a very limited continuation of the Italian wine trade. Dressel 20 amphorae, carrying olive oil from the southern Spanish province of *Baetica*, also began reaching the area at this time.

Mortaria were limited to a single, very well-worn vessel typical of the pre- to early Flavian period (Davies *et al.* 1994, 17, fig. 39, 205) from Jeavons Lane. No imported (eg, from north-west France or the Rhineland) forms were recorded, although these were available in Cambridge (Hartley 1999, 206, table ix.1). In the early Romano-British period in particular, the presence of mortaria has traditionally been interpreted as being indicative of the adoption of Romanised methods of food preparation and consumption. However, this view has recently been challenged (Cool 2006, 42–6), with the suggestion that, within early rural communities, these vessels were not used in the kitchen at all, but rather for the same purposes as the equally 'alien' large bowls of decorated samian and glass that were also becoming popular at this time (*ibid.*, 45). Whatever their function, it is clear that the inhabitants of the Cambourne farmsteads had little use for mortaria during the 1st century AD. The arm of an iron cauldron hanger (Fig. 46, 24), belonging to a type widespread in Europe in the Late Iron Age and into the 1st century AD (Manning 1985, 100–1, fig. 27, 1, pl. 45, P9), also stands witness to the continuation of traditional cooking methods.

Other elements of Roman culture were apparently more readily adopted by the inhabitants of the Cambourne settlements, or their uses at least adapted to fit in with local styles. Glass was available in small quantities, as indicated by two unstratified pieces, including part of a relief-decorated base from a square bottle, from Lower Cambourne; these shiny, translucent vessels must have represented very curious, exotic items to the residents of early Romano-British Cambridgeshire. Pieces of two copper alloy spoons, from Lower Cambourne and Jeavons Lane, dating from the mid-1st–2nd centuries, may have been used for eating items such as eggs, shell-fish, and/or snails (Crummy 1983, 69, type 1, fig. 73, 2008). An unusual early iron knife (Fig. 46, 33) was also found at Lower Cambourne. Copper alloy brooches, too, swiftly became popular, at least at Lower Cambourne where 22, all of early Romano-British date, were found. The earliest (Fig. 40, 1 and 2) date from the first half of the 1st century AD, although their occurrence in later 1st century deposits elsewhere in Britain means they do not necessarily represent pre-Conquest activity (Taylor 1985, 22). Others include Colchester one-piece brooches (Fig. 40, 3), Hod Hill types (Fig. 40, 4 and 5), penannular brooches (Fig. 40, 8 and 9), and a trumpet brooch with enamelled blue and red decoration (Fig. 40, 6); all common types. A horse and rider brooch (Fig. 40, 7) with parallels at Lode, Cambridgeshire (Taylor, 1985, fig. 12, 172), and in Norfolk and Suffolk (Hattatt 2000, 359, fig. 218, nos 158, 1174–5) belongs to one of the most common designs of zoomorphic brooches, although few are from securely dated contexts (Taylor 1985, 29). There is some suggestion that these brooches were associated with religious sites (Henig 1984).

2nd–3rd centuries (middle Romano-British)

Items characteristic of this period were restricted in both range and number. Even at Lower Cambourne, there is evidence from the pottery to suggest a sharp decline in the level of activity during the period from *c.* AD 150/160 into the early/mid-3rd century, although the reasons for this are far from clear.

Only pottery occurred in any quantity, although few discrete groups of this date were identified. The 2nd century witnessed several changes in ceramic supply. Early on, the use of grog-tempered coarsewares died out and, by the end of the century, the calcareous fabrics too had suffered a severe numerical decline (Hull and Pullinger 1999, 142; Gibson 2005, 34; Every 2006, 33). Both were replaced by sandy greywares from kilns to the north and east of Cambridge (Hull and Pullinger 1999, 141, fig. vii.1), the Nene Valley industry, West Stow, Wattisfield, Much Hadham, and the Caldecote kilns (Slowikowski and Dawson 1993). A distinctive flanged bowl (Fig. 39, 63) in a conspicuous white quartz-tempered fabric originating in the Milton Keynes area (Marney 1989, 82, fig. 33, 6) highlights

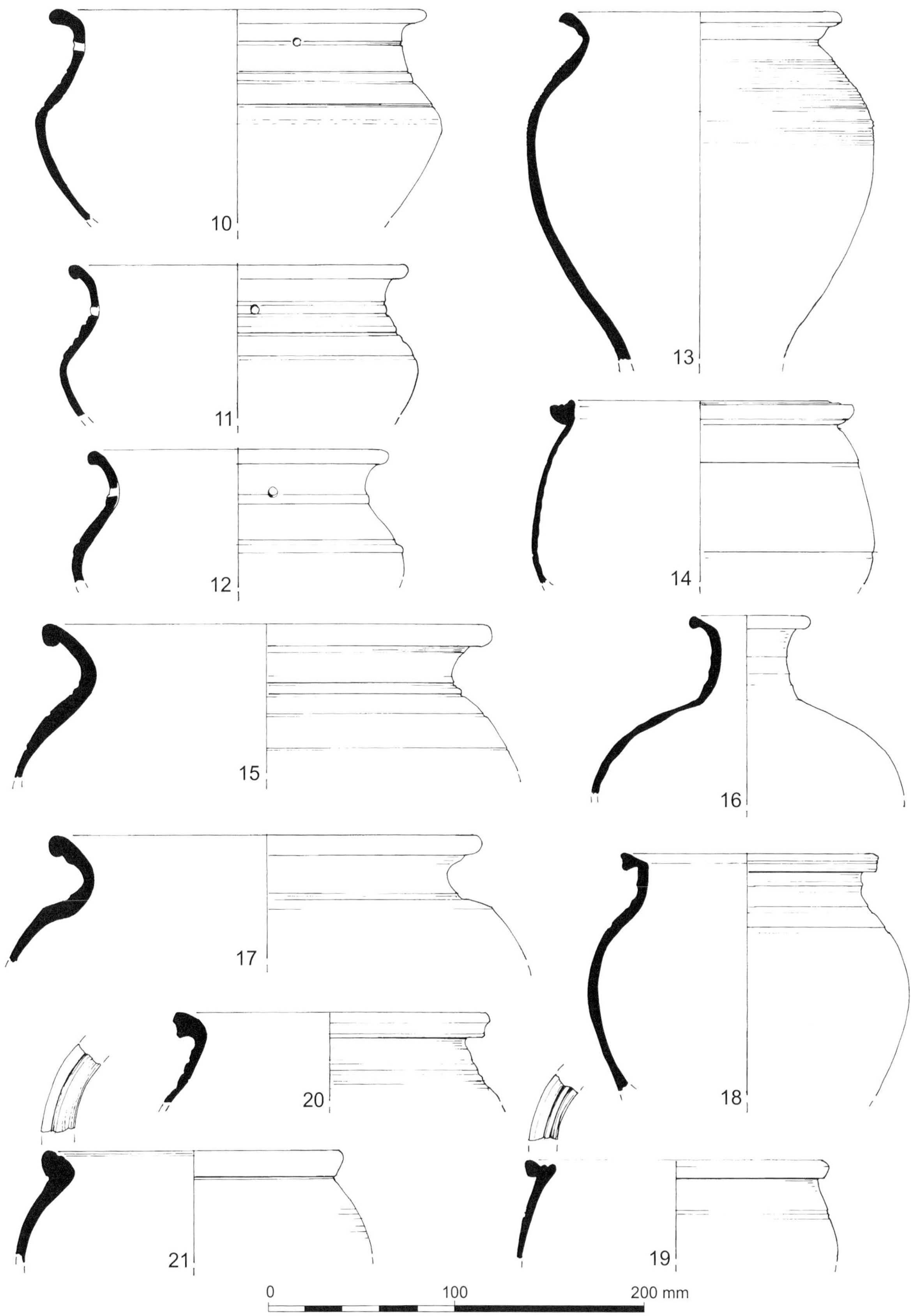

Figure 35 Romano-British pottery (see text for details)

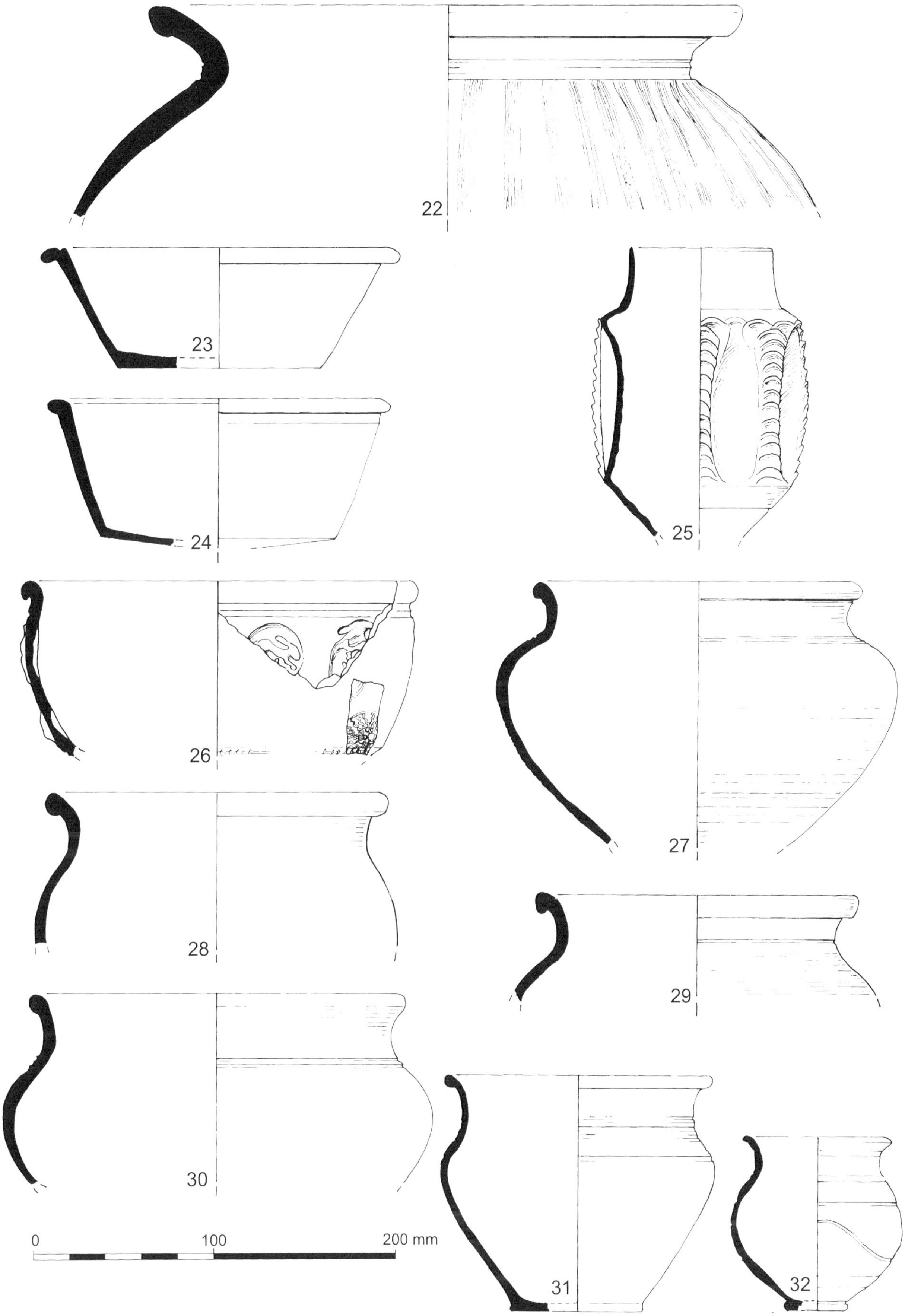

Figure 36 Romano-British pottery (see text for details)

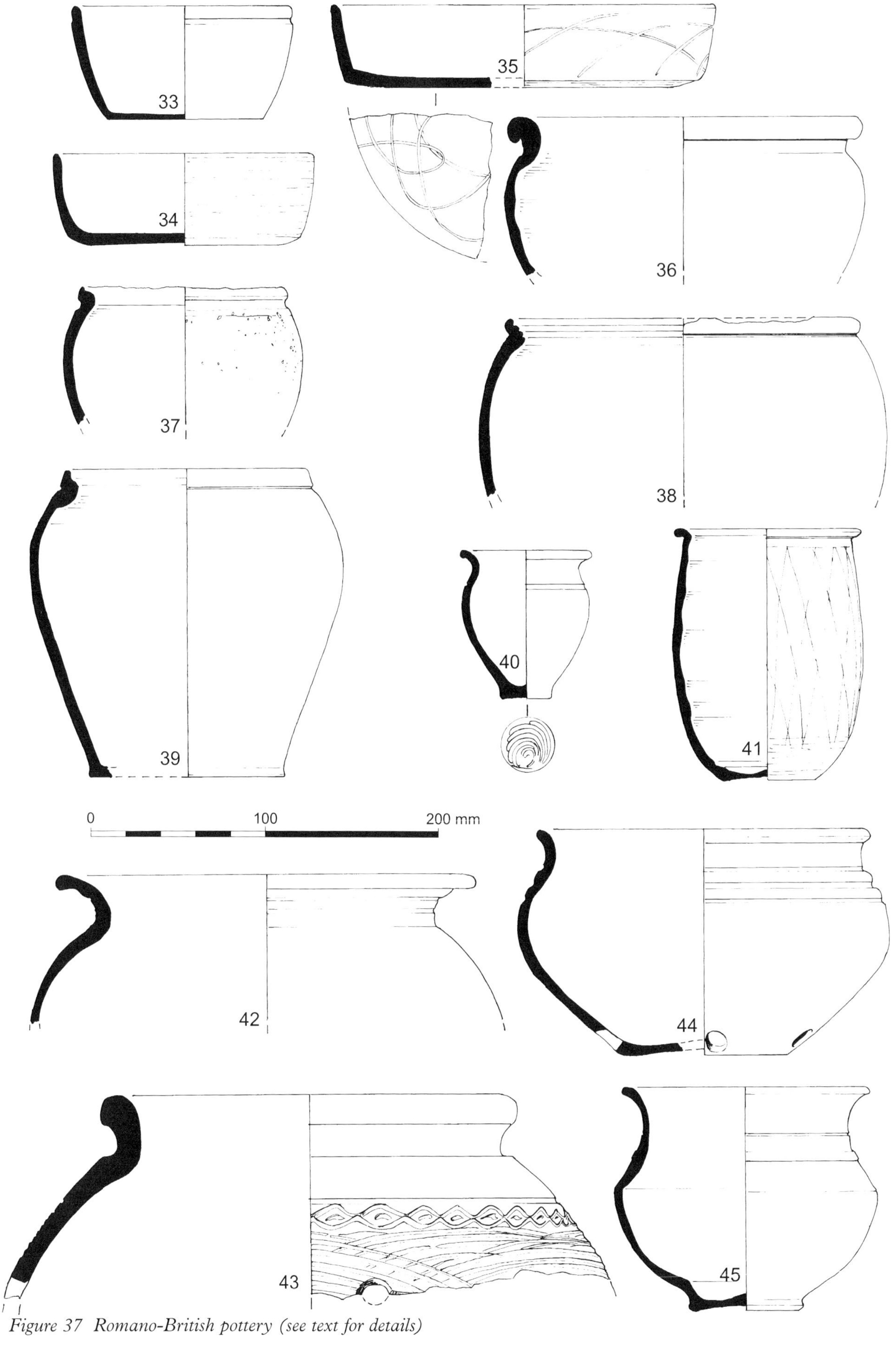

Figure 37 Romano-British pottery (see text for details)

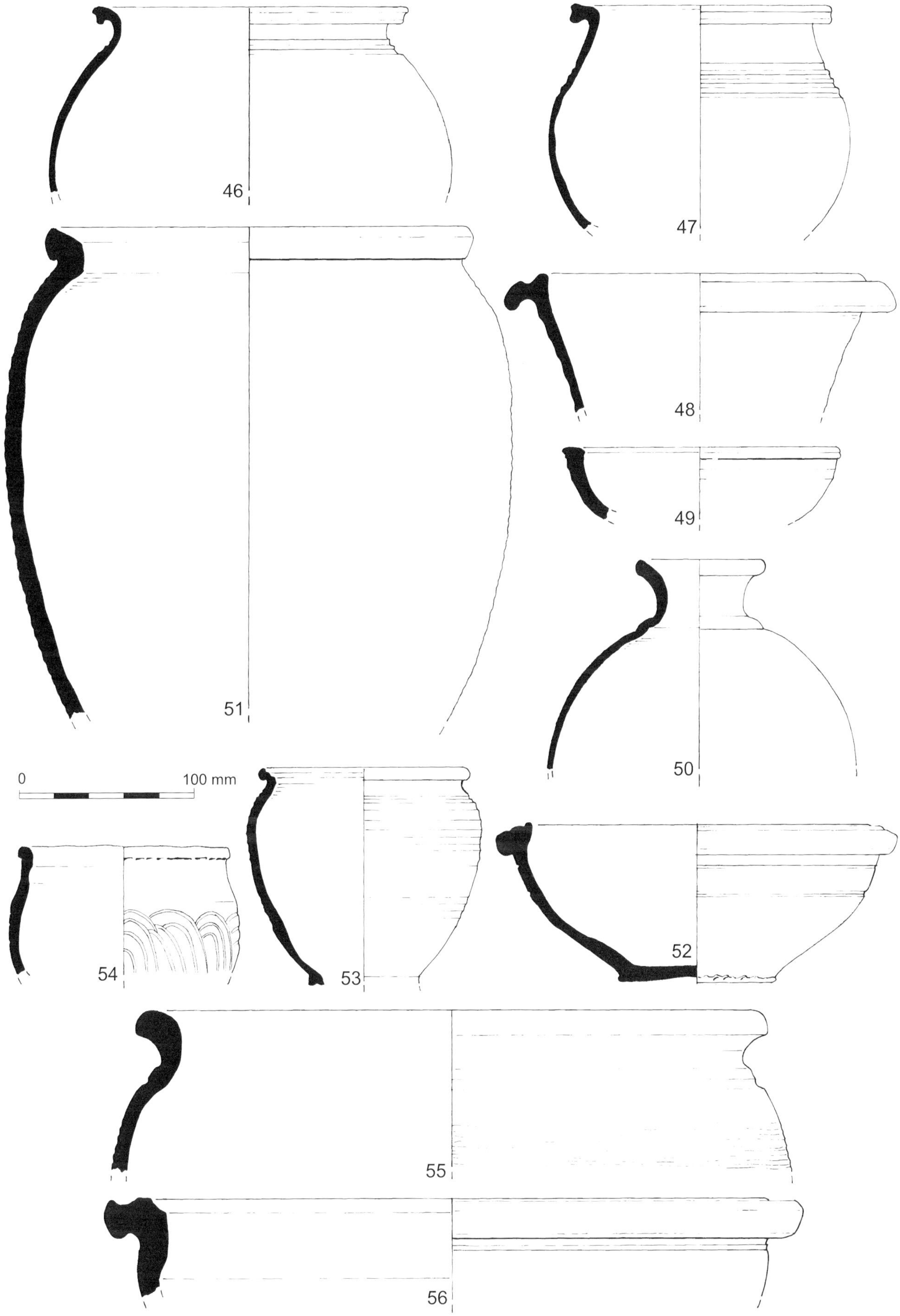

Figure 38 Romano-British pottery (see text for details)

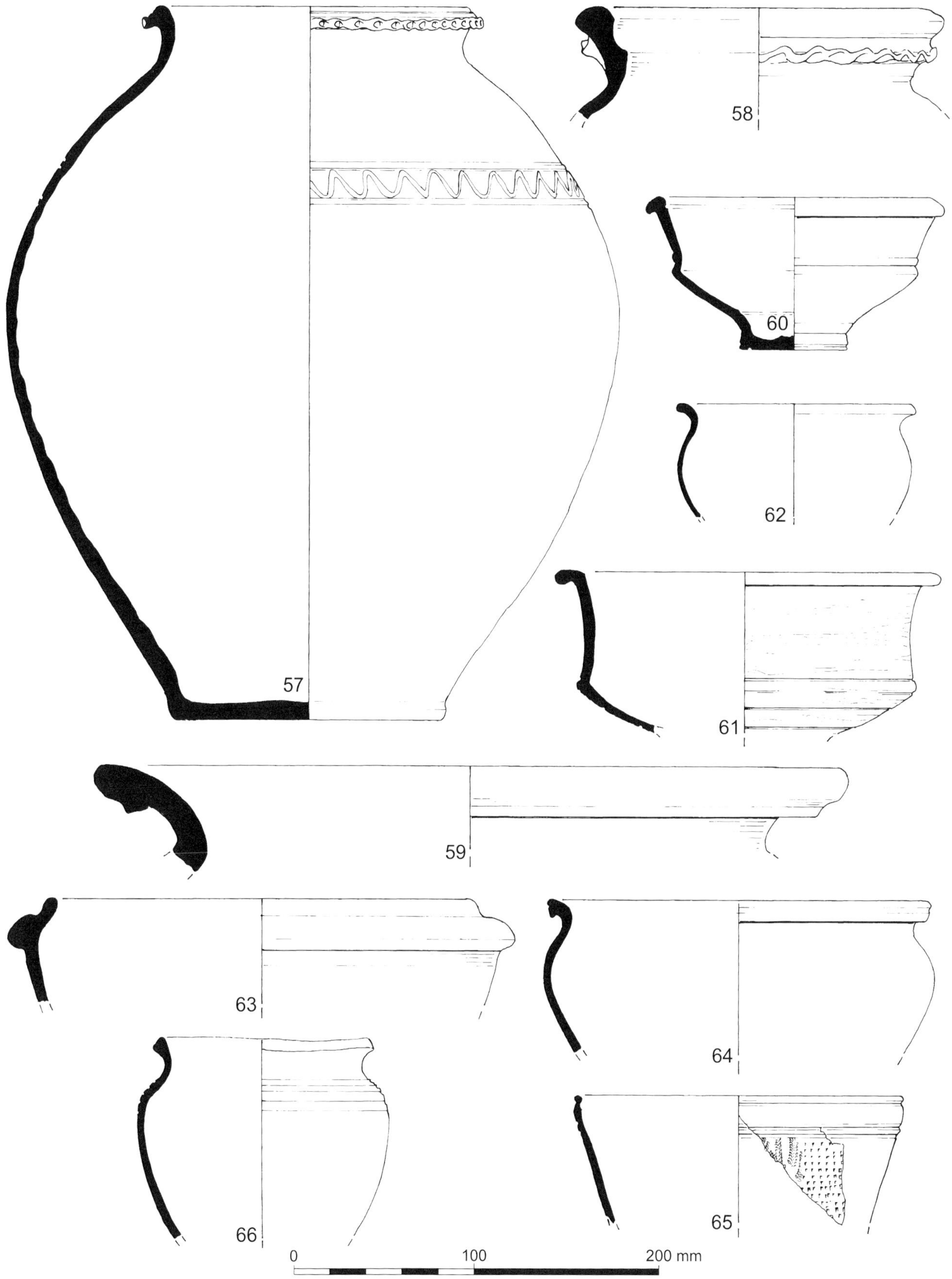

Figure 39 Romano-British pottery (see text for details)

the possibility of other, less diagnostic vessels from this area. Similarly, huge storage jars manufactured at Horningsea (eg. Fig. 36, 22; cf, Perrin 1999, 114, fig. 68, 383–5) from Lower Cambourne, Jeavons Lane, and Mill Farm may indicate other products from these kilns.

From the middle of the 2nd century onwards a much expanded range of forms was available. This included wide bag-shaped (Fig. 37, 41–2; Fig. 38, 53; and Fig. 39, 66) and narrow-necked (Fig. 35, 16; Fig. 38, 50; and Fig. 43, 67) jars and bowls (Fig. 39, 62 and 64), large storage jars, plain rimmed dishes, straight-sided bowls and dishes with flanged rims (Fig. 36, 23–4), poppy-head beakers, flagons, lids, and strainers. Flagons, jars, bowls, and dishes (Fig. 35, 14, 19–20; Fig. 38, 46, 47, 52), as well as strainers and a possible *tazza* in oxidised sandy fabrics also reached the area. Some were probably from the *Verulamium* region (M.G. Wilson 1984, fig. 93, 2244–6, 2249–51, 2254) but others may be local products. Marney (1989, 112) highlighted the difficulties of distinguishing between the white and pink sandy fabrics at Milton Keynes, and it is possible that a *Verulamium* region look-alike white ware was made in Northamptonshire (it occurred in very significant quantities at Stanwick) or possibly even at Godmanchester (R. Perrin pers. comm.), approximately 15 km north-east of Cambourne, during the 2nd century. Most were probably used at table, providing a range of medium-quality vessels between the coarse storage and food preparation vessels used in the kitchen, and the fine tablewares, which, after about AD 150, were mainly supplied by the Nene Valley industry (eg. Fig. 36, 25). By the 3rd century, the Nene Valley industry had become the dominant supplier.

Continental imports remained sparse, consisting of two tiny sherds from Moselkeramik beakers, from Lower Cambourne and Jeavons Lane, and greater quantities of samian platters, bowls, cups, and dishes from Central, and later, Eastern Gaulish sources. Dressel 20 amphorae indicate the continued use of Spanish oil but the inhabitants still showed little interest in mortaria, with only one *Verulamium* region form (M.G. Wilson 1984, 289, fig. 119, 99) present at The Grange. A certain level of sophistication at table is also implied by the presence of two pear-shaped spoons, dating from the first half of the 2nd century or later (Crummy 1983, 69, fig. 73, 2012–15) and part of a convex cup or beaker (Price and Cottam 1998, 103–4, fig. 39) in yellowish-green glass with self-coloured, unmarvered trailed decoration, both from Lower Cambourne.

In common with much of Britain, the fashion for brooches seems to have died out during this period, although personal ornament continued in other forms. A copper alloy hairpin (Fig. 41, 11) from Mill Farm dates from the early 2nd–3rd centuries (Crummy 1983, 29, type 2, fig. 27) and may indicate the adoption of more elaborate, Romanised styles of coiffure. Other items related to personal grooming included a spoon probe (Fig. 41, 19) and two pairs of tweezers (Fig. 41, 20). These were probably used for the removal of unwanted facial and body hair, while spoon probes may have served a number of purposes, including the extraction of cosmetics, perfumes, or medicinal ointments from small containers with the spoon end and their application with the probe (Crummy 1983, 60).

Limited evidence for iron smithing, predominantly associated with later 1st–3rd century pottery, was found at Lower Cambourne, suggesting that this was an occasional activity, perhaps for the repair of tools, etc. No other indications of metal working occurred at Cambourne, although a number of lead off-cuts indicate that this material was being utilised. Similarly small quantities of iron slag were found on two of the adjacent sites on the route of the A428 (Abrams and Ingham 2008, 50 and 55).

Later 3rd–5th centuries (late Romano-British)

Objects indicative of personal adornment and styles of dress were especially common among the larger assemblage from Lower Cambourne. Seven finger-rings were found, in addition to the two associated with a burial (see above). Most were very simple and plain; only two had decoration of any kind, one had terminals twisted into three running loops to form a decorative clasp (Fig. 41, 15), while another was decorated with transverse grooves (cf Crummy 1983, 49, fig. 50, 1770). Armlets too seem to have been worn by the inhabitants of the Cambourne settlements for the first time during the later 3rd or 4th centuries, despite being known in Roman Britain from the 1st century onwards (Swift 2000, 24). The five fragmentary examples from Lower Cambourne were all decorated with hatching, transverse grooves, and/or punched dot decoration (eg. Fig. 41, 12 and 14), while one crenellated example (Fig. 41, 13) seems to belong to a local style (Gardiner *et al.* 1999, pl. x, no. 88; Taylor 1985, 10, no. 56; Crummy 1983, 40, fig. 43, 1659), possibly of 4th century date. These items were found in a variety of pit and ditch fill contexts, probably representing casual losses while in use. The copper alloy hair pin (Fig. 41, 10) from Jeavons Lane belongs to a type more commonly found in East Anglia than elsewhere (Cool 1990, 151). Further evidence of hair-care comes from two highly fragmentary worked bone combs, both probably of 4th century date, from Lower Cambourne, and part of a bone hair pin from Jeavons Lane. Other hints at the personal possessions of the

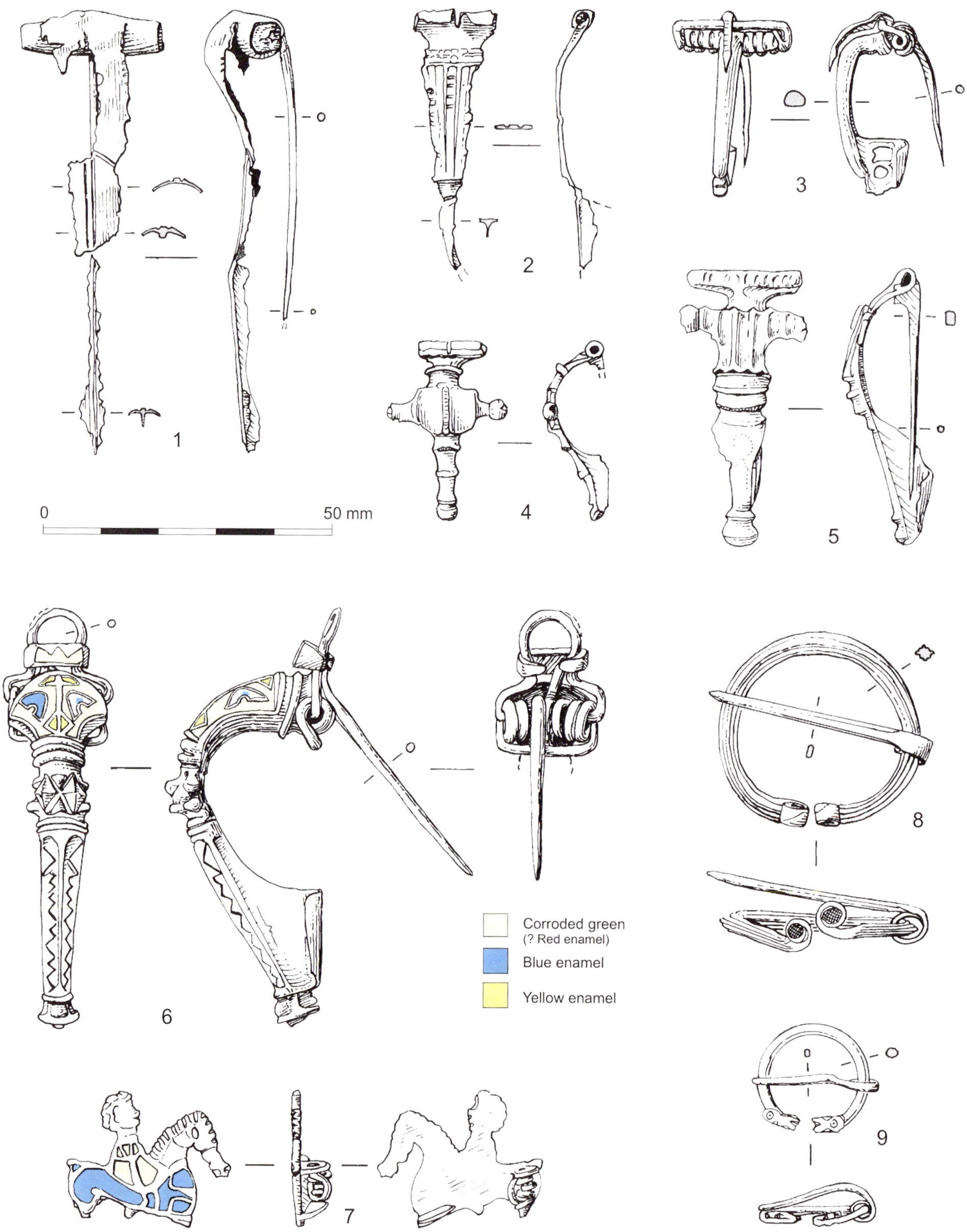

Figure 40 Metalwork. Personal objects: brooches (see text for details)

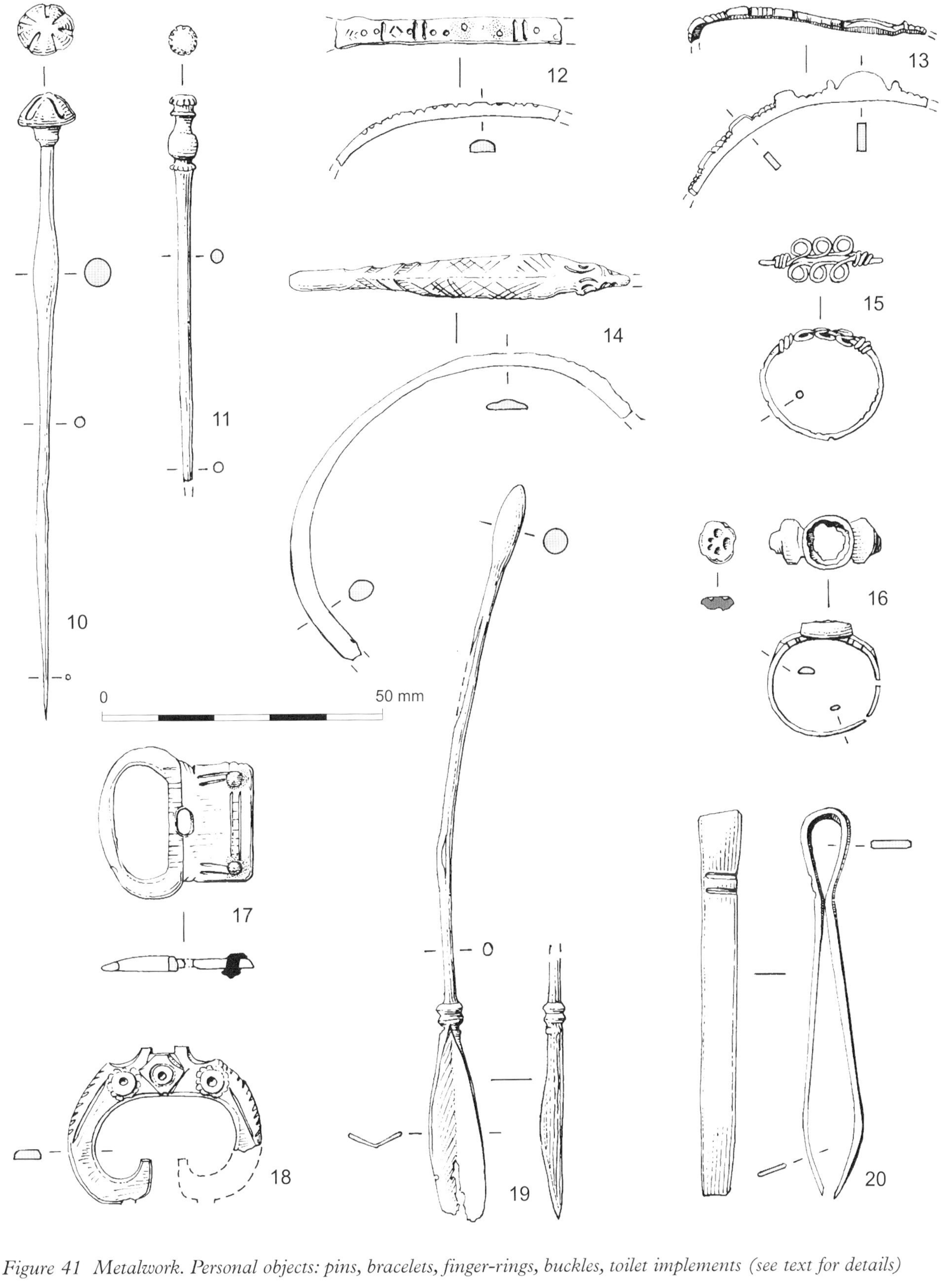

Figure 41 Metalwork. Personal objects: pins, bracelets, finger-rings, buckles, toilet implements (see text for details)

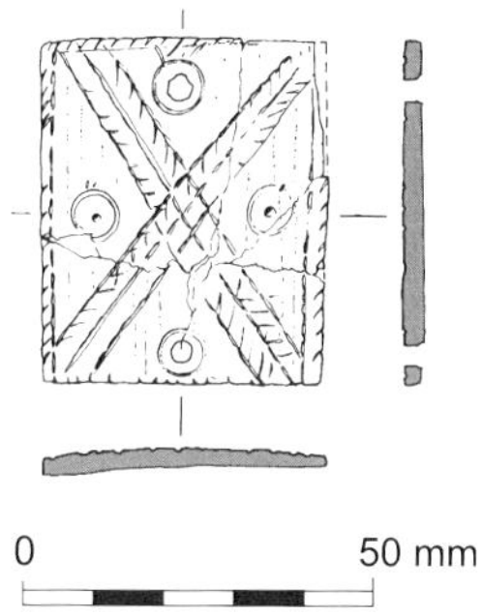

Figure 42 Worked bone plaque, possibly from a casket. Sf 501, Lower Cambourne, scoop 161

inhabitants of the Lower Cambourne settlement come from two small pieces of bone veneer or inlay (including Fig. 42). These probably derive from decorated caskets or other items of domestic furniture probably of later 3rd or 4th century date (Greep 2004, 275).

Within the Development Area, especially at Lower Cambourne, coin loss vastly increased during the later 3rd and 4th centuries, perhaps suggesting that people met here to exchange goods for money (Wells, Volume 2, 51–2). Although less precisely dated, an iron steelyard (see Fig. 46, 25) and lead weights (see Fig. 46, 26–9) from this site provided further evidence of such market-place activities. Overall, the patterns of coin loss at Cambourne were typical of the province as a whole, although peaks in two of the latest periods, between *c.* AD 364–378 and *c.* AD 388–402, may indicate continued activity into the early 5th century AD (Wells, Volume 2, 50).

A copper alloy buckle (Fig. 41, 18; Hawkes and Dunning 1961, 50, type IIa, fig. 18) from Lower Cambourne may also hint at some sort of military or official presence in the area. These buckles may have been from single-strap belts forming part of the uniform of a military force raised by the *vicarius* from, and serving within, the civilian zone from *c.* AD 350 (Clarke 1979, 286–91), perhaps continuing into the

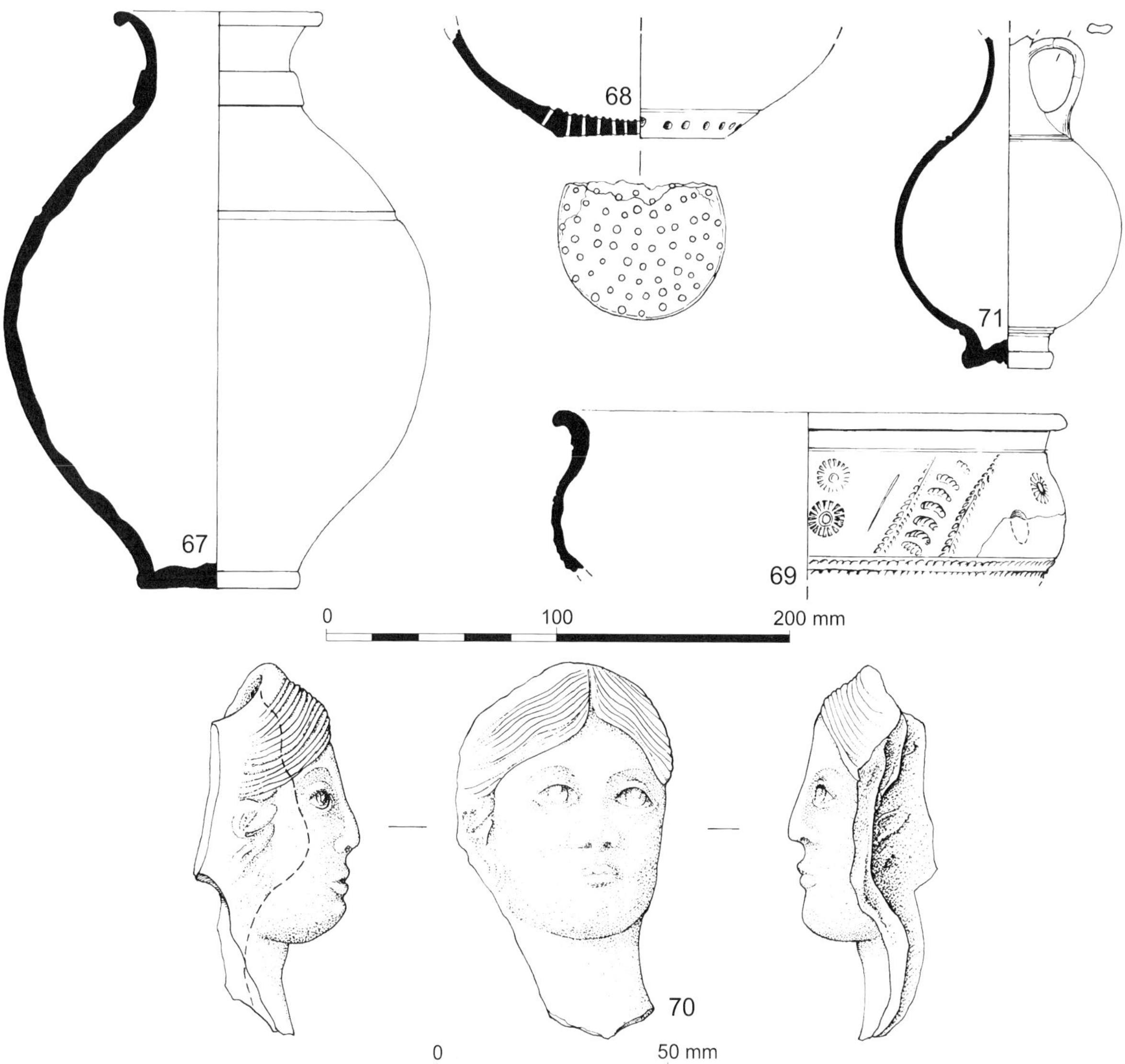

Figure 43 Romano-British pottery (see text for details)

early 5th century. It may be significant that a simple D-shaped buckle with a fixed plate (Fig. 41, 17) and fragments of two others were found at this site, while a small spearhead and a bell-shaped stud from Childerley Gate (site 5) on the A428 may also indicate 'military' connections, being more frequently found on Roman military sites than rural ones (Abrams and Ingham 2008, 60 and 100).

Further changes to, and re-organisations of, the regional trading networks during the late Romano-British period were attested by the ceramics. As at other sites in the region (Perrin 1996; Ellis *et al.* 1998, 79), the Nene Valley continued to dominate, by now supplying a wide range of multi-purpose, non-stick, oven-to-table wares in the colour-coated fabrics (Fig. 37, 34 and 36; Fig. 38, 48). More unusual 4th century vessels include a mould-decorated bowl (Fig. 36, 26) and a face mask from a flagon (Fig. 43, 70; Howe *et al.* 1980, fig. 8, 96). The calcareous wares (eg, Fig. 36, 28 and 29; Fig. 38, 56; Fig. 39, 57) enjoyed a resurgence of popularity at the expense of the sandy greywares (eg, Fig. 37, 33; Fig. 39, 58–9), falling within a widespread south Midlands tradition. The oxidised Hadham fabrics (including Fig. 43, 68 and 71) also increased in importance during the 4th century, although it is possible that a small volume of trade with this area began as early as the mid–late 2nd century (Marney 1989, 124). By the 4th century, too, the Oxfordshire industry was supplying a significant quantity of red colour-coated ware bowls (eg, Fig. 43, 69). However, it is possible that some of these products were made by a migrant Oxfordshire potter working the Obelisk kilns at Harston, to the south of Cambridge, during the second quarter of the 4th century (Pullinger and Young 1981, 8–9).

The 4th century also saw a surprising upswing in the desirability of mortaria. The Oxfordshire and Nene Valley potters more or less shared this market, a pattern also seen in Roman Cambridge (Hartley 1999, 206). Cool (2006, 44) has suggested that mortaria were being used for some specialised, perhaps non-culinary, function at this time.

Other products from well outside the locality included a small quantity of Black Burnished (BB) ware from the Wareham/Poole Harbour region of Dorset. This probably owed its presence to the movement of people and goods along Ermine Street, possibly even carried in the personal belongings of an individual or travelling piggy-back with some other commodity. The vessel forms (eg, Fig. 37, 35) all dated from the mid-2nd century onwards, although they were most common and widely distributed during the later 3rd–4th centuries. This low level of BB1 is also seen at other rural sites in the region (Marney 1989, 127; Hancocks *et al.* 1998, 45; Gibson 2005, 34) and it is not mentioned in the fabric list for the A428 sites.

'Placed deposits'

One unusual aspect of the lives of the inhabitants of the Cambourne area during the late Romano-British period was again demonstrated at Lower Cambourne

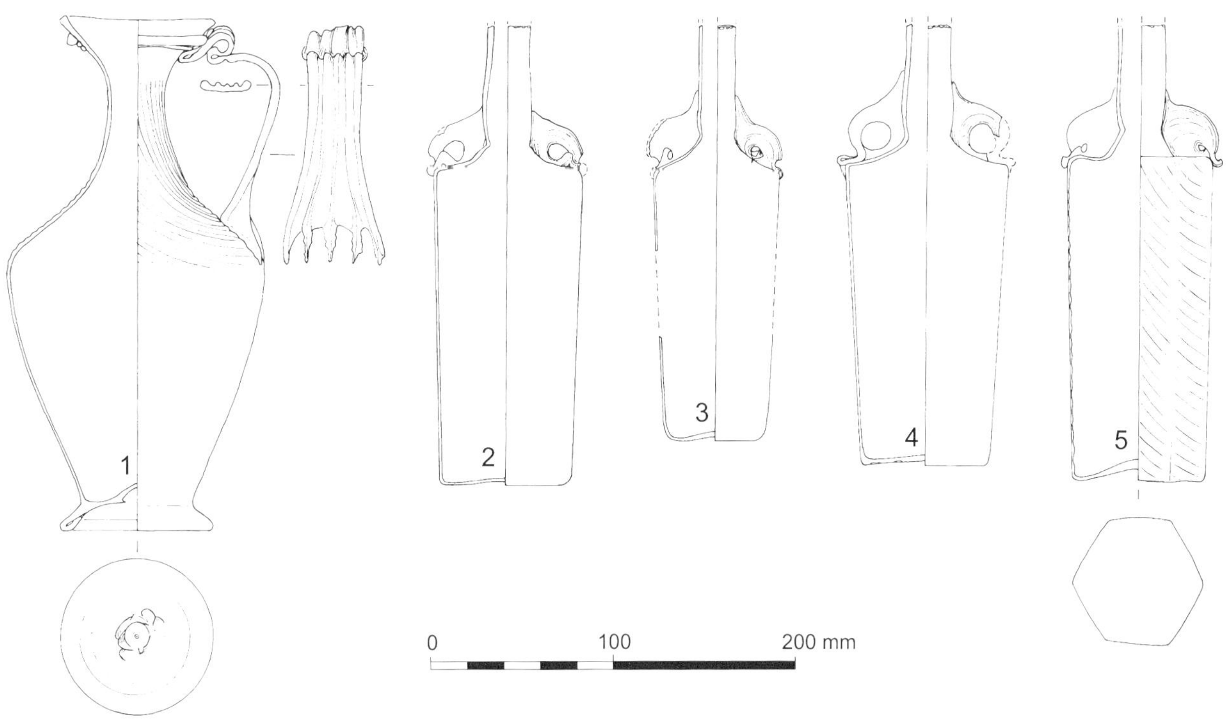

Figure 44 Group of 4th century glass bottles found inside a storage jar (Fig. 39, 57) in enclosure ditch 1001, Lower Cambourne

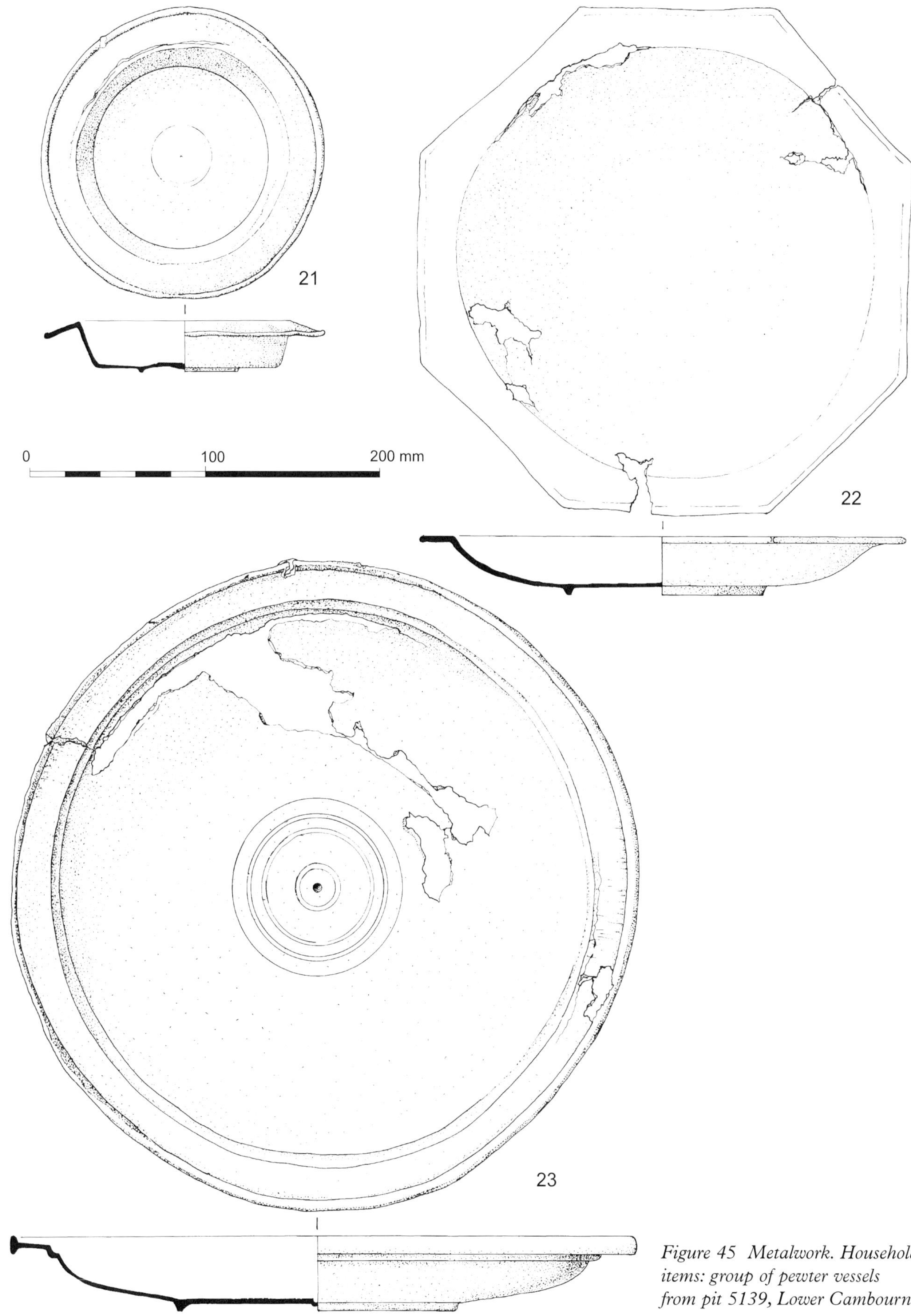

Figure 45 Metalwork. Household items: group of pewter vessels from pit 5139, Lower Cambourne

only. Here, three features (see Fig. 10) contained special, deliberately deposited items; all quite usable and seemingly of considerable value to their owners.

The first of these deposits consisted of five glass vessels, all of 4th century date, placed within a large, shell-tempered storage jar (Fig. 39, 57), found in ditch 1001 to the south of enclosure H. The jar was probably from a non-Harrold, but as yet unknown, source (Anna Slowikowski, pers. comm.) and broadly followed styles known in the area (eg, Pullinger *et al.* 1999, pl. cxxxvii, 1000–1) but the glass was much more exotic, only occurring as tiny scraps elsewhere at Cambourne. These complete glass vessels were probably intended for serving liquids, perhaps wine, at table. While the biconical jug (Fig. 44, 1) and cylindrical bottles (Fig. 44, 2–4) are relatively common late Romano-British forms (Price and Cottam 1998, 164 and 206), the hexagonal vessel (Fig. 44, 5) is much more unusual, Price and Cottam noting that no complete examples had ever been found in Britain and listing only nine very fragmentary examples (*ibid.*, 208).

Three pewter vessels, comprising a small, deep circular dish (Fig. 45, 21), an octagonal plate (Fig. 45, 22), and a large circular plate (Fig. 45, 23) had been deposited in pit 5139. The large circular plate has parallels in Chelmsford, Essex (Portable Antiquities Scheme ESS–A66FE2), and at *Verulamium*, where a similar vessel was one of three representing votive offerings found stratified in late Romano-British (*c.* AD 375–400) 'bog mud' (Frere 1984, fig. 27, 243).

The third unusual deposit consisted of an iron tanged bar share (see Fig. 47, 40; Rees 1979, 57–9, fig. 49, type 2a) and a coulter (see Fig. 47, 41; Manning 1985, 44, pl. 18: F6–7; Rees 1979, 59–61, fig. 69 and 70), found together in the base of ditch 5402. It is probable that such items were used together; the coulters cutting the sod vertically, in advance of the share, which cut it horizontally. Although not common finds, probably because iron is easily recycled and their 'scrap' value must have been considerable, the known distribution of these objects focuses on East Anglia and the south-east (*Rees* 1979, 70, map 4), while most are thought to be of 4th century date.

It is clear that these deposits cannot be the result of the deposition of normal domestic debris. Not only are all the items complete and in a usable condition but, by their intrinsic worth and, in two cases, their exotic nature, they stand out from the rest of the artefact assemblage. It is possible that these items were placed in locations that could easily be found again, perhaps suggesting that they were deposited in times of social and political unrest, with the intention of later recovery. It is certainly the case that Cambourne lies within the tight East Anglian group of 4th century metalwork hoards (Manning 1972, 5), while most Romano-British pewter vessels are also known from hoards, many of which cluster in the fens around Cambridge (Beagrie 1989, 175, fig. 3).

The recovery of groups of complete glass vessels in non-funerary contexts is highly unusual, although there is limited evidence for 4th century glass being brought together as hoards (Price 2000, 5). The Lower Cambourne finds are, therefore, in keeping with this pattern, and it may be of relevance that similar deposits containing a coulter, a pewter vessel, and a huge late 3rd century hoard of copper alloy coins were found Childerley Gate (site 5) on the A428 (Abrams and Ingham 2008, 70 and 90–2).

However, stemming from the work of Manning (1972), recent surveys of the practice of 'hoarding' (Johns 1996; Fulford 2001; Hingley 2006) have looked beyond this traditional interpretation of preservation during periods of personal or community danger with the intention of later recovery. They have focused instead on the possibility of more 'ritual' or 'religious' motives, even for items found in settlement contexts. It has been recognised that 'ritual' activities were not necessarily associated with cult buildings, burials, or even particular man-made or natural contexts, such as rivers, stream, and other wet places like deep pits and wells, especially at a time, and in a culture, where religion and its associated rites and rituals formed an intimate and inseparable part of daily life.

Is it possible, then, that the Lower Cambourne finds represent some form of religious activity? If so, the intrinsic worth of the items and, in the case of the plough share and coulter, their direct relevance to the daily lives of the inhabitants, as well as the lack of any other evidence for wealthy individuals living in the immediate vicinity, perhaps suggests that these offerings were made collectively, on behalf of the whole community. Such a religious focus and associated communal gatherings may go some way to explain the wide range and large quantity of other artefacts present on this site, especially the increased evidence for market-place activities and the possibility of an official presence, compared with others within the development area.

Interestingly, Childerley Gate (site 5), *c.* 5 km east of Lower Cambourne, also produced the greatest range and quantity of Romano-British finds (Abrams and Ingham 2008). It is even possible that these 'placed deposits' were made to mark the abandonment of the settlement; during the late Romano-British period in particular, Hingley (2006, 230) notes the preferential deposition of iron objects in late contexts within the sequence of site development, suggesting that these may mark beliefs about particular moments in time.

1st–4th centuries (general Romano-British)

Throughout the Late Iron Age–Romano-British period, evidence for buildings, with the exception of roundhouses, was sparse. No stone building materials (ashlar blocks or roof tiles) were recovered, while the quantities of ceramic building materials, found only at Lower Cambourne and Jeavons Lane, were insufficient to suggest any substantive use of these materials. Similarly small quantities of ceramic building material were found on the adjacent A428 sites, especially to the east of Childerley Gate (site 5) (Abrams and Ingham 2008, appendix 9). Small pieces of window glass were also found at Lower Cambourne. Overall, this material may suggest that a substantial building of considerable sophistication, with glazed windows, a tiled roof, and underfloor heating, existed somewhere in the general vicinity of Cambourne, although the possibility that this material was brought in as hardcore or with manuring material for the fields cannot be excluded.

Within the Development Area, it is likely the buildings were of post, wattle, or timber-framed construction with reed-straw thatched roofs. This need not imply any great impoverishment however, as, at all times, the highest quality timber-framed buildings, resting on sill-beams and of jointed construction, leave very few archaeological traces. Small, often featureless fragments of sand and chalk-tempered fired clay were common finds at Lower Cambourne, Knapwell Plantation, Jeavons Lane, Poplar Plantation, and Broadway Farm. Although few were large enough to preserve wattle impressions, it is probable that most represent daub, and it may be significant that, at Knapwell Plantation, concentrations were found in association with later Iron Age roundhouses 60321 and 60245, structure 60799, and curving gully 60197. At Lower Cambourne concentrations of similar material were found associated with roundhouse 1155 (Phase 2C) and structure 5443 (Phase 2B).

Numerous iron fastenings and fittings were discovered on all the excavated sites. These consisted predominantly of round-headed, hand-made nails in a variety of sizes, together with strip fragments, some with nail/rivet holes, an iron collar, loop-headed spikes, hooks, hinges, and binding fragments. Significant concentrations were found in deposits associated with possible building A at Jeavons Lane and building 3158 at Lower Cambourne. A barb spring padlock key and L-shaped lift key (see Fig. 47, 38) were also recovered from possible building A, while two other lift keys (see Fig. 47, 36–7) from Lower Cambourne were associated with presumed buildings, perhaps suggesting that these structures, or their contents, were of some significance to their occupants.

Hipposandals (Fig. 46, 30) from Jeavons Lane, a jointed snaffle bit (Fig. 46, 31) from Knapwell Plantation and a bit link from Lower Cambourne attest to the importance of horses, and their use as riding animals, in this area. This may be tied in with evidence from the Ermine Street sites to the south of Peterborough, which suggests that horses may have been bred in the region for use in the fenlands and exported north and south along Ermine Street, perhaps even as part of the official transport system, providing fresh horses at one or more rest stations (Ellis *al.* 1998, 109).

Aside from agriculture, evidence for industries, crafts, and other activities was relatively sparse. Part of an iron stylus from Jeavons Lane could suggest a certain level of literacy in the area, perhaps connected with military or civilian officialdom. Few recognisable iron tools were recovered but an unstratified drill bit (Fig. 46, 34) and a possible mortice chisel (Fig. 46, 35) were probably used by carpenters. An iron knife (Fig. 46, 32) and a cleaver (Manning 1985, 120), probably for butchering meat, were also found at Lower Cambourne. Other agricultural tools consisted only of a broken ploughshare from Jeavons Lane, a ferrule or goad, and part of a sickle or reaping hook, both unstratified finds. The long, socketed tool from Jeavons Lane (Fig. 47, 43) could represent part of a hearth tool, such as a poker or the handle of a fire shovel (Manning 1985, 12–13, pl. 6, A40–42), a pruning hook (Champion 1916, pl. iii, 15894), or even a shovel or spatula used when cooking in cauldrons (*ibid.*, pl. xi, 28987). Whetstones (Fig. 32, 7–9) used for sharpening knives and other metal tools, mostly made from the local Woburn Sands sandstone, were found in Romano-British contexts at Lower Camborne and Jeavons Lane.

Spinning was attested by two spindle-whorls made from sherds of pottery, a shale lathe core (Fig. 48) probably used as a spindle-whorl, and two worked bone spindles from Lower Cambourne. The shale spindle-whorl originated from the Purbeck region of Dorset and belonged to the standard Romano-British type, dated by Lawson (1976, 272) to the late 3rd century. Triangular loomweight fragments from Lower Cambourne and Knapwell Plantation suggest that weaving was also taking place. A pair of iron shears (Fig. 47, 39) could also have been used for tasks such as cutting cloth (Manning 1985, 34, type 2), although such items would be equally appropriate in more agricultural contexts, for shearing sheep, for instance. Numerous burnt flints and burnt fragments of unworked local greensand in the assemblages from most of the sites may have functioned as pot-boilers, perhaps providing further evidence of the cooking methods used.

The communities, or certain individuals within them, seem to have been careful with their possessions, adapting or repairing them once broken. A copper alloy finger-ring from Lower Cambourne, for instance, may have been made from a broken armlet. Sherds from a Southern Gaulish samian vessel had been trimmed to form a flat, sideless dish or plate, while five vessels had been repaired with glue made from birch bark tar (Wicks forthcoming). Small, post-firing perforations on 12 other vessels (eg. Fig. 35, 10–12) indicate repair with metal staples (lead or copper alloy) or perhaps leather laces, while one Central Gaulish samian dish had been repaired with both glue and staples. Six lead-plug type pot-mends may have filled holes made in vessel walls (eg. Fig. 37, 43–4) but, unfortunately, none of the perforated sherds was from the same contexts as the lead pot-mends (Brown, Volume 2, 40). Repaired vessels were most common from Lower Cambourne, probably as a result of its larger assemblage size, but also occurred at Knapwell Plantation, Mill Farm, Jeavons Lane, and The Grange. Most involved vessels of mid-/late 1st century date, possibly extending into the early 2nd century, although all the repaired samian was of 2nd century date, while two triangular-rimmed jars of 4th century date indicate that the practice occurred, at least sporadically, throughout the Romano-British period.

Traditionally, the repair of pottery vessels has been associated with inadequate supplies (Marsh 1981, 227), or particularly impecunious residents unable to afford new vessels, but this need not have been the case. As pottery studies shift their focus away from quantification and shopping-lists of fabrics and forms, the reported incidences of repair in antiquity have increased. Similar glue repairs have recently been noted, for example, at Asthall, Oxfordshire (Booth 1997, 123), West Cotton, Northamptonshire (Dudd and Evershed 1999), Staines (McKinley 2004b, 31), Manor Farm, Guildford (English 2005), and on a range of forms of 1st–early 2nd century date from Springhead Roman town, near Gravesend (Seager Smith *et al.* forthcoming) and from near Margate (Jones forthcoming), Kent. Other evidence for the re-use of broken pottery sherds comes from a single counter or gaming piece found at The Grange, and two slightly larger discs probably representing counters or weights from Lower Cambourne. Items such as these form part of the standard range of artefacts found on most Late Iron Age and Romano-British sites and represent perhaps the only evidence of leisure activities.

At Lower Cambourne, Jeavons Lane, Knapwell Plantation, Mill Farm, and The Grange cereals were ground into flour using rotary querns, probably on a household basis, as and when required. The querns, made from Millstone Grit, Hertfordshire Puddingstone, conglomerates and coarse sandstones from the Upper Devonian Basal Conglomerate, Niedermendig Lava, and basic and acid igneous rocks, further indicate trading links. Most had been transported over considerable distances; the Millstone Grit, for example, from Derbyshire, some 160 km to the north-west, while the Devonian Sandstones came from the Forest of Dean, 200 km to the west. Puddingstone was brought from Hertfordshire and Buckinghamshire, 70 km to the west, and the German Lavastones travelled at least 500 km from the Rhineland.

These distances reflect both the central geographic position of the Cambourne sites, close to Ermine Street and, perhaps, Car Dyke, 20 km to the north-east, engendering favourable communication links, and the unsuitability of the softer local materials (Lower Greensand and Kimmeridge Shale). As Peacock noted: 'it is desirable that the surface should not wear smooth, but that it should retain a rough texture which will continue to cut the grain' (1987, 61). Querns from similar sources have been found on other contemporaneous rural sites in the region, such as Vicar's Farm, Cambridge (Lucas and Whittaker 2001) and Earith (Heywood, in prep), but compared with these, the quantities from Cambourne, especially of Millstone Grit, were small. The size, shape, and battered surfaces of two quartzite cobbles (Fig. 32, 5–6) from The Grange and one from Broadway Farm suggest that they had been utilised for pecking/ hammering or rubbing/grinding, perhaps in association with the querns. The general absence of mortaria and comparative abundance of quern fragments may be a reflection of the crop-processing/ storage methods employed (see Stevens, below)

Throughout the Late Iron Age and Romano-British period, the material culture of the Development Area reflected the predominantly rural agricultural nature of the excavated sites. With the exception of the three 4th century 'placed deposits' from Lower Cambourne, which may have been related to, and symbolic of, the whole community, the distribution, condition, and nature of the artefacts are consistent with the deposition and redeposition of domestic debris from rural farming communities. There is nothing to suggest any great wealth in the area or, indeed, any great impoverishment either.

It seems likely that, for most of this period, the inhabitants of the Cambourne settlements could be regarded as of lower middling status. They were able to acquire at least limited quantities of samian and amphora-borne commodities, occasional glass vessels, and the more basic sorts of personal adornment, but most of their needs were met locally, perhaps without much recourse to the monetary economy, at least until the late Romano-British period, and they did not have the means or status to build fine, elaborately decorated homes.

The vagaries of an agricultural economy suggest that, at times, the population went hungry and their

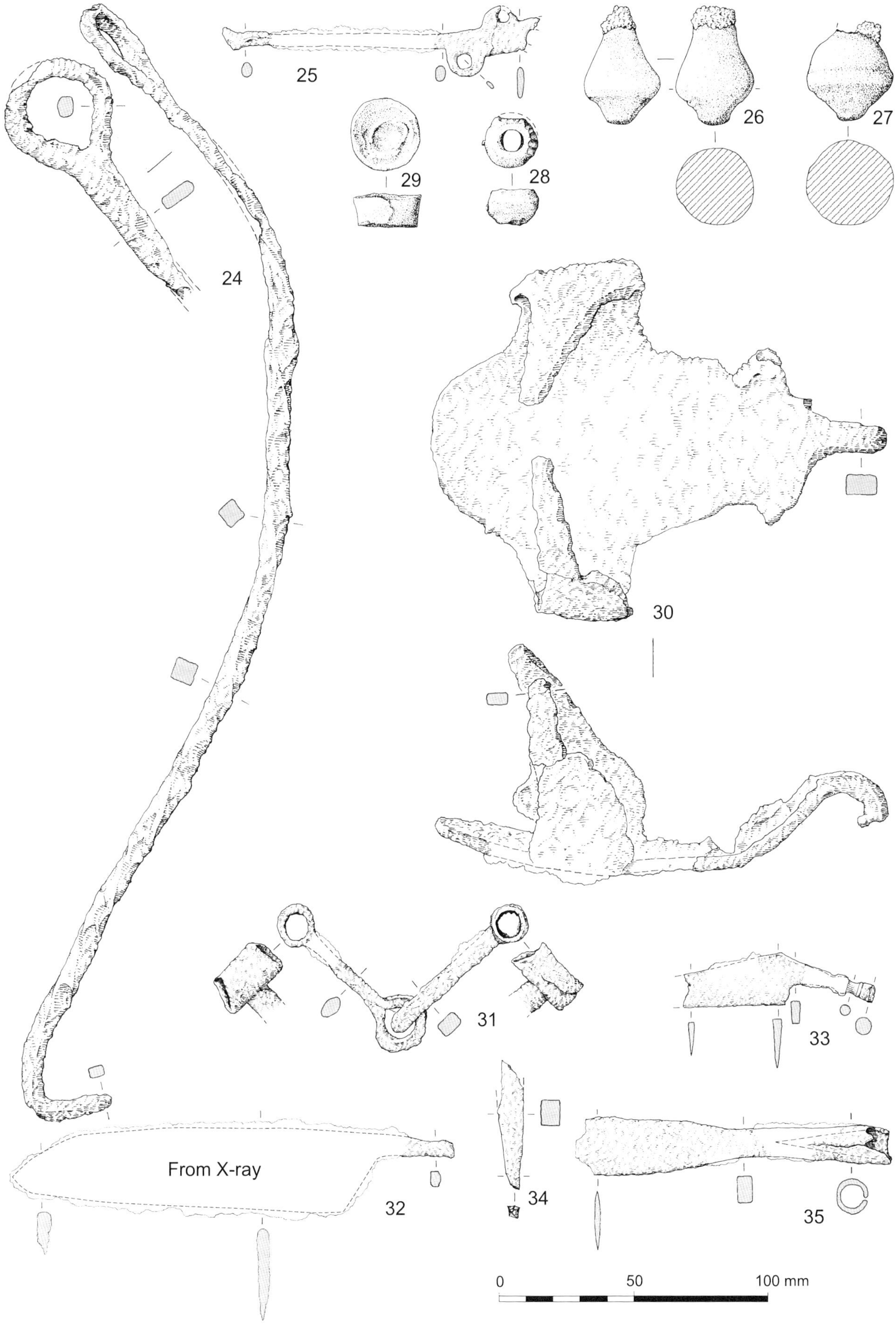

Figure 46 (above) Metalwork. Items concerned with weighing, measuring, transport, and household use
Figure 47 (opposite) Metalwork. Items of household, agricultural, military, and unknown use

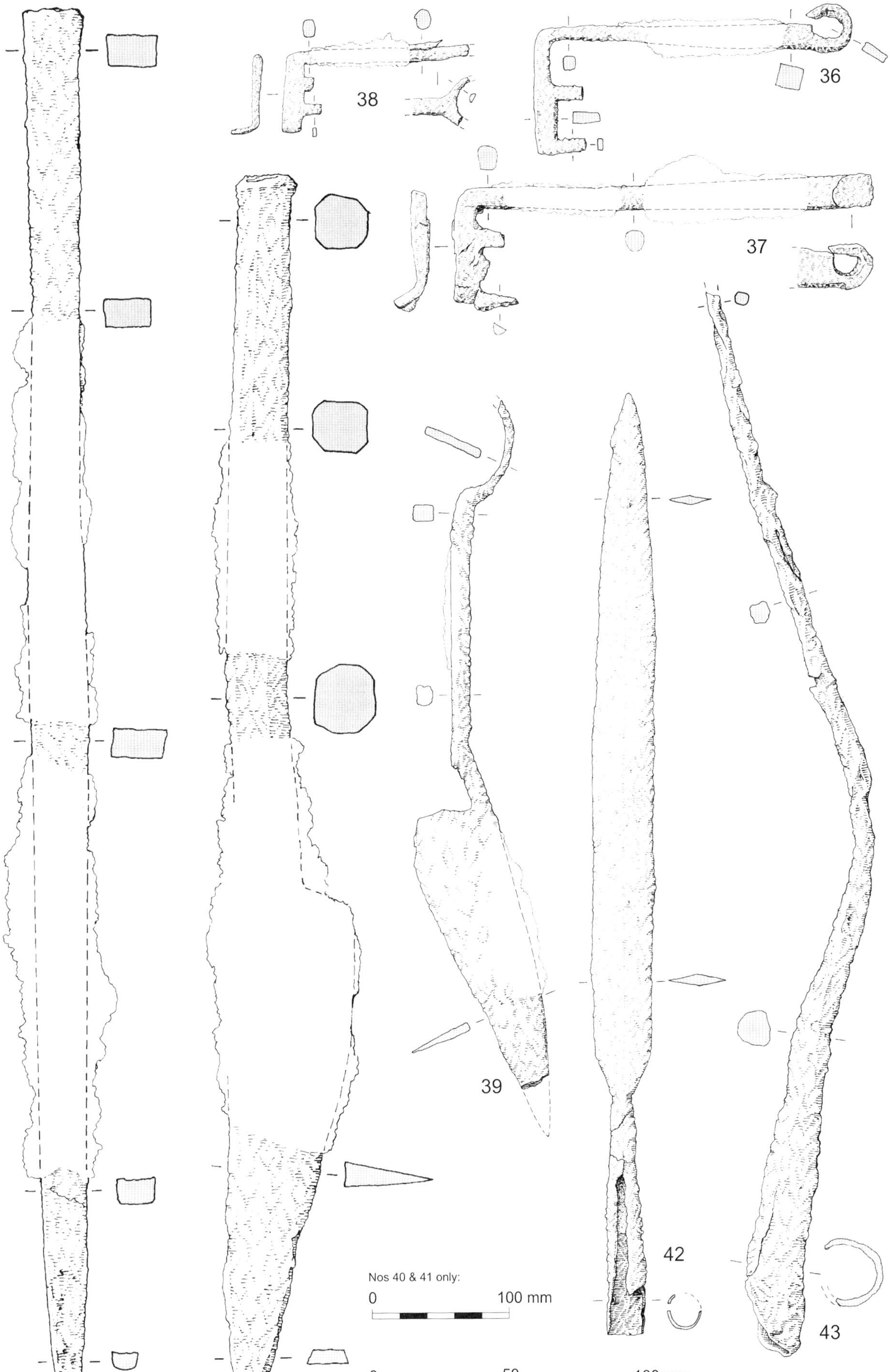
38
36
37
39
42
43
40
41
Nos 40 & 41 only:
0
100 mm
0
50
100 mm

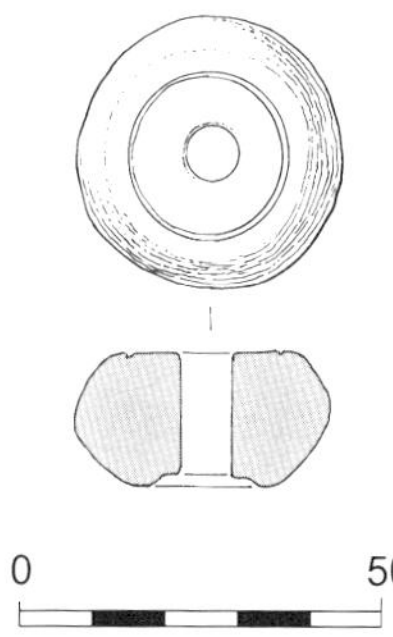

Figure 48 Shale lathe core probably used as a spindle-whorl. Sf141, Lower Cambourne, ditch 1055

low-lying, clayland environment was prone to both seasonal waterlogging and drought, so much of their time may have been spent in water management. The few skeletons show that they worked hard and were physically robust and while their ethnicity is unknown, it is likely that the successive generations of the same families lived quietly in this area throughout the period with only limited influence from outside.

The Romano-British agricultural economy

by Chris J. Stevens

In general, economic evidence relating to both the growing and consumption of crops and animal husbandry is better represented in this period than in the Iron Age. Charred plant remains came from seven sites with Romano-British evidence. Lower Cambourne produced by far the largest assemblage of this date, while The Grange and Jeavons Lane produced moderate-sized assemblages. Smaller assemblages were examined from North Caxton Bypass, Great Common Farm, Knapwell Plantation, and Mill Farm. At all of these sites preservation of charred plant material was generally very good in comparison to the Iron Age. Animal bones were well represented on only three Romano-British sites: Knapwell Plantation, Jeavons Lane, and Lower Cambourne. A small assemblage of marine molluscs was also recovered from Lower Cambourne.

Charred plant remains

The main crop grown at Cambourne in the Romano-British period was spelt wheat (*Triticum spelta*), represented mainly by glumes, as seen for other sites in the region (eg, van der Veen 1991). It is probable that barley persisted as a crop, although little evidence is present, and it is possible that little material would become charred if it was used mainly as a fodder crop. Emmer wheat (*T. dicoccum*), while still present, appears to have been reduced to a minor element since the Iron Age, and might be regarded as a contaminant of spelt fields at this time rather than a crop in its own right.

Remains of other crop species include celtic bean (*Vicia faba* var. *minor*), seeds of which came from Lower Cambourne and The Grange. A single sample from The Grange also produced a number of seeds of garden pea (*Pisum sativum*). No other remains of these crops were recovered, although it should be noted that crops such as flax, especially if grown for their fibre, rarely become charred.

A further possible cultigen was beet (*Beta vulgaris*), a single seed of which was recovered from a late Romano-British enclosure ditch at Lower Cambourne. It is unlikely that the plant would have been growing wild but it is possible that such remains may represent the cultivation of the wild form of seabeet (*Beta vulgaris* ssp. *maritima*) that grows naturally along the English coast, rather than the cultivated variety (eg, *B. vulgaris* ssp. *vulgaris*; *B. vulgaris* ssp. *cicla*). However, seabeet does grow as a weed of crops cultivated close to the coast on saline or partially saline soils (Hanf 1983). Given the quite high numbers of orache seeds, and the reclamation of parts of the fenlands during this period, this should be considered as a possibility and may indicate the exchange of crops brought in from the fenland.

While grains of oats (*Avena* sp.) were recovered, all the floret bases that could be identified as wild or cultivated were of the wild form, with the characteristic 'horseshoe-shaped' scar.

Crop husbandry

The weed flora represented across all the sites is broadly similar. It is probable that most differences can be related to richer assemblages from some sites producing a wider range of species rather than to any differences in the type of soil or methods of cultivation conducted at each settlement.

Evidence for cereals probably being cultivated locally comes from pollen sequences at both Jeavons Lane and The Grange. However, as cereal pollen is also released during processing, such evidence cannot be taken as definitive evidence for the presence of cereal fields around the sites. Nevertheless, it might be noted that pollen from a number of potential weed species was also recorded, including cornflower (*Centaurea nigra*) at Jeavons Lane, and *Sinapis* type and knotgrass at The Grange (Scaife, Volume 2, 217–8). Unlike the Iron Age samples, the Romano-British assemblages contained seeds of more ecologically specific species, mainly because the richer assemblages produced a wider array of species.

In comparison with Iron Age sites to the east and north-east, wetland species are still poorly represented proportionally to species of lighter, drier, slightly calcareous soils. While not necessarily specific to such soils, a number of species that together may be associated with drier calcareous soils are represented; these include brome-grass (*Bromus* sp.), black medick (*Medicago* sp.), campion (*Silene* sp.), small scabious (*Scabious columbaria*), self-heal (*Prunella vulgaris*), mallow (*Malva sylvestris*), red bartsia (*Odontites vernus*), ribwort plantain (*Plantago lanceolata*), corn gromwell (*Lithospermum arvense*), and field madder (*Sherardia arvensis*). Seeds of species recorded from drier, circum-neutral to acid soils were also recovered; for example, scarlet pimpernel (*Anagallis arvensis*), scentless mayweed (*Tripleurospermum inodorum*), and annual knawel (*Scleranthus annuus*), while blinks (*Montia fontana* ssp. *chondrosperma*) grows in wetter areas of spring flushes on such soil types.

Wetland species are better represented in some of the richer assemblages, for example, Lower Cambourne, where spikerush (*Eleocharis palustris*), marsh bedstaw (*Galium palustre*), and sedges (*Carex* sp.) are all present. Seeds of buttercup (*Ranunculus acris/repens/bulbosus*), which may be taken to represent the cultivation of damper soils, are common on many of the sites.

Finally, and also of interest, are the occasional finds of stinking mayweed (*Anthemis cotula*), a species associated with clay soils. Seeds of this species were recovered from Lower Cambourne, Jeavons Lane, and Great Common Farm. The species has also been recovered from other Romano-British sites in the area: to the north at Paston (Smith 2001), to the west at Eaton Socon (Stevens and Clapham 2005), and to the east at Childerley Gate (site 5) on the A428 (Giorgi 2008), with much greater numbers from Vicarage Farm on the western edge of Cambridge (Ballantyne, pers. comm.). The significance of this species is that it is associated with the cultivation of heavy clay soils, possibly linked to the introduction of iron shares and asymmetrical ploughs (Jones 1981). It is first recorded in England from occasional middle–later Romano-British sites but subsequently becomes one of the most common and characteristic species recovered from Saxon and medieval assemblages. Significantly, it might be seen as being more common on possibly more Romanised settlements, in Oxfordshire (Jones 1975; 1986; Stevens 1996; Pelling 2002) and at Gloucester (Clarke 1971), Milton Keynes (M.K. Jones 1987), York (Hall and Kenward (1990), Lancaster (Buxton *et al.* 2000), and in Kent (Stevens 2006). Such a distribution might further lend weight to its association with a change from the ard to asymmetrical ploughs. On this issue the finds of iron plough coulters from Lower Cambourne (Brown, Volume 2, 43) and Childerley Gate (site 5) (Duncan 2008) may have some significance.

To summarise, the general indication is that most of the fields under cultivation at Cambourne in the Romano-British period were located on drier, circum-neutral soils that perhaps spread onto damp and occasionally wet or flooded areas. While it appears that some heavier clay soils were under cultivation, seeds of stinking mayweed were not as well represented as on other sites in the region. This may, however, be a reflection of processing (see below). As in the Iron Age, it is probable that the proportion of annuals to perennials that can be used to gauge the level of soil disturbance (cf, Behre 1981; van der Veen 1992; Wilkinson and Stevens 2003) is likely to be skewed by the effects of processing. As such, whether tillage is more likely to have been conducted by ard or asymmetrical shares within the earlier Romano-British period is difficult to establish on the basis of the weed flora alone. Furthermore, like the Iron Age, it is also difficult to establish whether crops were sown in spring or autumn. It is possible that, as with modern farming and as recorded in the medieval period, both were practised, although the damp or wet ground conditions at Cambourne in the winter may have generally precluded autumn sowing.

As in the Iron Age it appears that harvesting was likely to have been by sickle and, along with seeds of clover (*Trifolium* sp.), those of self-heal, annual knawel, marsh bedstraw, and scarlet pimpernel all suggest that culms were cut low to the ground. Legumes, unlike cereal crops, are usually harvested either by picking pods by hand or by uprooting the whole plant. That the one sample containing higher numbers of seeds of pea from Lower Cambourne also contained swollen culm internodes of onion-couch grass suggests harvesting by uprooting.

Crop processing

Many of the weed seeds recorded are from large-seeded species or species whose seeds, by virtue of appendages, are difficult to separate from the grain. In the former group we can include large-seeded grasses, oats and brome grass, as well as many common arable weeds, knotgrass (*Polygonum aviculare*), black bindweed (*Fallopia convolvulus*), vetches/wild pea, and cleavers. In the latter group are the slightly smaller than grain-sized seeds of species whose seed remains in the spikelet or pod, such as perennial rye-grass (*Lolium perenne*) and black medick, respectively. The latter group also includes seeds of small seeded species that are often easily separated from their appendages, but during threshing some may still remain intact to contaminate the grain. Examples of these include docks (*Rumex* sp.) and orache (*Atriplex* sp.), whose seeds are released within grain-sized bracteoles.

Seeds of smaller-seeded weed species dominated only occasional samples from Caxton By-Pass, Lower Cambourne, Jeavons Lane, and Knapwell Plantation. In some cases such dominance was caused by over-representation of seeds of a single species, for example tormentil (*Potentilla* sp.) and red bartsia, or in others by seeds of orache, dock, and/or perennial rye grass. It was notable that within these same samples weed seeds generally outnumbered grains. Otherwise grain either dominated or was in approximately equal proportions to weed seeds.

Cereal crops ripen from mid–late summer depending on the time of sowing and the type of soils under cultivation. Within this narrow window of ripening, crops must be harvested, processed, and stored as dry as possible to prevent mould infection and germination. As such, there is a demand on agricultural labour during this time that is in part dependent on the amount of processing conducted before storage.

The processing of the harvested crop to obtain clean grain can be split into two parts: those stages that are conducted alongside harvesting in late summer and those carried out routinely throughout the year as crops are taken from storage as and when clean grain is required. Most charred assemblages have been demonstrated to relate to this second phase of processing that is conducted after storage, with the waste discarded on the fire (Stevens 2003a). As such, charred assemblages can be used to investigate how crops were stored, how much processing was conducted prior to storage, and to provide some indication of the demand on agricultural labour and organisation of such labour to perform these tasks.

The assemblages demonstrated that cereal crops, comprising mainly spelt wheat, were stored as semi-clean spikelets, as they had been in the Iron Age. In many cases samples contained more grain, and/or a greater proportion of weed seeds of large seeded species. As such it seems that at least threshing, winnowing, and coarse and fine sieving were conducted prior to storage. It would also seem probable than the scale and nature of organisation of agricultural labour seen in the Iron Age continued into the Romano-British period. Cambourne shows some affinity in this respect with sites to the west, such as Eaton Socon, where a similar pattern was noted (Stevens and Clapham 2005), while a site at Little Thetford, to the north-east, demonstrated a shift between the Iron Age and Romano-British period towards the storage of crops in a less-processed state (Stevens 1996c; 2003b, fig. 67).

In contrast to the Iron Age, there are a substantial number of samples that contain relatively few cereal grains or weed seeds but which are dominated by large quantities of glumes bases. The main explanation proffered for this pattern is that cereals were taken from storage and dehusked en masse, with pounding, further winnowing, and sieving conducted to rid a large portion of the crop of the bulk of its glumes. It is possible that some changes in technology may have facilitated such processing practices. While dehusking is usually conducted in mortars – which are comparatively rare among the Cambourne sites (see Seager Smith, above) – it might also be achieved by the use of rotary millstones (which are present in some abundance on the sites reported here, see below) with a slightly larger spacing between the stones. More significantly, it is probable that the development of corn-driers may be associated with such practices (cf. van der Veen 1989; van der Veen and O'Connor 1998). The relatively small numbers of weed seeds, especially larger weed seeds, might suggest that hand-sorting was not conducted at the same time or place as this mass dehusking.

Why this change in operations took place is a matter of speculation. One possibility is that, as seen in the Saxon and medieval periods, it became desirable to take larger amounts of grain at a single time to a local miller who would mill it to flour in return for a proportion of the grain. However, it might be noted that both saddle querns and rotary querns were present on the sites during this period, though some of the former may be residual Iron Age objects. A second alternative is that such processing was conducted to produce flour for use in exchange and trade. Such glume-rich assemblages are not unique to Cambourne but are seen on a number of Romano-British settlements, from Ilchester and Catsgore, Somerset (Stevens 1999; Hillman 1982), to Droitwich and Wilderspool, Worcestershire (de Moulins 2006; Hillman 1992) and to Bower Road, Kent (Stevens 2006).

In Cambridgeshire such a deposit was also recovered from a roadside ditch in Cambridge itself (Ballantyne pers. comm.). Such remains have also been frequently associated with Romano-British corn-driers, in particular those on villa or manorial farming estates (van der Veen 1989). Such exchange may have been driven by a requirement or desire to supply local towns and markets as part of the general changes seen from the 2nd–5th centuries (Fulford 1989, 189).

Rotary quern-stones were recovered from a number of Romano-British contexts from Lower Cambourne, Mill Farm and Jeavons Lane. Lava stone deriving from rotary quern-stones came from several of these Cambourne sites (Haywood, Volume 2, 59) and it is probable that examples from both Bourn Airfield (site 3) and Childerley Gate (site 5) on the A428 are also from rotary querns (Duncan 2008). Rotary quern-stones are also known from other Romano-British sites in Cambridgeshire, such as Paston (Bevan 2001).

Malting

The final difference in crop husbandry practices between the Romano-British period and the Iron Age concerns the high presence of germinated grains and coleoptiles from the Romano-British samples. Again, while such assemblages are rare from Iron Age sites they are relatively common from what might be considered more Romanised settlements. In many of these cases it has also been suggested by numerous authors that such evidence may relate to the malting of spelt wheat for use in beer (Hillman 1992; van der Veen 1989; Monckton 2002; Stevens 1999).

On several of the Cambourne sites, particularly Lower Cambourne, Great Common Farm, Mill Farm, and The Grange, glume bases in some samples numbered into the thousands and many of these samples also contained cereal coleoptiles: the sprouted or germinated embryos. Although such remains generally rarely survive charring, in several instances they outnumbered cereal grains, indicating that, with the glume bases, they had probably been separated during dehusking, by sieving and winnowing. Finds of germinated hulled wheat grains, mainly of spelt type, were also common in the same samples. In some cases the coleoptiles have either been charred away or become detached so that only a distinctive groove running along the dorsal side of the grain is visible. Further it is noted that many grains have other morphological characteristics in keeping with the charring of germinated or malted grain.

There is, then, some suggestion that the sites were involved in the production of beer. While this may have been for local consumption, such evidence often predominates on sites close to Roman roads and within Roman towns and beer production was probably driven, in part, to supply such needs to traveller and town dweller alike. Given the location of Cambourne, close to Ermine Street and also to the minor Roman Road 231, it is possible that the settlements at Cambourne produced some surplus production of beer for travellers along these routes. The latter road also passes through a small possible market centre at Vicarage Farm (*Current Archaeology* 2002) 10 km to the east.

The animal economy

Throughout the Romano-British period across Britain it is noticeable that cattle often seem to predominate over sheep and goat (King 1978; Grant 1989), including within this part of East Anglia (Hammon and Albarella 2001; Rielly 2008; King 1988; 1996). However, this was less apparent along the Ermine Street sites to the north of Cambourne, where, in general, cattle were also slightly more numerous in the Late Iron Age (Albarella 1998), while sheep predominated at Grandford near March and Stonea (Stallibrass 1982; 1996). Such a change, from sheep/goat to cattle, is seen to an extent at Cambourne where, at all three sites producing adequate bone samples bones of cattle predominate over sheep (see Hamilton-Dyer, Volume 2, 86). At Lower Cambourne the dominance of cattle is much less, possibly a result of the reworking of older, Iron Age material. At Jeavons Lane it might be noted that the later Iron Age phase also has high numbers of cattle bone, which may indicate that the transition from sheep/goat to cattle in this region took place before the Roman Conquest.

There is some evidence for a small increase in the size of cattle in the Romano-British period at Cambourne (Hamilton-Dyer, Volume 2, 88), and a similar possible increase was noted on sites to the east (Rielly 2008) and also to the north at Paston (Hammond and Albarella 2001) and the Ermine Street sites (Albarella 1998).

As with the Iron Age material it is probable that most if not all of the sheep/goat remains are of sheep, and no certain goat bones have been identified in the Romano-British assemblages (Hamilton-Dyer, Volume 2, 92). This corresponds with other sites in the region where a clear predominance of sheep is seen (cf. Hammon and Albarella 2001; Albarella 1998; King 1988; Stallibrass 1996).

Pigs seem even less frequent than in the Iron Age (Hamilton-Dyer, Volume 2, 94), and this is a pattern seen at a number of other Romano-British sites in the area, for example Haddon (Baxter 2000) and Paston, where pig was noted to decline in 3rd–4th century deposits (Hammon and Albarella 2001)

Horse, as in the Iron Age, appears to be relatively unimportant. This compares well with Romano-British sites in general, although horse bones were well represented on sites to the north in the region (cf. Albarella 1998). Dog is again present although rarely frequent, while cat is also present for the first time.

Butchery and age distributions

At Cambourne there is some suggestion that, by comparison with the Iron Age, cattle were more frequently slaughtered at a younger age, under 4 years, while a greater proportion of sheep were slaughtered at a slightly older age of 4–8 years (Hamilton-Dyer, Volume 2, 87, 93). This contrasts with the evidence from the sites to the east where there is a trend towards older cattle (Rielly 2008), while on the sites along Ermine Street there were reasonable numbers of immature sheep mandibles (Albarella 1998).

Differences in butchery marks on Romano-British sites have been noted by Maltby (1989) with knife marks more frequent on rural sites and those of cleaver more frequent in towns. As seen in the Iron

Age, it is probable that butchery at Cambourne was conducted by both knife and cleaver and, furthermore, no discernable differences were noted between Iron Age and Romano-British butchery practices at the sites on the A428 (Rielly 2008). Knife and cleaver marks have been observed in generally equal numbers on several other Romano-British sites in the region (Hammon and Albarella 2001; Albarella 1998). At Cambourne only two bones from Romano-British deposits were seen to have knife marks while a number have cleaver or axe marks, in particular a scapula from Jeavons Lane. Such marks are typical of Romano-British assemblages (see Hamilton-Dyer 2001b; 2005) and are thought to be related to the separation and curing of shoulders (Hamilton-Dyer, Volume 2, 87). Cleaver marks were also more common at Bourn Airfield (site 3) and Childerley Gate (site 5) on the A428 (Rielly 2008).

Indication of the use of cattle as either cart or plough animals was confined to just two bones, and the size of one of these from Jeavons Lane hints that it may have come from a bull or castrate (Hamilton-Dyer, Volume 2, 88).

Marine molluscs

A number of marine mollusc shells were recovered from Lower Cambourne, with both mussel (*Mytilus edulis*) and oyster (*Ostrea edulis*) present (Wyles, Volume 2, 134). Oyster was also seen at Paston (Hammond and Albarella 2001), while Tort Hill East had oyster, cockle, and mussel. It is of interest to note that at Tort Hill a tentative south coast origin for the oysters was suggested (Winder 1998).

6. The Saxon and Medieval Periods

The local and wider Saxon and medieval landscape

by Chris J. Stevens

By the end of the Romano-British period, and into the Saxon and medieval periods, settlement of much of the fens was restricted to the fen-edge and the drier islands, but there is very little evidence for the local environment around Cambourne at this time. Molluscs (particularly the presence of *Vallonia pulchella*) at Bourn Airfield (site 3) on the A428 appear to indicate increased wetness of the area, although some patches of drier grassland appear to have survived (Pipe 2008). It is notable that mollusc samples from post-Roman deposits at Lower Cambourne indicate a generally similar environment with long, dank, grassland (Allen, Volume 2, 190–2). At Lower Cambourne an unusually large sample of charcoal was recovered from one of the upper fills of a Phase 4 enclosure ditch (1365), provisionally attributed to the Saxon period, and this consisted predominantly of blackthorn (*Prunus spinosa*) and the hawthorn/*Sorbus* group (Pomoideae), but also included oak (*Quercus* sp.).

Following the abandonment of the Romano-British farmsteads, it is likely that much of the area reverted to scrub and woodland. Some of the local place-names refer to areas of ancient woodland and, at *Domesday* (1086), wood for fencing and building was recorded for both Bourn Parish and the adjacent Caxton Parish (*VCH* Cambridge V, 4, 26; Rackham 2001, 62, 63, 195, fig. 22c). The village of Caxton probably originated as a late Scandinavian settlement in a wooded area (*ibid.*, 26). By 1086, however, both parishes were at least partly under cultivation

Anglo-Saxon settlement

by James Wright

There is no certain evidence for continuity of occupation on any of the sites at Cambourne after AD 410, though it is probable that at least some activity continued in the 5th century, particularly at Lower Cambourne (Fig. 49). On the adjacent A428 there is only one site, at Childerley Gate (site 5), that has any hint of sub-Roman (5th and 6th century) activity (Abrams and Ingham 2008, 101). This is a situation common to much of East Anglia (Wade 2000, 23) when what happened during the 5th century remains unclear.

Settlements and industries were in decline from the middle of the 4th century and various changes took place from the beginning of the 5th. It seems certain that there was a decline in population and that the social hierarchy became less structured, with fewer high status buildings and structures less substantial; arable land was abandoned and pasture increased. The overall effect of this in archaeological terms is that settlement became less enclosed and more open, and consequently more difficult to identify and, because the material culture became more restricted, there is substantially less artefactual evidence. Therefore, the small amount of evidence that can be identified assumes a greater importance than might initially appear.

Earthworks associated with the Romano-British enclosures would have survived and at some sites there were deposits of 'dark earth' in the tops of some of the larger features. Early Saxon material, principally pottery, was present in small quantities on five sites in various parts of the Development Area (at Lower Cambourne, Knapwell Plantation, Jeavons Lane, Monk Field Farm, and The Grange), often in the 'dark earth', and usually mixed with Romano-British material. This is similar to the evidence recorded in many Romano-British towns (Dark and Dark 1997, 120). It is possible that all five sites had enclosures in use during the 4th century and these may have provided foci for continued settlement in the 5th century.

A few pits or, more probably, wells were dug at Lower Cambourne, while ditch 26, a substantial Phase 4 feature forming a small C-shaped enclosure, may have remained sufficiently open to form a useable enclosure in the 5th century. One well, 2409, seems to have been provided with a partial shelter. Early Saxon pottery was present over an area measuring 140 m east-west and 100 m north-south, centred on the Phase 3B late Romano-British enclosure. Although it was not possible to identify any contemporaneous structures, a single Saxon sherd was recovered from Romano-British building 1325, and perhaps here we have reasonably secure evidence for the survival of a farmstead into the 5th century and possibly beyond. The only other feature at

Cambourne which might be attributed to the Saxon period was what has been interpreted as a hedgeline at Monk Field Farm.

There is generally little evidence of Early Saxon settlement in the vicinity of Cambourne with, for example, no features or finds of this date recorded from any of the sites on the A428 (Abrams and Ingham 2008) and only low-levels of Saxon activity at Bassingbourn to the east (Ellis *et al.* 2001, 123). However, sunken-featured buildings associated with pits and gullies, all dated to the 5th–7th centuries, were present at Eynesbury, near St Neots in the Great Ouse valley just a few kilometres to the west (Ellis 2004), and a cemetery of broadly similar date is also known at St Neots (Spoerry 2000). Closer to Cambourne there was an Early Saxon cemetery at Haslingfield, near the mouth of the Bourn valley. The paucity, in particular of settlement evidence, at Cambourne and in the immediately surrounding areas is to be expected, for settlement, more than at most periods, will have been concentrated in the valleys, and will have rarely occurred on the clay uplands when there was no pressure to occupy them. Place names have been used to demonstrate an Early Saxon presence along the Bourn valley (Oosthuizen 2008), with most settlements sited in the valley, with cemeteries on higher, more prominent locations above, and the clay uplands used principally for pasture.

After the 6th or possibly 7th century there is a gap in the archaeological record at Cambourne and elsewhere on the surrounding clay uplands, with an absence of artefacts and features until the appearance, probably in the 12th century, of the ubiquitous ridge and furrow agriculture. *Domesday* records that a large part of Bourn parish was held in 1086 by the sheriff of Cambridge, and there is evidence of a severe economic decline following the Norman Conquest. The lack of archaeological evidence for this later Saxon-early Norman period is, therefore, not surprising.

Anglo-Saxon material culture

by Rachael Seager Smith

Artefactual evidence is limited to a few sherds of pottery and two individual objects. The first of these, a copper alloy girdle hanger, a type most frequently found in graves (Malim and Hines 1998, fig. 3.66, 37) and dated to the 6th century, was found in the top of a ditch at The Grange (Pl. 26, above). An iron split socketed spearhead of 6th–7th century date (Swanton 1973, 87, fig. 29) comes from Lower Cambourne (Fig. 47, 42). Finds of Early/Middle Saxon pottery occurred more widely, at Lower Cambourne, Knapwell Plantation, Jeavons Lane, Monk Field Farm, and The Grange, although usually in small quantities alongside Romano-British sherds, incorporated into the latest fills of earlier features. Vessel forms are rare and the few sherds can only be broadly dated to the 5th–7th centuries. Most were locally made, the raw materials being obtained from the Boulder Clay. Only a granitic fabric may have had a non-local origin; such wares are well-known across the East Midlands (Mepham 2004, 53–4, table 13) and may derive from the Charnwood Forest area of Leicestershire (Williams and Vince 1997). Although traditionally viewed as the characteristic Early/Middle Saxon pottery type, organic-tempered wares are poorly represented, in common with other parts of the south-east Midlands (Blinkhorn 1996/7, 72, Mepham 2004, 53).

The Anglo-Saxon agricultural economy

by Chris J. Stevens

There is little to no evidence for charred plant remains dating to the Saxon period. Some cereal remains were recovered from contexts at Lower Cambourne, but it is possible, given their low density, that such remains were reworked. Both free-threshing wheat and rye are recorded from other sites in East Anglia (Murphy 1985) and across England as a whole in the Early Saxon period. These crops are absent though from the post-Roman contexts at Cambourne, and while hulled wheats are present, such remains may be residual (Greig 1991)

No animal bones were recovered from the Saxon contexts at Lower Cambourne. However, it is notable that at Childerley Gate (site 5 on the A428) pig was slightly more frequent in the final stages of the late Romano-British/Early Saxon period, while sheep and goat also increased, and there was a tendency towards more adult cattle; there is also the first evidence for goose (Rielly 2008).

However, what little evidence there is can at least provide a modicum of support to the suggested change of emphasis from a mixed agricultural regime on the clay uplands in the Romano-British period to one that was predominantly, perhaps exclusively, pastoral in the Anglo-Saxon period.

Medieval settlement and agriculture

by James Wright

The evidence from Cambourne and elsewhere demonstrates an even lower density of settlement on the clay uplands of western Cambridgeshire during the medieval period than was seen in the Saxon period. However, increasing population, concentrated in the valleys, resulted in extensive areas of what was probably considered marginal land being brought into arable cultivation, with large, open fields established.

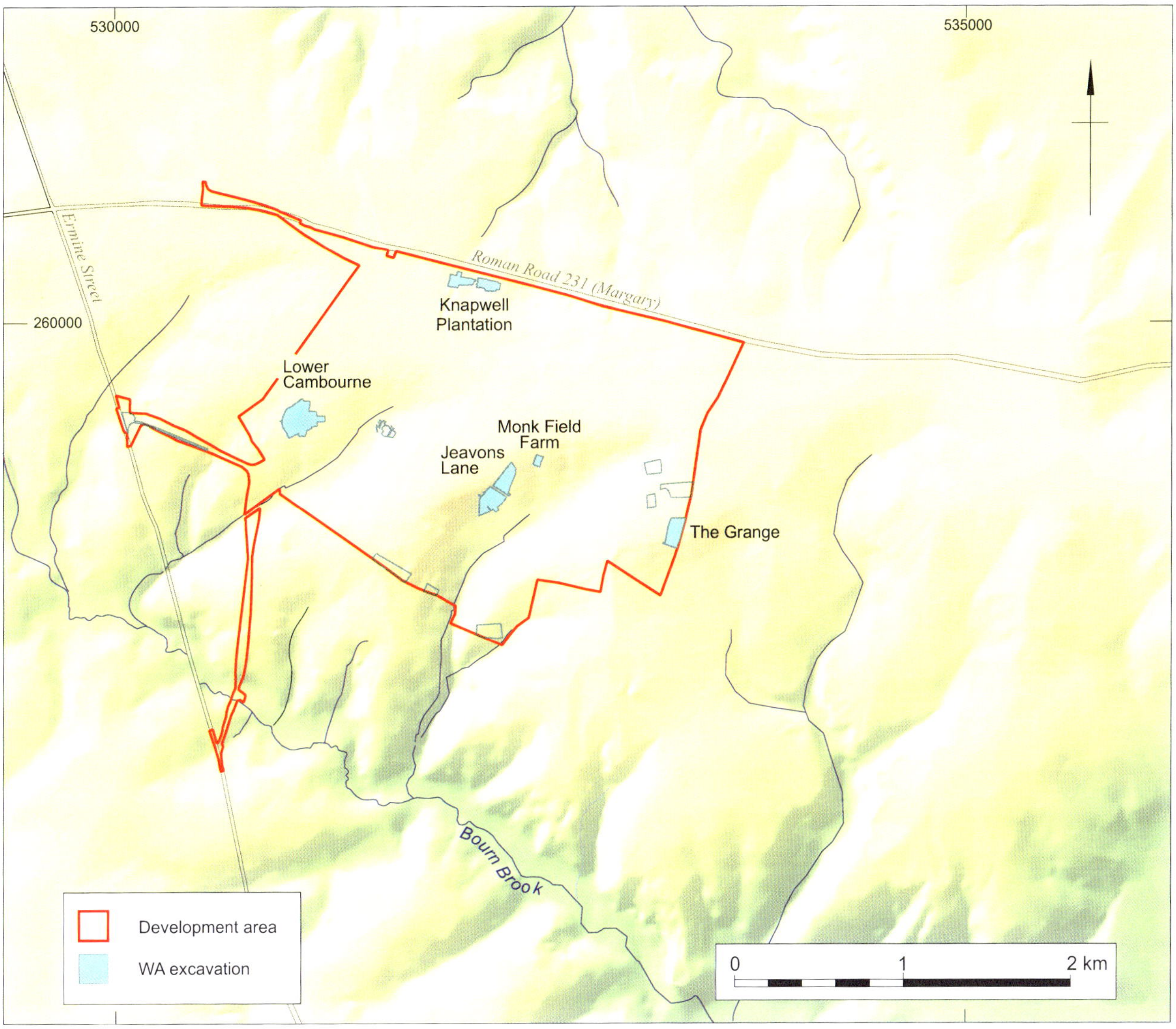

Figure 49 Terrain model of Cambourne: sites with Saxon (Phase 4) features

These survive today in the form of ridge and furrow earthworks where not ploughed flat, as at Cambourne, by 20th century agriculture. The land along the north side of the Bourn valley was probably always regarded as unsuitable for arable agriculture and only cultivated when the demand for food could not be fulfilled by what could be produced in the arable fields in the lower part of the valley alone. The parish of Hardwick, 3 km to the east of Cambourne, was referred to as 'Hungry Hardwick' during the 19th century (*VCH*, Cambridgeshire IV, 99), presumably an indicator of poor harvests or crop failures.

Evidence for medieval ridge and furrow was recorded on all of the excavated sites, represented by broad, shallow furrows cutting the subsoil and underlying Boulder Clay. Much of the overall pattern within the Development Area and the immediately surrounding land could be plotted from air photographs (see Fig. 1). This shows a patchwork of mainly large fields of differing shapes and sizes with various alignments of ridge and furrow.

The ridge and furrow landscape of western Cambridgeshire is similar to that of the East Midlands, which saw the most highly developed form of the 'planned' medieval landscape (Williamson 2003, 62), with nucleated settlements practising two- or three-field cultivation, interspersed with occasional woods and enclosures, small hamlets and isolated farms. Such a medieval, agricultural landscape has been termed 'south-eastern champion' by Williamson (2003, 62) to distinguish it from its East Midlands counterpart.

In some parts of western Cambridgeshire elements of pre-medieval field systems and land boundaries can be seen to have survived in the medieval layout (*ibid.*, 74), but there is no evidence for this at Cambourne, unless the junction of four fields at Lower Cambourne in some way reflects the

Saxon presence here several centuries earlier. When precisely the land at Cambourne was brought into cultivation is unknown, though Williamson (2006, 52) has remarked that 'in the course of the 10th, 11th and 12th centuries, cultivation expanded on to the heavier soils of the interfluves …', and at Cambourne a date towards the end of this range is most likely, reflecting a peak in medieval population in the 12th–13th centuries.

The Bourn valley has been the subject of an extensive landscape survey by Susan Oosthuizen (2006), combining archaeological data, field-name, and cartographic evidence, which has provided a detailed picture of the agricultural economy from the Late Saxon period onwards. This has shown that for most of this time the higher ground was pasture and the lower ground, towards the valley bottom, was arable. However, for a relatively short period, in the 12th and 13th centuries, the demand for food led to the arable use of areas that had probably remained uncultivated since towards the end of the Romano-British period, and then not on such an extensive scale. Following this, as the population declined and with it the demand for food, the area reverted to pasture, resulting in the preservation of the extensive ridge and furrow earthworks. Grazing now was predominantly for sheep as wool became a very significant part of the rural economy in this area and more generally.

Although no medieval settlement evidence was found on any of the Cambourne sites, Ermine Street, to the west, survived from the Romano-British period and became one of four main highways in medieval England, the Great North Road (Hindle 2002, 6). It attracted settlement in the 12th–13th centuries, resulting in the depopulation of some villages in the vicinity, including Caxton (Williamson 2003, 78). Immediately to the north of Cambourne, Roman Road 231 also survived as a route, though somewhat narrowed, from its earlier broader, meandering course, by the arable fields which encroached on either side. Later, when the arable fields had been replaced by pasture, it widened again and in the early post-medieval period it became a green-way with common grazing rights (*ibid.*, 75). However, it was subsequently narrowed under the pressures of enclosure in the early 19th century, though continuing as the main route between Cambridge and St Neots and also acting as the boundary between a number of parishes to the north and south – at Cambourne between Knapwell and Bourn, respectively. In contrast, Ermine Street ran across a string of parishes, but nowhere did it form a boundary between parishes.

There were no substantial settlements within approximately 1.5 km of the former Roman Road 231. All of the present villages to the south, which developed from nucleated settlements in the Late Saxon period, were located in the valley bottom of the Bourn Brook, between the various tributary valleys and often just below the spring line. Hamlets and farmsteads surrounded these villages and further, isolated farmsteads including, at Cambourne, Little Common Farm, Great Common Farm, Monk Field Farm, and Mill Farm, lay on the higher ground. Some of these farmsteads may have had late medieval origins but no evidence for this came from the excavations at Cambourne.

From around the beginning of the 20th century the marginal clay uplands at Cambourne and along the north side of the Bourn valley were once again brought into cultivation, obliterating the medieval ridge and furrow. Subsequently, the development of Cambourne New Settlement at the end of the 20th century, and the recent upgrading of the A428, represent both changes and a continuation of the sequence of settlement which can be traced back 2500 years to the Middle Iron Age and possibly earlier. The A428 has its origins in a probable prehistoric trackway along the northern edge of the Bourn valley, whilst Cambourne represents the first major settlement on the clay uplands in this area.

Bibliography

This incorporates references cited in the specialist reports on the CD

Abbreviations

RCHM(E) 1968: Royal Commission on Historic Monuments in England, West Cambridgeshire

VCH: Victoria County History of England, Cambridgeshire I–X

Abrams, J. and Ingham, D. (eds), 2008 *Farming on the Edge: archaeological evidence from the clay uplands to the west of Cambridge*, Cambridge: E. Anglian Archaeol. 123

Adams, J.C., 1986 *Outline of Orthopaedics*, London: Churchill Livingstone

Adams, J.C., 1987 *Outline of Fractures*, London: Churchill Livingstone

Albarella, U., 1995 Depressions in sheep horncores, *J. Archaeol. Sci.* 22, 689–704

Albarella, U., 1997 *Iron Age and Roman animal bones excavated in 1996 from Norman Cross, Tort Hill East, Tort Hill West and Vinegar Hill, Cambridgeshire*, London: Anc. Monum. Lab. Rep. 108/1997

Albarella, U., 1998 The animal bones, in Ellis *et al.* 1998, 99–104

Allen, M.J., 1995 Land molluscs, in Wainwright, G. and Davies, S., *Balksbury Camp, Hampshire, Excavations 1973 and 1981*, 92–100, London: English Heritage Archaeol. Rep. 4

Allen, T.G. and Robinson, M.A., 1993 *The Prehistoric and Iron Age Enclosed Settlement at Mingies Ditch; Hardwick-with-Yelford, Oxfordshire*, Oxford: Thames Valley Landscapes: the Windrush Valley 2

Alexander, J. and Pullinger, J., 1999 *Roman Cambridge: excavations on Castle Hill 1956–1988, Proc. Cambridge Antiq. Soc.* 88

Aufderheide, A.C. and Rodríguez-Martín, C., 1998 *The Cambridge Encyclopaedia of Human Palaeopathology*, Cambridge: Univ. Press

Ballantyne, R.M., 2004a Plant remains, in Regan *et al.* (eds) 2004, 52–6

Ballantyne, R.M. 2004b A cross-disciplinary investigation of Iron Age pit deposition, 53–7, in French, C. (ed.), Evaluation survey and excavation at Wandlebury Ringwork, Cambridgeshire, 1994–7, *Proc. Cambridge Antiq. Soc.* 93, 15–66

Bass, W.M., 1987 *Human Osteology*, Columbia: Missouri Archaeol. Soc.

Baxter I.L., 1998 *Animal, Bird and Amphibian Bone from Landewade Road, Fordham, Cambridgeshire*, Cambridge: Co. Counc. Archaeol. Fld Unit unpubl. archive rep.

Baxter I.L., 1999 *Mammal, Bird, amphibian and fish bones from Greenhouse Farm, Fen Ditton, Cambridgeshire*, Cambridge: Co. Counc. Archaeol. Fld Unit unpubl. archive rep.

Baxter, I.L., 2000 *Report on the Mammal and Bird Bones from Haddon Lodge Farm, Cambridgeshire*, Cambridge: Co. Counc. Archaeol. Fld Unit unpubl. archive rep.

Baxter I.L., 2001 *Mammal, Bird and Amphibian Bones from Tunbridge Lane, Bottisham, Cambridgeshire*, Hertford: Hertfordshire Archaeol. Trust unpubl. archive rep.

Beagrie, N., 1989 The Romano-British pewter industry, *Britannia* 20, 169–92

Beek, G.C. van, 1983 *Dental Morphology: an illustrated guide*, London: Wright PSG

Behre, K.E., 1981 The interpretation of anthropogenic indicators in pollen diagrams, *Pollen et spores* 23(2), 225–45

Bennett, K.D., Whittington, G. and Edwards, K.J., 1994 Recent plant nomenclatural changes and pollen morphology in the British Isles, *Quat. Newslet.* 73, 1–6

Berry, A.C. and Berry, R.J., 1967 Epigenetic variation in the human cranium, *J. Anat.* 101(2), 261–379

Bevan, L., 2001 The finds, in Ellis *et al.* 2001, 35

Birley, M., 1988 Iron Age, 79–84, in Moss-Eccardt, J., Archaeological investigations in the Letchworth Area, 1958–1974: Blackhorse Road, Letchworth; Norton Road, Baldock; Wilbury Hill, Letchworth, *Proc. Cambridge Antiq. Soc.* 77, 35–104

Blinkhorn, P., 1996/7 Early/Middle Saxon pottery, 71–3, in Soden, I., Saxon and medieval settlement remains at St John's Square, Daventry, Northamptonshire, July 1994–February 1995, *Proc. Northamptonshire Archaeol.* 27, 51–99

Boessneck J., 1969 Osteological differences between sheep (*Ovis aries* Linné) and goat (*Capra hircus* Linné), in Brothwell, D. and Higgs, E.S., *Science in Archaeology*, 331–58, London: Thames and Hudson

Boon, G.C. and Savory H.N., 1975 A silver trumpet-brooch with relief decoration, parcel-gilt, from Carmarthen, and a note on the development of the type, *Antiq. J.* 55(1), 41–61

Booth, P.M., 1997 *Asthall, Oxfordshire: Excavations in a Roman 'Small Town'*, Oxford: Thames Valley Landscapes 9

Bower, M., 2000 Environmental remains, in Regan, R. and Evans, C. (eds), *Excavations at Colne Fen,*

Earith, Sites III & IV, 40–9, Cambridge: Cambridge Archaeol. Unit Rep. 398

Boylston, A., 2000 Evidence for weapon trauma in British archaeological examples, in Cox, M. and Mays, S. (eds), *Human Osteology* 357–80, London: Greenwich Medical Media

Bradley, R.J., 1984 *The Social Foundations of Prehistoric Britain*, Harlow: Longman

Brothwell, D. and Zakrzewski, S., 2004 Metric and non-metric studies of archaeological human remains, in Brickley, M. and McKinley, J.I. (eds), *Guidelines to the Standards for Recording Human Remains*, 24–30, Bradford: Brit. Assoc. Biol. Anthrop. Osteoarchaeol./Inst. Fld Archaeol.

Brown, A., 1994 A Romano-British shell-gritted pottery and tile manufacturing site at Harrold, Bedfordshire, *Bedfordshire Archaeol.* 21, 19–107

Brown N. and Murphy, P., 1997 Neolithic and Bronze Age, in Glazebrook (ed.) 1997, 12–22

Brown, N. and Glazebrook, J., (eds) 2000 *Research and Archaeology: a framework for the eastern counties 2: research agenda and strategy*, Norwich: E. Anglian Archaeol. Occas. Pap. 8

Brown, N. and Murphy, P., 2000 Neolithic and Bronze Age, in Brown and Glazebrook (eds) 2000, 9–13

Bryant, S., 1997 Iron Age, in Glazebrook (ed.) 1997, 23–34

Bryant, S., 2000 The Iron Age, in Brown and Glazebrook (eds) 2000, 14–18

Bryant, S.R. and Niblett, R., 1997 The late Iron Age in Hertfordshire and the north Chilterns, in Gwilt, A and Haselgrove, C. (eds), *Reconstructing Iron Age Societies; new approaches to the British Iron Age*, 270–81, Oxford: Oxbow Monogr. 71

Buckley, D.G. and Major, H., 1983 Quernstones, in Crummy 1983, 73–6

Buikstra, J.E. and Ubelaker, D.H., 1994 *Standards for Data Collection from Human Skeletal Remains*, Arkansas: Arkansas Archaeol. Surv. Res. Ser. 44

Burleigh, G.R., 1993 Some aspects of burial types in the cemeteries of the Romano-British settlement at Baldock, Hertfordshire, in Struck, M. (ed.), *Römerzeitliche Gräber als Quellen zu Religion Bevölkerungsstruktur und Sozialgeschichte*, 41–9, Mainz: Archäologische Schriften des Instituts für Vor- und Frühgeschichte der Johannes Gutenberg Universität Mainz 3

Buxton, K., Howard-Davis, C. and Huntley, J., 2000 Phase 1; the establishment of the Roman fort and settlement; Phase 2: renewal of the fort and rearrangement of the extramural area; Phase 3: demolition and rebuilding; Phase 4: the military fabricia and extramural annex, in Buxton, K. and Howard-Davis, C. (eds), Bremetenacum: *excavations at Roman Ribchester 1980, 1989–1990*, Lancaster Imprints Ser. 9, 25–49, 51–75, 77–101, 103–26

Callender, M.H., 1965 *Roman Amphorae with Index of Stamps*, Oxford: Univ. Press

Cameron, R.A.D. and Morgan-Huws, D.I., 1975 Snail faunas in the early stages of a chalk grassland succession, *Biol. J. Linnean Soc.* 7, 215–29

Campbell, G., 1992 Bronze Age plant remains, in Moore, J. and Jennings, D. (eds), *Reading Business Park: a Bronze Age Landscape*, 103–110, Oxford: Thames Valley Landscapes 1

Campbell, G. 2000 Plant utilisation: the evidence from charred plant remains, in Cunliffe, B., *The Danebury Environs Programme The prehistory of a Wessex Landscape Volume 1: Introduction*, 45–59, Oxford: Engl. Herit./Oxford Univ. Comm. Archaeol. Monogr. 48

Carruthers W.J., 1989 The carbonised plant remains, in Fasham P.J., Farwell D.E. and Whinney R.J.B., *The Archaeological Site at Easton Lane, Winchester*, 131–4, Winchester: Hampshire Fld Club Archaeol. Soc. Monogr. 6

Casey, P.J., 1986 *Understanding Ancient Coins*, London: Batsford

Champion, B., 1916 Utils en fer du musée de Saint-Germain, *Revue Archéologique* 3 (Ser. 5), 211–46

Champion, T., 1994 Socio-economic development in eastern England in the first millennium BC, in Kristiansen, K. and Jenson, J. (eds), *Europe in the First Millennium BC*, 125–44, Sheffield: Sheffield Archaeol. Monogr. 6

Chappell, H.G., Ainsworth, J.F., Cameron, R.A.D. and Redfern, M. 1971 The effect of trampling on a chalk grassland ecosystem, *J. Applied Ecol.* 8, 869–82

Clarke H.H., 1971 The plant remains. Analysis of vegetable matter from the corn drier, in Fowler P.J. and Walthew C.V., Archaeology and the M5. 1st report, 1969, *Trans. Bristol Gloucestershire Archaeol. Soc.* 90, 22–63

Coates, G., Hancocks, A. and Ellis, P., 2001 A Romano-British site at Paston, Peterborough: Archaeological Investigations 1996–7, in Ellis *et al.* 2001, 26–61

Condron, F., 1995 When is a town not a town? Small towns on the Nene and Welland in their context, in Brown, A.E. (ed.), *Roman Small Towns in Eastern England and Beyond*, 103–18, Oxford: Oxbow Monogr. 52

Conolly A.P., Levy J.F. and Dalby D.H., 1971 Appendix 1: plant remains, wood, mosses, ferns, 47, in Greenfield, E., *The Roman Villa at Denton, Lincolnshire*, Lincolnshire Hist. Archaeol. 6, 29–57

Cool, H.E.M., 1990 Roman metal hair pins from southern Britain, *Archaeol. J.* 147, 148–82

Cool, H.E.M., 2006 *Eating and Drinking in Roman Britain*, Cambridge: Univ. Press

Cool, H.E.M. and Price, J., 1995 *Roman Vessel Glass from Excavations in Colchester*, Colchester: Colchester Archaeol. Rep 8

Cox, C. and Deegan, A., 1996 *Cambourne New Village, Cambridgeshire. Aerial Photographic Assessment: Archaeology*, Air Photo Services, unpubl. client rep.

Crummy, N., 1983 *The Roman Small Finds from Excavations in Colchester 1971–79*, Colchester: Colchester Archaeol. Rep. 2

Current Archaeology, 2002 Vicar's Farm, Cambridge; Government estate or rural marketplace?, *Curr. Archaeol.* 15(12), 180

Dark, K. and Dark, R., 1997 *The Landscape of Roman Britain*, Stroud: Sutton

Davies, B., Richardson, B. and Tomber, R., 1994 *The Archaeology of Roman London Volume 5: a dated corpus of early Roman Pottery from the City of London*, York: Counc. Brit. Archaeol. Res. Rep. 98

Davies, M.S. and Hillman, G.C., 1988 Effects of soil flooding on growth and grain yield of populations of tetraploid and hexaploid species of wheat, *Annals Bot.* 62, 597–604

Davies S.J.M., 1999 *Animal Bones from the Iron Age Site at Wardy Hill, Coveney, Cambridgeshire, 1991 Excavations*, Portsmouth: Anc. Monum. Lab. Rep. 47/1999

Davies, S.J.M., 2003 Animal bone, in Evans 2003, 122–32, 135

Dawson, M. (ed.), 2000 *Prehistoric, Roman and Post-Roman Landscapes of the Great Ouse Valley*, York: Counc. Brit. Archaeol. Res. Rep. 119

Dawson, M., 2000 The Iron Age and Romano-British period: a landscape in transition, in Dawson 2000, 57–88

Deegan, A., 1996 *Cambourne New Village, Cambridgeshire. Aerial Photographic Assessment: Archaeology. Supplement to May 1996 Report*, Air Photo Services unpubl. client rep. 967/06

Dobney K.M., Jaques S.D. and Irving B.G., 1996 *Of Butchers and Breeds, Report on Vertebrate Remains from Various Sites in the City of Lincoln*, Lincoln: Lincoln Archaeol. Stud. 5

Dobney K., 2001 A place at the table: the role of vertebrate zooarchaeology within a Roman research agenda for Britain, in James S. and Millett, M. (eds), *Britons and Romans: advancing an archaeological agenda*, 36–45, York: Counc. Brit. Archaeol. Res. Rep. 125

Driesch A. von den, 1976 *A Guide to the Measurement of Animal Bones from Archaeological Sites*, Cambridge, Massachusetts: Peabody Mus. Bull. 1

Driesch A. von den, and Boessneck J., 1974 Kritische Anmerkungen zur Widerristhöhenberechnung aus Längenmaßen vor- und frühgeschichtlicher Tierknochen, *Säugetierkundliche Mitteilungen* 22, 325–48

Drury, P.J. (ed.), 1982 *Structural Reconstruction: approaches to the interpretation of the excavated remains of buildings*, Oxford: Brit. Archaeol. Rep. 110

Dudd, S.N., and Evershed, R.P., 1999 Unusual triterpenoid fatty acyl ester components of archaeological birth bark tars, *Tetrahedron Letters* 40(2), 359–62

Duncan, H., 2008 Appendix 3: other artefacts, CD-Rom, in Abrams and Ingham 2008

Egan, G., 1992 *Leaden Cloth Seals*, Finds Research Group 700–1700, Datasheet 3

Egan, G., 1998 *The Medieval Household, Daily Living c. 1150–1450*, London: Museum of London

Ellis, A.E. 1969 *British Snails; the non-marine Gastropoda of Great Britain and Ireland*, Oxford: Clarendon

Ellis, C.J., 2004 *A Prehistoric Ritual Complex at Eynesbury, Cambridgeshire; Excavation of a Multi-Period Site in the Great Ouse Valley, 2000–2001*, Norwich: E. Anglian Archaeol. Occas. Pap. 17

Ellis, P., Hughes, G., Leach, P., Mould, C. and Sterenberg, J., 1998 *Excavations alongside Roman Ermine Street, Cambridgeshire, 1996*, Oxford: Birmingham Univ. Fld Archaeol. Unit Monogr. 1/Brit. Archaeol. Rep. 276

Ellis, P., Coates, G., Cuttler, R. and Mould, C., 2001 *Four Sites in Cambridgeshire: Excavations at Pode Hole Farm, Paston, Longstanton and Bassingbourn, 1996–7*, Oxford: Birmingham Univ. Fld Archaeol. Unit Monogr. 4/Brit. Archaeol. Rep. 322

Ellis, P., Mould, C., and Rátkai, S., 2001 Saxon and Medieval occupation in Bassingbourn, Cambridgeshire: archaeological investigations in Church Close, 1997, in Ellis *et al.* 2001, 105–24

Elsdon, S.M., 1989 *Later Prehistoric Pottery in England and Wales*, Princes Risborough: Shire

Elsdon, S.M., 1992 East Midlands Scored Ware, *Trans. Leicestershire Archaeol. Hist. Soc.* 66, 83–91

Elsdon, S.M., 1993 *Iron Age Pottery in the East Midlands: a handbook*, Nottingham: Univ. Nottingham

English, J., 2005 Two examples of Roman pottery repair in antiquity, *Surrey Archaeol. Collect.* 92, 263–5

Esmonde Cleary, S., 2000 Putting the dead in their place: burial location in Roman Britain, in Pearce, J., Millet, M. and Struck, M. (eds), *Burial, Society and Context in the Roman World*, 127–42, Oxford: Oxbow

Evans, C., 1992a Iron Age research priorities, *Fenland Res.* 7, 8–10

Evans, C., 1992b Commanding gesture in lowlands: the investigation of two Iron Age ringworks, *Fenland Res.* 7, 16–26

Evans, C., 1997 Hydraulic communities: Iron Age enclosure in the East Anglian Fenlands, in Gwilt, A. and Haselgrove, C. (ed.), *Reconstructing Iron*

Age Societies, 216–27, Oxford: Oxbow Monogr. 71

Evans, C., 2003 *Power and Island Communities: excavations at the Wardy Hill Ringwork, Coveney, Ely*, Cambridge: E. Anglian Archaeol. 103

Evans, C. and Knight, M., 2000 A fenland delta: Later prehistoric land-use in the lower Ouse reaches in Dawson (ed.) 2000, 89–106

Evans, C. and Knight, M., 2001 The 'Community of Builders': the Barleycroft post alignment, in Brück, J. (ed.), *Bronze Age Landscapes: tradition and transformation*, 83–98, Oxford: Oxbow

Evans, C. and Hodder, I., 2006 *Marshland Communities and Cultural Landscapes: the Haddenham Project. Volume 2*, Cambridge: McDonald Inst. Monogr.

Evans, J.G., 1972 *Land Snails in Archaeology*, London: Seminar

Evans, J.G., 1984 Stonehenge – the environment in the Late Neolithic and Early Bronze Age and a Beaker burial, *Wiltshire Archaeol. Natur. Hist. Soc. Mag.*, 7–30

Every, R., 2006 Roman pottery, 32–5, in Andrews, P., Romano-British and medieval saltmaking and settlement in Parson Drove, *Proc. Cambridge Antiq. Soc.* 95, 25–48

Farrar, R.A.H., Hull, M.R. and Pullinger, J., 1999 The Iron Age pottery, in Alexander and Pullinger 1999, 117–30

Finnegan, M., 1978 Non-metric variations of the infracranial skeleton, *J. Anat.* 125(1), 23–37

Foster, J., 1986 Querns, in Stead, I.M. and Rigby, V., *Baldock: the excavation of a Roman and pre-Roman settlement, 1968–72*, 179–82, London: Britannia Monogr. 7

Fowler, E 1960 The origins and development of the penannular brooch in Europe, *Proc. Prehist. Soc.* 26, 149–77

Fox, C., 1923 *The Archaeology of the Cambridge Region*, Cambridge: Univ. Press

French, C.A.I., 2003 *Geoarchaeology in Action: studies in soil micromorphology and landscape evolution*, London: Routledge

French, C.A.I. and Pryor, F., 1992 Floodplain gravels: buried Neolithic and Bronze Age landscapes along the Fen margins, in Fulford, M. and Nichols, E. (eds), *Developing Landscapes in Lowland Britain: the archaeology of the British gravels: a review*, 63–77, London: Soc. Antiq. London Occas. Pap. 14

French, C.A.I. and Wait, G.A., 1988 *An Archaeological Survey of the Cambridgeshire River Gravels*, Cambridge: Co. Counc.

French, C.A.I., Macklin, M.G. and Passmore, D.G., 1992 Archaeology and palaeochannels in the Lower Welland and Nene valleys: alluvial archaeology at the fen-edge, eastern England, in Needham, S. and Macklin, M.G. (eds), *Alluvial Archaeology in Britain*, 169–76, Oxford: Oxbow Monogr. 27

Frere, S.S., 1972 *Verulamium Excavations I*, Oxford: Rep. Res. Comm. Soc. Antiq. London 28

Frere, S.S., 1984 *Verulamium Excavations III*, Oxford: Oxford Univ. Comm. Archaeol. Monogr. 1

Fulford, M., 1989 The Economy of Roman Britain, in Todd, M. (ed.), *Research on Roman Britain 1960–89*, 175–201, London: Britannia Monogr. 11

Fulford, M.G., 2001 Links with the past: pervasive 'ritual' behaviour in Roman Britain, *Britannia* 32, 199–218

Gale, R. 2008 Appendix 16: charcoal, CD-Rom, in Abrams and Ingham 2008

Gardiner, F., Henig, M. and Pullinger, J., 1999 The small finds, in Alexander and Pullinger 1999, 85–106

Gibson, C.A., 2005 A Romano-British rural site at Eaton Socon, Cambridgeshire, *Proc. Cambridge Antiq. Soc.* 94, 21–38

Gibson, C. and Knight, S., 2007 A Middle Iron Age Settlement at Weston Down Cottages, Weston Colley near Winchester, *Hampshire Stud.* 62, 1–34

Giorgi, J., 2006 The plant remains from White Horse Stone, in Giorgi, J. (ed.), *Palaeoenvironmental Evidence from Section 1 of the Channel Tunnel Rail Link, Kent*, CTRL Scheme-wide Spec. Rep. Ser., Archaeology Data Service

Giorgi, J. 2008 Appendix 15: charcoal, CD-Rom, in Abrams and Ingham 2008

Glazebrook, J. (ed.), 1997 *Research and Archaeology: a framework for the eastern counties, 1. resource assessment*, Norwich: E. Anglian Archaeol. Occas. Pap. 3

Godwin, H., 1984 *History of the British Flora* (2 edn), Cambridge: Univ. Press

Grant A., 1982 The use of tooth wear as a guide to the age of domestic ungulates, in Wilson, B., Grigson, C. and Payne, S., *Ageing and Sexing Animal Bones from Archaeological Sites*, 251–4, Oxford: Brit. Archaeol. Rep. 109

Grant, A., 1984a Animal husbandry in Wessex and the Thames Valley, in Cunliffe, B. and Miles, D. (eds), *Aspects of the Iron Age in Central Southern Britain*, 102–19, Oxford: Oxford Univ. Archaeol. Monogr. 3

Grant, A., 1984b Survival or sacrifice? A critical appraisal of animal burials in Britain in the Iron Age, in Clutton-Brock, J. and Grigson, C., *Animals in Archaeology 4: husbandry in Europe*, 221–8, Oxford: Brit. Archaeol. Rep. S227

Grant, A., 1989 Animals in the Roman Britain, in Todd, M. (ed.), *Research on Roman Britain, 1960–89*, 135–46, London: Britannia Monogr. 11

Green, H.J.M., 1982 The origins and development of cruck construction in Eastern England, in Drury 1982, 87–100

Greep, S., 2004 Bone and antler veneer, in Cool, H.E.M., *The Roman Cemetery at Brougham, Cumbria, excavations 1966–67*, 273–82, London: Britannia Monogr. 21

Greig, J.R.A., 1991 The British Isles, in Zeist, W. van, Wasylikowa, W. and Behre, K-E. (eds), *Progress in Old World Palaeoethnobotany*, 299–334, Rotterdam: Balkema

Guest, P., 1998 Discussion of the distribution of coins in and around the town, in Holbrook, N. (ed.), *Cirencester: the Roman town defences, public buildings and shops*, 262–8, Cirencester: Cirencester Excav. 5

Guiraud, H., 1989 Bagues et anneaux à l'époque romaine en Gaule, *Gallia* 46, 173–211

Gurney, D., 1986 *Settlement, Religion and Industry on the Fen-edge; three Romano-British sites in Norfolk*, Gressenhall: E. Anglian Archaeol. 31

Hall, A.R. and Kenward H.K., 1990 *Environmental Evidence from the Colonia: General Accident and Rougier Street*, London: Archaeol. York 14(6), 289–434 and fiche 1–9

Hall, D. and Coles, J., 1994 *Fenland Survey: an essay in landscape and persistence*, London: Engl. Herit. Archaeol. Rep. 1

Halstead, P. and Collins, P., 2002 Sorting the sheep from the goats: morphological distinctions between the mandibles and mandibular teeth of adult *Ovis* and *Capra*, *J. Archaeol. Sci.* 29, 545–53

Hambleton, E., 1999 *Animal Husbandry Regimes in Iron Age Britain*, Oxford: Brit. Archaeol. Rep. 282

Hamilton-Dyer, S., 2001a The faunal remains, in, Peacock D.P.S. and Maxfield V.A., *Mons Claudianus, Survey and Excavation: Vol. II Excavations Part 1*, 249–310, Cairo: Institut Français d'Archéologie Orientale Documents de Fouilles 43

Hamilton-Dyer, S., 2001b *The animal bones, Tilly's Lane and Two Rivers, Staines*, unpubl. rep. for Wessex Archaeol.

Hamilton-Dyer, S., 2003 *Fish and bird bone notes, Tunbridge Lane, Bottisham, Cambridge*, unpubl. notes for Cambridge Co. Counc. Archaeol. Fld Unit

Hamilton-Dyer, S., 2005 *The Animal Bones, 60–63 Fenchurch Street, City of London EC3*, unpubl. rep. for Wessex Archaeol.

Hammon, A. and Albarella, U., 2001 The animal bones, in Ellis *et al.* 2001, 47–52

Hancocks, A., Evans, J. and Woodward, A., 1998 The prehistoric and Roman pottery, in Ellis *et al.* 1998, 34–72

Hanf, M., 1983 *Weeds and their Seedlings*, Ipswich: B.A.S.F.

Harcourt R.A., 1974 The dog in prehistoric and early historic Britain, *J. Archaeol. Sci.* 1, 151–76

Harden, D.B., 1939 Romano-British Remains, B. Roads; C. Settlement Sites; D. Industries, in *The Victoria History of the Counties of England: Oxfordshire 1*, 271–305

Harding, D.W., 1975 The pottery, 69–84, in Jackson, D.A., An Iron Age site at Twywell, Northamptonshire, *Northamptonshire Archaeol.* 10, 31–93

Harman, M., Molleson, T.I. and Price, J.L. 1981 Burials, bodies and beheadings in Romano-British and Anglo-Saxon cemeteries, *Bull. Brit. Mus. Natur. Hist. (Geol.)* 35(3), 145–88

Hartley, K.F., 1999 The mortaria, in Alexander and Pullinger 1999, 201–8

Haselgrove, C., 1979 The significance of coinage in pre-Conquest Britain, in Burnham, B.C. and Johnson, H.B. (eds), *Invasion and Response; the case of Roman Britain*, 197–209, Oxford: Brit. Archaeol. Rep. 73

Haselgrove, C., 1996 Iron Age coinage: recent work, in Champion, T.C. and Collis, J.R. (eds), *The Iron Age in Britain and Ireland: recent trends*, 67–85, Sheffield: Univ. Sheffield

Hattatt, R., 2000 *A Visual Catalogue of Richard Hattat's Ancient Brooches*, Oxford: Oxbow

Havis, R. and Brooks, H., 2003 *Excavations at Stansted Airport, 1986–91, Volume 1: Prehistoric and Romano-British*, Chelmsford: E. Anglian Archaeol. 107

Hawkes, S.C. and Dunning, G.C., 1961 Soldiers and settlers in Britain, 4th–5th century, with a catalogue of animal ornamented buckles and related belt fittings, *Medieval Archaeol.* 5, 1–70

Henig, M., 1984 *Religion in Roman Britain*, London: Batsford

Hill, J.D., 1995 *Ritual and Rubbish in the Iron Age of Wessex*, Oxford: Brit. Archaeol. Rep. 242

Hill, J.D. and Braddock, P., 2006 Iron Age pottery, in Evans and Hodder 2006, 148–94

Hillman, G.C., 1981 Reconstructing crop husbandry practices from charred remains of crops, in Mercer, R.J. (ed.), *Farming Practice in British Prehistory*, 123–62, Edinburgh: Univ. Press

Hillman, G., 1982 Crop husbandry at the medieval farmstead Cefn Graeonog, 904–7, in Kelly, R.S. (ed.), The excavation of a Medieval farmstead at Cefn Graeonog, Clynnog, Gywnned, *Bull. Board Celtic Stud.* 29(4)

Hillman, G., 1984 Interpretation of archaeological plant remains: the application of ethnographic models from Turkey, in Zeist, W. van and Casparie, W.A. (eds), *Plants and Ancient Man: studies in palaeoethnobotany*, 1–42, Rotterdam: Proc. 6th Symp. Int. Work Grp Palaeoethnobot.

Hillman, G., 1992 Crop processing at 3rd century AD Wilderspool, in Hinchcliffe, J. and Williams, J.H. (eds), *Excavations at Wilderspool 1966–1968*, 167–9, Cheshire Co. Counc. Monogr.

Hillson, S.W., 1979 Diet and dental disease, *World Archaeol.* 2(2), 147–62

Hindle, P., 2002 *Medieval Roads and Tracks*, Aylesbury: Shire

Hingley, R., 2006 The deposition of iron objects in Britain during the later prehistoric and Roman periods: contextual analysis and the significance of iron, *Britannia* 37, 213–57

Hodgson, J.M., 1976 *Soil Survey Field Handbook*, Harpenden: Soil Surv. Tech. Monogr. 5

Holmes, E.F., 1985 *Sewing Thimbles*, Finds Res. Group 700–1700, Datasheet 9

Holmes, M., 2007 Animal bone, in Timby, J., Brown, R., Hardy, A., Leech. S., Poole, C. and Webley, L. (eds), *Settlement on the Bedfordshire Claylands: Archaeology along the A421 Great Barford Bypass*, 329–63, Bedford: Bedfordshire Archaeol. Monogr. 8

Hooley, D., 2001 Copper alloy and silver objects, in Anderson, A.S., Wacher, J.S. and Fitzpatrick, A.P., *The Romano-British 'Small Town' at Wanborough, Wiltshire*, 75–116, London: Britannia Monogr. 19

Howe, M.D., Mackreth, D.F. and Perrin, J.R., 1980 *Roman Pottery from the Nene Valley: a guide*, Peterborough City Mus. Occas. Pap. 2

Hull, M.R. and Pullinger, J., 1999, The Roman pottery, in Alexander and Pullinger 1999, 141–4

Hunt, G., 2006 Waterlogged plant remains, in Evans and Hodder 2006, 255–60

Isings, C., 1957 *Roman Glass from Dated Finds*, Groningen

Johns, C., 1996 The classification and interpretation of Romano-British treasures, *Britannia* 27, 1–16

Jones, A., 2001 A Romano-Celtic shrine and settlements at Little Paxton Quarry, Diddington, Cambridgeshire, *Proc. Cambridge Antiq. Soc.* 90, 5–27

Jones, G.E.M., 1984 Interpretation of plant remains: ethnographic models from Greece, in Zeist, W. van and Casparie, W.A. (eds), *Plants and Ancient Man: studies in palaeoethnobotany*, 43–61, Rotterdam: Proc. 6th Symp. Int. Work Grp Palaeoethnobot.

Jones, G.E.M., 1987 A statistical approach to the archaeological identification of crop processing, *J. Archaeol. Sci.* 14, 311–23

Jones, G.E.M., 1992 Weed phytosociology and crop husbandry: identifying a contrast between ancient and modern practice, in Pals, J.P., Buurman, J. and Veen, M. van der (eds), *Festschrift for Professor van Zeist/Rev. Palaeobot. Palynol.* 73, 133–43

Jones, G.E.M, 2006 Cereal processing, household space and crop husbandry, Overview discussion: cereals – the evidence for local cultivation, in Evans and Hodder 2006, 248–55, 263

Jones, G.E.M. and Halstead, P., 1995 Maslins, mixtures and monocrops: on the interpretation of archaeobotanical crop samples of heterogeneous composition, *J. Archaeol. Sci.* 22(1), 1103–14

Jones, G.P. forthcoming The Iron Age and Romano-British pottery, in Egging Dinwiddy, K. and Schuster, J., Thanet's longest excavation, in Andrews, P., Egging Dinwiddy, K., Ellis, C., Hutcheson, A., Phillpotts, C., Powell, A.B. and Schuster, J. *Kentish Sites and Sites of Kent*, Salisbury, Wessex Archaeol. Rep. 24

Jones, M.K., 1975 Seed report, 50–2, in Parrington, M. and Balkwill C., Excavations at Broad Street, Abingdon, *Oxoniensia* 40, 5–58

Jones, M.K., 1981 The development of crop husbandry, in Jones, M.K. and Dimbleby, G. (eds), *The Environment of Man, The Iron Age to the Anglo-Saxon Period*, 95–127, Oxford: Brit. Archaeol. Rep. 87

Jones, M.K., 1986 The carbonised plant remains, in Miles, D. (ed.), *Archaeology at Barton Court Farm, Abingdon, Oxfordshire*, Fiche 9: A1–9: B5, London: Counc. Brit. Archaeol. Res. Rep. 50

Jones, M.K., 1987 Carbonised grain, in Mynard, D. (ed.), *Roman Milton Keynes: excavations and fieldwork 1971–82*, 192–3, Buckinghamshire Archaeol. Soc. Monogr. 1

Jones, M.K., 1988a The phytosociology of early arable weed communities with special reference to southern England, in Küster, H. (ed.), *Der prähistorische Mensch und seine Umwelt*, 43–51, Stuttgart: Forschungen und Berichte zur Vor-und Frühgeschichte in Baden-Württemberg 31

Jones, M.K., 1988b The arable field: a botanical battleground, in Jones, M.K. (ed.), *Archaeology and the Flora of the British Isles*, 86–91, Oxford: Oxford Univ. Comm. Archaeol.

Kenney, S., 2007 A banjo enclosure and Roman farmstead: excavations at Caldecote Highfields, Cambridgeshire, in Mills, J. and Palmer, R. (eds), *Populating Clay Landscapes: Recent Advances in Archaeology on Difficult Soils*, Stroud: Tempus

Kerney, M.P., 1999. *Atlas of the Land and Freshwater Molluscs of Britain and Ireland*, Colchester: Harley

King, A., 1978 A comparative survey of bone assemblages from Roman sites in Britain, *Bull. Inst. Archaeol. London* 15, 207–32

King, A., 1988 Villas and animal bones, in Branigan, K. and Miles, D. (eds), *Villa Economies (Economic Aspects of Romano-British Villas)*, 51–9, Sheffield: Dept Archaeol. Prehist., Univ. Sheffield

King, J., 1988 Animal bones, 146–9, in Mackreth, D.F., Excavation of an Iron Age and Roman enclosure at Werrington, Cambridgeshire, *Britannia* 19, 59–151

King, J., 1996 The animal bones, in Mackreth, D.F., *Orton Hall Farm: a Roman and early Anglo-Saxon farmstead*, 216–18, Cambridge: E. Anglian Archaeol. 76

Knight, D., 1984 *Late Bronze and Iron Age Settlement in the Nene and Great Ouse Basins*, Oxford: Brit. Archaeol. Rep. 130

Knüsel, C. 2000 Activity related changes, in Fiorato, V., Boylston, A. and Knüsel, C. (eds), *Blood Red Roses: The archaeology of the mass grave from the battle of Towton AD 1461*, 103–18, Oxford: Oxbow

Lambrick, G.H., 1992a The development of late prehistoric and Roman farming on the Thames gravels, in Fulford, M. and Nichols, E. (eds), *Developing Landscapes of Lowland Britain. The Archaeology of the British Gravels: a review*, 23–38, London: Soc. Antiq. London Occas. Pap. 14

Lambrick, G., 1992b Alluvial archaeology of the Holocene in the Upper Thames basin 1971–1991: a review, in Needham, S. and Macklin, M.G. (eds), *Alluvial Archaeology in Britain*, 209–29, Oxford: Oxbow Monogr. 27

Lambrick, G. and Robinson, M., 1979. *Iron Age and Roman Riverside Settlements in Farmoor, Oxfordshire*, London: Counc. Brit. Archaeol. Res. Rep. 32/Oxford Archaeol. Unit Rep. 2

Lane, T. and Morris, E.L. (eds) 2001 *A Millennium of Saltmaking: prehistoric and Romano-British salt production in the Fenland*, Sleaford: Lincolnshire Archaeol. Herit. Rep. 4

Lauwerier R.C.G.M., 1988 *Animals in Roman Times in the Dutch Eastern River Area*, Amersfoort: Nederlandse Oudheden 12/Project Oostelick Rivierengebied 1

Lawson, A.J., 1976 Shale and jet objects from Silchester, *Archaeologia* 105, 241–75

Leith, S., 1997 *Late Iron Age, Roman, and Medieval Enclosures and Settlement Features at Highfields, Caldecote: an archaeological excavation*, Cambridge: Co. Counc. Archaeol. Fld Unit unpubl. client rep. 144

Levine, M.A., 1982 The use of crown height measurements and eruption-wear sequences to age horse teeth, in Wilson, B., Grigson, C. and Payne, S., *Ageing and Sexing Animal Bones from Archaeological Sites*, 223–50, Oxford: Brit. Archaeol. Rep. 109

Liversidge, J., 1973 *Britain in the Roman Empire*, London: Cardinal

Liversidge, J., 1977 Roman burials in the Cambridge area, *Proc. Cambridge Antiq. Soc.* 47, 11–38

Liversidge, J., 1999 The glass, in Alexander and Pullinger 1999, 107–8

Lucas, G., 2003 Worked stone, in Evans 2003, 189–90

Lucas, G., 2006 Worked and unworked stone, in Evans and Hodder 2005, 201–5

Lucas, G. and Whittaker, P., 2001 *Vicar's Farm, Cambridge: post-excavation assessment report*, Cambridge: Cambridge Archaeol. Unit Rep. 425

Lyons, A., nd *A Technical Report for the Romano-British pottery from the A428 Caxton to Hardwick Improvement Scheme, Cambridgeshire*, unpubl.

Malim, T., 1997 Prehistoric and Roman remains at Edix Hill, Barrington, Cambridgeshire, *Proc. Cambridge Antiq. Soc.* 86, 13–56

Malim, T., 2000, The ritual landscape of the Neolithic and Bronze Age along the middle and lower Ouse valley, in Dawson 2000, 58–90

Malim, T., 2001, Place and space in the Cambridgeshire Bronze Age in Brück, J. (ed.), *Bronze Age Landscapes; tradition and transformation*, 9–22, Oxford: Oxbow

Malim, T. and Hines, J., 1998 *The Anglo-Saxon Cemetery at Edix Hill (Barrington A), Cambridgeshire*, York: Counc. Brit. Archaeol. Res. Rep. 112

Maltby, J.M., 1985a The animal bones, in Fasham, P.J., *The Prehistoric Settlement at Winnall Down, Winchester*, 97–112, Winchester: Hampshire Fld Club Archaeol. Soc. Monogr. 2

Maltby, J.M., 1985b Patterns in faunal assemblage variability, in Barker, G. and Gamble, C., *Beyond Domestication in Prehistoric Europe*, 33–74, London: Academic

Maltby, J.M., 1989 Urban-rural variations in the butchering of cattle in Romano-British Hampshire, in Serjeantson, D. and Waldron, T. (eds), *Diet and Crafts in Towns: the evidence of animal remains from the Roman to the post-medieval periods*, 75–106, Oxford: Brit. Archaeol. Rep. 199

Maltby, J.M., 1994 The meat supply in Roman Dorchester and Winchester, in Hall, A.R. and Kenward, H.K., *Urban-Rural Connexions: perspectives from environmental archaeology*, 85–102, Oxford: Oxbow Monogr. 47/Symp. Assoc. Environ. Archaeol. 12

Manchester, K., 1983 *The Archaeology of Disease*, Bradford: Univ. Press

Manning, W.H., 1972 Ironwork hoards in Iron Age and Roman Britain, *Britannia* 3, 224–50

Manning, W.H., 1985 *Catalogue of Romano-British Iron Tools, Fittings and Weapons in the British Museum*, London: Brit. Mus.

Margary, I.D., 1973 *Roman Roads in Britain* (3 edn), London: John Baker

Marney, P.T., 1989 *Roman and Belgic Pottery from Excavations in Milton Keynes 1972–1982*, Milton Keynes: Buckinghamshire Archaeol. Soc. Monogr. 2

Marsh, G., 1981 London's samian supply and its relationship to the development of the Gallic samian industry, in Anderson, A.C and Anderson, A.S. (eds), *Roman Pottery Research in Britain and North-west Europe. Papers Presented to*

Graham Webster, 173–238, Oxford: Brit. Archaeol. Rep. S13

Martin, E. and Murphy, P., 1988 West Row Fen, Suffolk: a Bronze Age fen-edge settlement site, *Antiquity* 62, 353–8

McAvoy, F., 2000 The development of a Neolithic monument complex at Godmanchester, Cambridgeshire, in Dawson 2000, 51–6

McKinley, J.I. 1993a *Baldock Project [unburnt] human bone report*, unpubl. rep. for Letchworth Mus.

McKinley, J.I., 1993b A decapitation from the Romano-British cemetery at Baldock, Hertfordshire, *Int. J. Osteoarchaeol.* 3(1), 41–4

McKinley, J.I., 2004a Compiling a skeletal inventory: disarticulated and co-mingled remains, in Brickley, M. and McKinley, J.I. (eds), *Guidelines to the Standards for Recording Human Remains*, 13–16, Bradford: British Assoc. Biol. Anthrop. Osteoarchaeol./Inst. Fld Archaeol.

McKinley, J.I., 2004b Welcome to *Pontibus* ... gateway to the West, *Surrey Archaeol. Collect.* 91, 1–70

Mepham, L.N., 2004 Saxon pottery, in Ellis 2004, 53–7

Molleson, T.I., 1993 The human remains, in Farwell, D.E. and Molleson, T.I., *Poundbury Volume 2: The Cemeteries*, 142–214, Dorchester: Dorset Natur. Hist. Archaeol. Soc. Monogr. 11

Monckton, A., 2002 Charred plant remains from Bronze Age to Roman contexts, including Roman corndriers, from the Wing to Whatborough pipeline, Rutland, in Beamish, M., *Excavations on the Wing to Whatborough Anglian Water pipeline*, Univ. Leicester Archaeol. Serv. archive rep.

Moore, P.D. and Webb, J.A. 1978 *An Illustrated Guide to Pollen Analysis*, London: Hodder & Stoughton

Moore, P.D., Webb, J.A. and Collinson, M.E., 1991 *Pollen Analysis* (2nd edn), London: Hodder & Stoughton

Morris, E. L., 1994 *The Analysis of Pottery*, Salisbury: Wessex Archaeol. Guideline 4

Morris, E.L., 2001 Briquetage, in Lane and Morris (eds) 2001, 33–63

Moulins, D. de, 2006. Charred plant remains, in Hurst, D. (ed.), *Roman Droitwich: Dodder Hill fort, Bays Meadow villa, and roadside settlement*, 69–75, York: Counc. Brit. Archaeol. Res. Rep. 146

Murphy, P.J., 1985 The cereals and crop weeds, in West, S. (ed.), *West Stow: the Anglo-Saxon Village*, 100–8, Ipswich: E. Anglian Archaeol. 24

Murphy, P.J., 1991a Early crop production and wild plant resources in the coastal area of Essex, England, in Renfrew, J.M. (ed.), *New Light on Early Farming*, 329–48, Rotterdam: Proc. 7th Symp. Int. Work Grp Palaeoethnobot.

Murphy, P.J., 1991b Cereals and crop weeds, 31–5 in Bedwin, O., Asheldham Camp – an early Iron Age hill fort: the 1985 excavations, *Essex Archaeol. Hist.* 22, 13–37

Murphy P.J., 1997 Environment and economy, 30–1 in Bryant, S., Iron Age, in Glazebrook (ed.) 1997, 23–34

Murphy, P.J., 2003 Plant macrofossils and molluscs, insects and pollen, in Evans 2003, 84–114

Oakey, N., 1996. *Iron Age and Romano-British Field Systems at Highfields, Caldecote. An Archaeological Evaluation*, Cambridge: Co. Counc. Archaeol. Fld Unit unpubl. rep. 125

O'Connor T.P., 1986 The animal bones, in Zienkiewicz, J.D., *The Legionary Fortress Baths at Caerleon, II. The Finds*, 225–48, Cardiff: Nat. Mus. Wales

O'Connor, T.P., 1988 Slums, puddles and ditches: are molluscs useful indicators, in Murphy, P. and French, C. (eds), *The Exploitation of Wetlands*, 61–8, Oxford: Brit. Archaeol. Rep. 186

O'Connor T.P.,1989 *Bones from Anglo-Scandinavian levels at 16–22 Coppergate*, London: Archaeol. York 15/3

Olsen, S.L., 1994 Exploitation of mammals at the Early Bronze Age site of West Row Fen, Mildenhall, Suffolk, England, *Annals Carnegie Mus.* 63(2), 115–53

Ordnance Survey, 1978 *Roman Britain* (3 edn), Southampton: Ordnance Surv.

Oosthuizen, S., 2006 *Landscapes Decoded: the origins and development of Cambridgeshire's medieval fields*, Hertford: Explor. Local Regional Hist. 1

Oosthuizen, S., 2008 Field names in reconstructing Late Saxon agricultural land-use in the Bourn Valley, West Cambridgeshire, in Chadwick, A. (ed.), *Recent Approaches to the Archaeology of Land Allotment*, 337–54, Oxford: Brit. Archaeol. Rep. S1875

Palmer, R., 1996 A further case for the preservation of earthwork ridge-and-furrow, *Antiquity* 70, 436–9

Paradine P., 1984 Plant macrofossils from the well, in Ellis, P., Catsgore, 1979, *Further Excavation of the Romano-British Village*, 40–1 and fiche D11–14, Taunton: Western Archaeol. Trust Excav. Monogr. 7

Payne S., 1985 Morphological distinctions between the mandibular teeth of young sheep, *Ovis*, and goats, *Capra*, *J. Archaeol. Sci.* 12, 139–47

Peacock, D.P.S., 1987 Iron Age and Roman quern production at Lodsworth, West Sussex, *Antiq. J.* 67, 59–85

Peacock, D.P.S. and Williams, D., 1986 *Amphorae and the Roman Economy; an introductory guide*, London: Longman

Pelling, R., 2002 Charred plant remains, in Booth, P.M., Evans, J. and Hiller, J., *Excavations in the Extramural Settlement of Roman Alchester, Oxford-*

shire, 1991, 418–22, Oxford: Oxford Archaeol. Monogr. 1

Percival, J., 1921 *The Wheat Plant*, London: Duckworth

Perrin, J.R., 1996 The Roman pottery, in Mackreth, D.F., *Orton Hall Farm: a Roman and Early Anglo-Saxon farmstead*, 114–204, Cambridge: E. Anglian Archaeol. 76

Perrin, J.R., 1999 Roman pottery from excavations at and near to the Roman Small Town of *Durobrivae*, Water Newton, Cambridgeshire, 1956–58, *J. Roman Pott. Stud.* 8

Perrin, J.R., and Webster, G., 1990 Roman pottery from excavations in Normangate Field, Castor, Peterborough, 1962–3, *J. Roman Pott. Stud.* 3, 35–62

Pfleger, V. and Chatfield, J., 1988 *A Guide to Snails of Britain and Europe*, London: Hamlyn

Philpott, R., 1991 *Burial Practices in Roman Britain; a study of grave treatment and furnishing A.D. 43–410*, Oxford: Brit. Archaeol. Rep. 219

Pipe, A., 2008 Appendix 14: molluscan remains, CD-Rom, in Abrams and Ingham 2008

Potter, T.W., 1981 The Roman occupation of the central fenland, *Britannia* 12, 79–133

Prehistoric Ceramics Research Group [PCRG], 1997 *The Study of Later Prehistoric Pottery: general policies and guidelines for analysis and publication*, Southampton: Prehist. Ceram. Res. Grp Occas. Pap. 1/2

Price, J., 2000 Late Roman glass vessels in Britain and Ireland from AD 350 to 410 and beyond, in Price, J. (ed.), *Glass in Britain and Ireland AD 350–1100*, 1–32, London: Brit. Mus. Occas. Pap. 127

Price, J. and Cottam, S. 1998, *Romano-British Glass Vessels: a handbook*. York: Counc. Brit. Archaeol. Pract. Handbk Archaeol. 14

Pringle, S., 2002 The building materials, in Drummond-Murray, J. and Thompson, P. with Cowan, C., *Settlement in Roman Southwark: archaeological excavations (1991–8) for the London Underground Limited Jubilee Line Extension Project*, 151–61, London: Mus. London Archaeol. Serv. Monogr. 12

Pryor, F. (ed.), 1984 *Excavation at Fengate, Peterborough, England: the fourth report*, Northampton/Toronto: Northamptonshire Archaeol. Soc. Monogr. 2/Roy. Ontario Mus. Archaeol. Monogr. 7

Pryor, F., 2001 *The Flag Fen Basin: archaeology and environment in the Lower Welland Valley*, London: English Herit.

Pullinger, J. and Young, C.J., 1981 Obelisk Kilns, Harston, *Proc. Cambridge Antiq. Soc.* 71, 1–24

Pullinger, J., Burnham, B.C., Rotherham, A. and White, P. 1999 Roman pottery illustrations, in Alexander and Pullinger 1999, 145–99

Rackham, O., 2001 *Trees and Woodland in the British Landscape* (rev. edn), London: Orion

Reece, R., 1987 *Coinage in Roman Britain*, London: Seaby

Reece, R., 1995 Site finds in Roman Britain, *Britannia* 26, 179–206

Rees, S.E., 1979 *Agricultural Implements in Prehistoric and Roman Britain*, Oxford: Brit. Archaeol. Rep. 69

Regan, R., Evans C. and Webley, L., 2004 *The Camp Ground Excavations, Colne Fen, Earith* 1, Cambridge: Cambridge Archaeol. Unit Rep. 654

Reid-Henry, D. and Harrison C., 1988 *The History of the Birds of Britain*, London: Collins

Reynolds, P.J., 1981 Deadstock and livestock, in Mercer, R. (ed.), *Farming Practice in British Prehistory*, 97–122, Edinburgh: Univ. Press

Rielly, K., 2008 Appendix 13: animal bone, CD-Rom, in Abrams and Ingham 2008

Roberts, C. and Manchester K., 1997 *The Archaeology of Disease*, Stroud: Sutton

Roberts, C. and Cox, M., 2003 *Health and Disease in Britain from Prehistory to the Present Day*, Stroud: Sutton

Robinson, M., 1981 Roman waterlogged plant and invertebrate evidence, 90–106, in Hinchcliffe, J. and Thomas, R., Archaeological investigations at Appleford, *Oxoniensia* 45, 9–111

Robinson, M., 1988 Molluscan evidence for pasture and meadowland on the floodplain of the upper Thames basin, in Murphy, P. and French, C. (eds), *The Exploitation of the Wetlands*, 101–12, Oxford: Brit. Archaeol. Rep. 186

Robinson, M., *Unpubl. Draft Report 3.4 The invertebrate and waterlogged plant remains from Claydon Pike*, www.oxfordarch.co.uk/microsites/cotswoldweb/text/fcp_environmental.pdf

Robinson, M.A. and Wilson, R., 1987 A survey of environmental archaeology in the South Midlands, in Keeley, H.C.M. (ed.), *Environmental Archaeology: a regional review*, 16–100, London: Hist. Build. Monum. Comm. Engl. Occas. Pap. 1

Rogers, J. and Waldron, T., 1995 *A Field Guide to Joint Disease in Archaeology*, Chichester: Wiley

Rudge, E.A., 1968 Interim report on the distribution of the puddingstone quern, *Trans. Essex Archaeol. Soc.* 1, 247–9

Scaife, R.G., 1988 Pollen analysis of the Mar Dyke sediments, in Wilkinson, T.J., *Archaeology and Environment in South Essex*, 109–14, Chelmsford: E. Anglian Archaeol. 42

Scaife, R.G., 1992 Flag-Fen: the vegetation environment, *Antiquity* 66, 462–6

Scaife, R.G., 1993 Pollen analysis at Crowtree Farm, and Pollen analysis at Oakhurst Farm, in French, C. and Pryor, F., *The South-west Fen Dyke Survey*

Project 1982–86, 48–51, 54–9, Cambridge: E. Anglian Archaeol. 59

Scaife, R.G., 1998 Pollen analyses, in Pryor, F., Etton: *Excavations at a Neolithic Causewayed Enclosure near Maxey, Cambridgeshire, 1982–7*, 301–10, London: Engl. Herit. Archaeol. Rep. 18

Scaife, R.G., 2001 The vegetation and environment, in Pryor, F. (ed.) 2001, 351–81

Scaife, R.G., 2008 Appendix 17: pollen, CD-Rom, in Abrams and Ingham 2008

Scheuer, L. and Black, S., 2000 *Developmental Juvenile Osteology*, London: Academic

Scott, E., 1993, *A Gazetteer of Roman Villas in Britain*, Leicester: Leicester Archaeol. Monogr. 1

Seager Smith, R., Brown, K. and Mills, J., forthcoming The [Late Iron Age–Roman] pottery from Springhead, in Andrews, P., Biddulph, E. and Hardy, A., *Settling the Ebbsfleet Valley: CTRL excavations at Springhead and Northfleet, Kent – the Late Iron Age, Roman, Saxon and medieval landscape*, Salisbury: Oxford-Wessex Archaeol. Rep.

Serjeantson, D., 2006 Animal remains, in Evans and Hodder 2006, 288–91

Shackley, M.L., 1976 The Danebury project: an experiment in site sediment recording, in Davidson, D.A. and Shackley, M.L. (eds), *Geoarchaeology: earth science and the past*, 9–21, London: Duckworth

Sickle, W.H.H. van, 1995 *Caxton and Bourn, Cambridgeshire. Summary of Site History*, unpubl. rep.

Simms, J., 2006 Pollen analysis, in Evans and Hodder 2006, 260–3

Slowikowski, A.M. and Dawson, M., 1993, An early Roman period pottery kiln at Warren Villas Quarry, Upper Caldecote, Bedfordshire, *J. Roman Pott. Stud.* 6, 37–50

Smith, W., 2001 The charred plant remains, in Ellis *et al.* 2001, 53–5

Snow D.W. and Perrins C.M., 1998 *The Birds of the Western Palearctic, Concise edn*, Oxford: Univ. Press

Soil Survey, 1984 *Soils and Their Use in South-East England*, Rothamsted: Soil Surv.

Sparks, B.W., 1961 The ecological interpretation of Quaternary non-marine Mollusca, *Proc. Linnean Soc. London* 172, 71–80

Spoerry, P., 2000 Estate, village, town? Roman, Saxon, and medieval settlement in the St Neots area, in Dawson 2000, 45–60

Stace, C., 1997 *New Flora of the British Isles*, Cambridge: Univ. Press

Stallibrass, S., 1982 The faunal remains, in Potter T. and Potter, C. (eds), *A Romano-British Village at Grandford, March, Cambridgeshire*, 98–122, London: Brit. Mus. Occas. Pap. 35

Stallibrass, S., 1996 Animal bones, in Jackson, R. and Potter, T. (eds), *Excavations at Stonea, Cambridgeshire 1980–85*, 587–612, London: Brit. Mus. Press

Stead, I.M. and Rigby, V., 1989 Verulamium: *the King Harry Lane site*, London: Engl. Herit. Archaeol. Rep. 12

Stevens, C.J., 1996 *Iron Age and Roman Agriculture in the Upper Thames Valley: Archaeobotanical and Social Perspectives*, unpubl. PhD thesis, Cambridge Univ.

Stevens, C.J. 1997a The charred plant remains, in Mortimer, R. and Evans, C., *Archaeological Excavations at 138 Huntingdon Road, Cambridge*, Cambridge: Cambridge Archaeol. Unit Rep. 203

Stevens, C.J., 1997b Molluscs and plant remains, in Mortimer, R. *The Iron Age settlement at Greenhouse Farm, Fen Ditton, Cambridge: A Trench Assessment*, 40–4, Cambridge: Cambridge Archaeol. Unit Rep. 240

Stevens, C. J. 1997c Bulk environmental samples, in Evans, C. and Knight, M., *The Barleycroft Paddocks Excavations, Cambridgeshire*, 108–19, Cambridge: Cambridge Archaeol. Unit unpubl. client rep.

Stevens, C. J. 1998 Botanical remains, in Regan, R. and Evans C. (ed.), *Excavations at Colne Fen Earith, Site 1*, 42–52. Cambridge: Cambridge Archaeol. Unit Rep. 273

Stevens, C.J. 1999 Plant remains, 156–65, in Broomhead, R.A., Ilchester, Great Yard Archaeological Excavations 1995, *Proc. Somerset Archaeol. Natur. Hist. Soc.* 142, 139–91

Stevens, C.J. 2003a An investigation of consumption and production models for prehistoric and Roman Britain, *Environ. Archaeol.* 8, 61–76

Stevens, C.J., 2003b Agricultural processing: an overview, in Evans 2003, 138–44

Stevens, C.J., 2005 *Three later Iron Age sites, Colne Fen Earith: agricultural practises and landuse as seen from the plant remains*, unpubl. rep. for Cambridge Archaeol. Unit/Wessex Archaeol. client rep. 60060

Stevens, C.J., 2006 Charred plant remains from Saltwood Tunnel, in Giorgi, J. (ed.) *Palaeoenvironmental Evidence from Section 1 of the Channel Tunnel Rail Link, Kent*, CTRL Scheme-wide Spec. Rep. Ser., Archaeol. Data Serv.

Stevens, C.J., in press a Agricultural practises and landuse as seen from the plant remains, in Evans, C., Appleby, G. Lucy, S. and Regan, R. (eds), *Prehistoric and Roman Fen-edge Communities at Colne Fen, Earith. The Archaeology of the Lower Ouse Valley* 1, Cambridge: McDonald Inst.

Stevens, C.J., in press b Charred and waterlogged plant remains from Broom Hill Quarry, in Edmonds, M. and Cooper, A., *Past and Present.*

Excavations at Broom, Bedfordshire, Oxford: Oxbow

Stevens, C.J., and Clapham, A.J., 2005 Charred and waterlogged plant remains, internet report, in Gibson, C.A., Romano-British rural site at Eaton Socon, Cambridgeshire, *Proc. Cambridge Antiq. Soc.* 94, 21–38

Stirland, A., 1984 A possible correlation between *Os acromialie* and occupation in the burials from the *Mary Rose*, *Proc. 5th European Meeting Palaeopath. Assoc.*, 327–34

Stockmarr, J., 1971 Tablets with spores used in absolute pollen analysis, *Pollen et Spores* 13, 614–21

Swanton, M.J., 1973 *The Spearheads of the Anglo-Saxon Settlements*, Leeds: Roy. Archaeol. Inst.

Swan, V.G, 1984 *The Roman Pottery Kilns of Roman Britain*, London: Roy. Comm. Hist. Monum. England Supple. Ser. 5

Swift, E., 2000 *Roman Dress Accessories*, Princes Risborough: Shire

Taylor, A., 1985 Prehistoric, Roman, Saxon and medieval artefacts from the southern Fen edge, Cambridgeshire, *Proc. Cambridge Antiq. Soc.* 74, 1–37

Taylor, M., 1996 Worked wood, 93–115 in Pollard, J., Iron Age riverside pit alignments at St Ives, Cambridgeshire, *Proc. Prehist. Soc.* 62, 93–116

Tebbutt, C.F., 1957 A Belgic and Roman Farm at Wyboston, Bedfordshire, *Proc. Cambridge Antiq. Soc.* 50, 75–84

Thomas, K.D., 1977 The Mollusca from an Iron Age pit at Winklebury, 70–4 in Smith, K., The Excavation of Winklebury Camp, Basingstoke, Hampshire, *Proc. Prehist. Soc.* 43, 31–130

Thompson, I., 1982 *Grog-tempered 'Belgic' pottery of South-eastern England*, Oxford: Brit. Archaeol. Rep. 108

Tilson, P., 1973 A Belgic and Romano-British site at Bromham, *Bedfordshire Archaeol. J.* 8, 23–66

Tilson, P., 1975 The excavation of an Iron Age hut circle at Bromham in 1971 with a note on two post-medieval finds from Clapham, *Bedfordshire Archaeol. J.* 10, 19–23

Tipper, J.B., 1994 A Late Iron Age/Romano-British settlement at Madingley, Cambridgeshire, *Proc. Cambridge Antiq. Soc.* 83, 23–30

Trotter, M. and Gleser, G.C., 1952 Estimation of stature from long bones of American whites and Negroes, *Amer. J. Phys. Anthropol.* 10(4), 463–514

Trotter, M. and Gleser, G.C., 1958 A re-evaluation of estimation of stature bases on measurements of stature taken during life and of long bones after death, *Amer. J. Phys. Anthropol.* 16(1), 79–123

Trow-Smith, R., 1957 *A History of British Livestock Husbandry to 1700*, London: Routledge and Kegan Paul

Veen, M. van der, 1989 Charred grain assemblages from the Roman-period corn driers in Britain, *Archaeol. J.* 146, 302–19

Veen, M. van der, 1991 Consumption or production? Agriculture in the Cambridgeshire Fen, in Renfrew, J.M. (ed.), *New Light on Early Farming*, 349–61, Edinburgh: Univ. Press

Veen, M. van der, 1992. *Crop Husbandry Regimes. An Archaeobotanical Study of Farming in Northern England 1000 BC–AD 500*, Sheffield: Sheffield Archaeol. Monogr. 3

Veen, M. van der and O'Connor, T., 1998 The expansion of agriculture in late Iron Age and Roman Britain, in Bayley, J. (ed.), *Science in Archaeology: an agenda for the future*, 127–43, London: Engl. Herit.

Wade, K., 2000 Anglo-Saxon and medieval (rural), in Brown and Glazebrook (eds) 2000, 23–6

Waller, M., 1994 *The Fenland Project No. 9: Flandrian Environmental Change in Fenland*, Cambridge: E. Anglian Archaeol. 70

Welfare, A.T., 1986 The milling-stones, in Bidwell, P.T., *The Roman Fort of Vindolanda*, 154–64, London: Hist. Build. Monum. Comm. Engl. Archaeol. Rep. 1

Wessex Archaeology, 1989 *Swansley Wood, Caxton, Cambridgeshire. Proposed New Settlement*, unpubl. client rep.

Wessex Archaeology, 2000 *Cambourne New Settlement, Cambridgeshire, Archaeological Mitigation; Research Aims and Methodology for Archaeological Mitigation – Excavation*, unpubl. client rep. 45978.1

Wessex Archaeology, 2003 *Cambourne New Settlement, Cambridgeshire. Archaeological Excavations at Lower Cambourne, Knapwell Plantation, Jeavons Lane, Poplar Plantation, Mill Farm, Broadway Farm, Great Common Farm, North Caxton Bypass and The Grange*, unpubl. client rep. 45973.1

Wessex Archaeology, 2004a *Cambourne New Settlement, Cambridgeshire. Archaeological Mitigation at The Fields*, unpubl. client rep. 45973.00

Wessex Archaeology, 2004b *Cambourne New Settlement, Cambridgeshire. Archaeological Excavations at Monk Field Farm and Little Common Farm: Interim Statement of Results*, unpubl. client rep. 45973.2

Wessex Archaeology, 2005 *Camborne New Settlement, Cambridgeshire. Proposal for a Programme of Archaeological Post-excavation Analysis and Publication*, unpubl. client rep. 45979.1

Wessex Archaeology, 2006 *Stilton, Cambridgeshire; Archaeological Evaluation and Assessment of Results*, unpubl. client rep. 62505.1

Whimster, R., 1981 *Burial Practices in Iron Age Britain*, Oxford: Brit. Archaeol. Rep. 90

Wicks, K., forthcoming Analysis of residues on Romano-British pottery by Fourier transform infrared spectroscopy and gas chromatography mass spectrometry, *J. Archaeol. Sci.*

Wilkinson, K.N. and Stevens, C.J., 2003 *Environmental Archaeology: approaches, techniques and applications*, Stroud: Tempus

Williams, P., 1979 Waterlogged wood remains, 71–7, in Smith, C.A., *Fisherwick: the reconstruction of an Iron Age landscape*, Oxford: Brit. Archaeol. Rep. 61

Williams, D. and Vince, A., 1997 The characterisation and interpretation of early to middle Saxon granitic-tempered pottery in England, *Medieval Archaeol.* 41, 214–20

Williamson, T.M., 1984 The Roman countryside: settlement and agriculture in N.W. Essex, *Britannia* 15, 225–30

Williamson, T.M., 2003 *Shaping Medieval Landscapes: Settlement, Society, Environment*, Macclesfield: Windgather

Willis, S., 2005 *Samian Pottery, a Resource for the Study of Roman Britain and Beyond: the results of the English Heritage funded Samian Project. An e-monograph*, http://intarch.ac.uk/journal/issue17/willis_index.html

Wilson B., 1996 *Spatial Patterning among Animal Bones in Settlement Archaeology: an English regional exploration*, Oxford: Brit. Archaeol. Rep. 251

Wilson, D.G., 1968 Plant remains from the Roman well at Bunny, Nottinghamshire, *Trans. Thoroton Soc.* 72. 42–9

Wilson, D.G., 1973 Plant and microfaunal remains, 6–10, in Davidson, I. and Curtis, G., An Iron Age site in the land of the Plant Breeding Institute, Trumpington, *Proc. Cambridge Antiq. Soc.* 64, 1–14

Wilson, D.G., 1978 Appendix I: Iron Age and Roman plant remains, in Drury, P.J., *Excavations at Little Waltham 1970–1971*, 142–5, London: Counc. Brit. Archaeol. Res. Rep. 26/Chelmsford Excav. Comm. Rep. 1

Wilson, G., 1984 A report on the plant macrofossils from Fengate, in Pryor 1984, MF 242–4

Wilson, M.G., 1984 The other pottery, in Frere 1984, 201–66

Wiltshire, P., 2003 Palynology, in Evans 2003, 71–84

Winder, J.M., 1998 Marine molluscs, in Ellis *et al.* 1998, 97–9

Wymer, J.J, 1977 *Gazetteer of Mesolithic sites in England and Wales*, London: Counc. Brit. Archaeol. Res. Rep. 20

Young, C.J., 1977 *The Roman Pottery of the Oxford Region*, Oxford: Brit. Archaeol. Rep. 43

Young, R. and Humphrey, J., 1999 Flint use in England after the Bronze Age: time for a re-evaluation?, *Proc. Prehist. Soc.* 65, 231–42

Zeder M.A., 2002 Reconciling rates of long bone fusion and tooth eruption and wear in sheep (*Ovis*) and goat (*Capra*), in Ruscillo, D. (ed.), *Recent Advances in Ageing and Sexing Animal Bones*, 87–118, Oxford: Oxbow

Zeepvat, R.J., 1987 Tiles, in Zeepvat, R.J., Williams, R.J. and Mynard, D.C., *Roman Milton Keynes Excavations and Fieldwork 1971–82*, 118–25, Aylesbury: Buckinghamshire Archaeol. Soc. Monogr. 1

Appendix: Cambourne client reports not referenced in text

Wessex Archaeology, 1996 *Cambourne New Settlement, Cambridgeshire. Archaeological Evaluation Phase 1,* Fieldwalking, rep. 33224

Wessex Archaeology, 1998a *Cambourne New Settlement, Cambridgeshire. Archaeological Evaluation, Site 1: A428 access,* rep. 33225a

Wessex Archaeology, 1998b *Cambourne New Settlement, Cambridgeshire. Archaeological Evaluation, Site 2: Rising main,* rep. 33225b

Wessex Archaeology, 1998c *Cambourne New Settlement, Cambridgeshire. Archaeological Evaluation, Site 3: Entrance park,* rep. 33227

Wessex Archaeology, 1998d *Cambourne New Settlement, Cambridgeshire. Archaeological Evaluation, Sub-phases 3–6,* rep. 33228

Wessex Archaeology, 1998e *Cambourne New Settlement, Cambridgeshire. Archaeological Evaluation, Site 13: Phasing one landscape – western boundary,* rep. 33220

Wessex Archaeology, 1999a *Cambourne New Settlement, Cambridgeshire. Archaeological Evaluation, Sub-phases 10–12,* rep. 45970

Wessex Archaeology, 1999b *Cambourne New Settlement, Cambridgeshire. Archaeological Evaluation, Plots 1000 and 2000,* rep. 45974

Wessex Archaeology, 1999c *Cambourne New Settlement, Cambridgeshire. Archaeological Evaluation, Sub-phase 13 (Site 26),* rep. 45976.1

Wessex Archaeology, 2000a *Cambourne New Settlement, Cambridgeshire. Archaeological Evaluation, August–December 1999,* rep. 45976.2

Wessex Archaeology, 2000b *Cambourne New Settlement, Cambridgeshire. Archaeological Evaluation, Lower Cambourne Green settlement centre roads,* rep. 45976.3

Wessex Archaeology, 2000c *Cambourne New Settlement, Cambridgeshire. Archaeological Evaluation, Country park and eastern landscaping (Monkfield Drive),* rep. 45976.4

Wessex Archaeology, 2000d *Cambourne New Settlement, Cambridgeshire. Archaeological Evaluation, Lower Cambourne Plots 6–15,* rep. 45976.5

Wessex Archaeology, 2000e *Cambourne New Settlement, Cambridgeshire. Archaeological Evaluation, Plots GC09–11, 17–20, 26 and the west of the golf course,* rep. 45976.7

Wessex Archaeology, 2001a *Cambourne New Settlement, Cambridgeshire. Archaeological Evaluation, Supplementary Report: Greater Cambourne Church and High Street,* rep. 45976.5

Wessex Archaeology, 2001b *Cambourne New Settlement, Cambridgeshire. Archaeological Evaluation, Land on proposed new route of A428, associated landscaping and Plots GC 29–30,* rep. 45976.6

Wessex Archaeology, 2001c *Cambourne New Settlement, Cambridgeshire. Archaeological Evaluation, Land (GC05, CR01, CR06), landscaping (Phases 4 and 5) and housing adjacent to Jeavons Lane (GC12, 13, 16, 22, 24, 27),* rep. 45976.8

Wessex Archaeology, 2001d *Cambourne New Settlement, Cambridgeshire. Archaeological Evaluation, Land along proposed new route of the South Caxton Bypass,* rep. 45976.9

Wessex Archaeology, 2001e *Cambourne New Settlement, Cambridgeshire. Archaeological Mitigation, Plots GC10 and 11 (Poplar Plantation),* rep. 45978.4

Wessex Archaeology, 2002a *Cambourne New Settlement, Cambridgeshire. Archaeological Evaluation, Elsworth turn, balancing pond at Monkfield Drive and landscaping around Great Common Farm,* rep. 45976.10

Wessex Archaeology, 2002b *Cambourne New Settlement, Cambridgeshire. Archaeological Evaluation, Lake 4 and landscaping,* rep. 45976.11

Wessex Archaeology, 2002c *Cambourne New Settlement, Cambridgeshire. Archaeological Evaluation, South Caxton Bypass: Power augering survey,* rep. 45976.12

Wessex Archaeology, 2000d *Cambourne New Settlement, Cambridgeshire. Archaeological Excavation, Interim report for Great Common Farm,* rep. 45978

Wessex Archaeology, 2003a *Cambourne New Settlement, Cambridgeshire. Archaeological Evaluation and Watching Brief, Phase 4 and 5 spine sewer, storm water drain and temporary haul road,* rep. 45975.2

Wessex Archaeology, 2003b *Cambourne New Settlement, Cambridgeshire. Archaeological Evaluation, Upper Cambourne (Housing phases 6–9) and GC23 and 26 (Housing phase 5),* rep. 45976.13

Wessex Archaeology, 2003c *Cambourne New Settlement, Cambridgeshire. Archaeological Evaluation, Lake 2 and landscaping,* rep. 45976.14

Wessex Archaeology, 2006 *Land adjacent to Knapwell Plantation Far East,* rep. 63121.2

Wessex Archaeology, 2007 *Cambourne New Settlement, Cambridgeshire. Archaeological Evaluation, Upper Cambourne allotments and village green car park,* rep. 63124

Index